INCA RELIGION AND CUSTOMS

Inca Religion and Customs

by Father Bernabe Cobo

Translated and edited
by Roland Hamilton
Foreword by John Howland Rowe

 UNIVERSITY OF TEXAS PRESS
AUSTIN

This project has been supported by the National Endowment
for the Humanities, a federal agency which supports the study
of such fields as history, philosophy, literature, and languages.

Third paperback printing, 1997

Requests for permission to reproduce material from this work
should be sent to Permissions, University of Texas Press,
Box 7819, Austin, TX 78713-7819.

⊗ The paper used in this publication meets the minimum
requirements of American National Standard for Information
Sciences—Permanence of Paper for Printed Library Materials,
ANSI Z39.48-1984.

LIBRARY OF CONGRESS
CATALOGING-IN-PUBLICATION DATA

Cobo, Bernabé, 1580–1657
  [Historia del Nuevo mundo. English. Selections]
  Inca religion and customs / by Bernabé Cobo ; translated
and edited by Roland Hamilton — 1st ed.
    p. cm.
  Translation of: Historia del Nuevo mundo.
  ISBN 0-292-73861-7 (alk. paper)
    1. Incas.   2. Incas—Religion and mythology.   3. Incas—
Social life and customs.   I. Hamilton, Roland,
1936– .   II. Title.
F3429.C58213 1990
985'.01—dc20   89-37604
                                                      CIP
                                                      Rev.

Contents

BOOK I: RELIGION

BOOK II: CUSTOMS

Foreword Bernabe Cobo described the political organization of the Inca Empire and its law and economy in the same book in which he gave an account of Inca history. Roland Hamilton's translation of that book was published in 1979. This volume contains the next two books of Cobo's great work. The first book presented here is an account of Inca religion, a subject in which our author, as a Jesuit scholar, had a professional interest. The following book is about other Inca manners and customs, completing Cobo's coverage of Inca culture.

The book on Inca religion is based almost entirely on earlier manuscript sources. The Inca state religion had been swept away in successive campaigns to convert the native population to Christianity, and by 1609, when Cobo's own observations began, there was very little left to observe.

Cobo's principal source on Inca religion was an extensive manuscript report written by Juan Polo de Ondegardo in 1559. Polo was trained as a lawyer and occupied important posts in the Spanish administration. He investigated many aspects of Inca administration, and other reports of his were used by Cobo for his treatment of Inca political administration and economy in the previous volume. Polo's manuscript on Inca religion is lost. We have some idea of what it covered, because a summary of it was published by the Third Provincial Council of Lima in 1585. On the basis of the summary, we can identify the sections of Cobo's text that are based on Polo's investigations. Cobo preserved more of Polo's material than the 1585 summary did. Polo's report was the most extensive and systematic record of Inca religious beliefs and practices made by anyone, and the investigations for it were carried out early enough that there were many older people available who could provide detailed information.

Cobo also used a manuscript account of certain aspects of Inca religion written in 1575 by a priest named Cristóbal de Molina. Molina was particularly interested in the rituals related to the calendar. A copy of Molina's manuscript has been preserved, so that we can compare it with what Cobo said about calendar rituals. Polo and Molina disagreed on important points, and Cobo had to reconcile them as best he could.

A prominent feature of Cobo's account of Inca religion is his inclusion of a catalogue of the *huacas* (*guacas*) or shrines of Inca Cuzco, over three hundred of which are included in the list. Both Polo and Molina collected information on these shrines, but Cobo's list appears to be derived from a source independent of both these writers. I have published my thoughts on this list elsewhere.[1] The reason that Cobo included the catalogue of shrines in his account of Inca religion was that he wanted to make the point that the Incas worshipped many and diverse things, including rocks and springs of water, and not just a few nature deities. The catalogue of the *huacas* of Cuzco is one of the most important items Cobo has transmitted to us, and we have no other copy of it.

As part of his account of Inca religion, Cobo described five great Inca holy places, the Temple of the Sun at Cuzco, the temple of Pachacama, the shrine of Titicaca near Copacabana, the ruins of Tiahuanaco, and the oracle of Apurima. His descriptions of three of these holy places are purely archaeological; he described the physical remains he could see. The Temple of the Sun at Cuzco was a Dominican monastery in Cobo's day; he examined the ruins that were standing before the great earthquake of 1650 but did not take measurements. He did make measurements at the ruins of Tiahuanaco and was the first to note that two kinds of building stone were used in them. He also made systematic measurements of the temple of Pachacama, which is the structure now identified as the Inca Temple of the Sun at Pachacamac, near Lima. The measurements help to convey the scale of the monuments described; we do not know whether Cobo intended to use them to draw plans of the sites as well. He seems to have made few inquiries of the local people about the myths and rituals associated with the sites he described.

For the other two holy places he had literary sources. He had visited the shrine of Titicaca near Copacabana himself, but he knew the description of it written by Alonso Ramos Gavilán, published in 1621. His account of the oracle at Apurima is taken from a manuscript by Pedro Pizarro.

As we have noted, the second book in this volume is about those Inca manners and customs not covered previously. The information in this book is based for the most part on Cobo's own observations rather than on the writings of others.

Cobo's ethnographic observations were casual ones, made in the course of his residence and travels in Peru. There is no indication that he followed a plan of investigation. For the most part, what he reports are observations in the most literal sense. He did not question people systematically about their customs, except sometimes when plants or animals were involved. Cobo was primarily a naturalist, interested in plants and animals, which he described in loving detail in ten books not translated for this project.

When he was talking about people, he recorded what he had seen, ordinary behavior involving the use of things, and not what people said or thought. For example, in his chapter on agriculture, Cobo described terraces and irrigation canals, discussed the hand tools used, and mentioned fertilizer, but he said nothing about crop rotation, which is something he would have had to ask about.

Cobo wanted to describe Inca culture as it was at the time the Spanish first arrived. His desire to do so is signaled by his use of the past tense in telling us about things that he evidently saw himself. He assumed, as ethnographers have commonly assumed in more recent times, that any customary behavior that is different from that of Europe represents the native culture as it was before European contact. The possibility that there had been changes in native culture not related to European influence did not occur to him. The assumption of cultural stability sometimes led him astray, as in the case of his treatment of Inca men's hair style. At the time of the arrival of the Spanish, Inca men wore their hair cropped very short, while by the time Cobo observed them, the men were wearing their hair longer and cut off squarely below the ears. Cobo described the hair style he observed and attributed it to pre-Spanish times. Guaman Poma knew that a change had taken place and showed the contrast in his illustrations.

Some Inca technology had been lost by Cobo's time, particularly in metal working. Since Cobo described the native metal work that he saw, his description fails to do justice to the technical skill reflected in surviving examples of Inca metallurgy.

As a good European, Cobo believed as strongly in the superiority of European medical science as he did in the superiority of his religion. The medical science of his time was based on the humoral pathology of Hippocrates, not discredited in Spain until the eighteenth century. Cobo remarked on how ignorant Inca medical practitioners were of what he considered the basic principles of medical science (Chapter 10 of the second book).

For the most part, however, Cobo wrote about the Incas with clarity and good judgment. His coverage is systematic and easy to follow. What he said about Inca religion is particularly important, because so much of it is based on Polo de Ondegardo's lost treatise on the subject. We are now privileged to have a translation of it in English.

John Howland Rowe

Introduction: Father Cobo and the Incas

Those interested in an accurate understanding of Inca culture must consult the sources, Spanish chronicles written in the sixteenth and seventeenth centuries. Although the Incas left no written records before the conquest, the Spanish chronicles are based on extensive interviews with Inca witnesses and on personal contact with those subjugated by the Incas. A surprisingly large number of these chronicles have survived and are used by all researchers in the field. Many of the documents contain vague and misleading passages which create great difficulties for the reader. One chronicle, however, stands out for its clarity and accuracy. I refer to the works of Father Bernabe Cobo. Completing his research in the first half of the seventeenth century, he produced what has become recognized as one of the most respected sources on the Incas.

In this introduction, I will give some of the highlights of Father Cobo's life, especially that part which relates to his research on the Incas. Then I will discuss the procedure I used to identify the original manuscript of Cobo's works on the Incas and give a resume of this manuscript. I will pay special attention to the section on Inca religion and customs contained in the present translation. Finally, I will comment on Father Cobo's scholarship and on his place among Inca sources.

Father Bernabe Cobo was born in Southern Spain, in the little town of Lopera, in 1580. Evidently he attended elementary school there. In 1595, he traveled to the large city of Seville, at the time a major port of call for ships going to and from America. Young Bernabe must have come to pray at the cathedral, the most prominent building in the city, before embarking on his journey to the New World. Little did he know that after his death his writings on the Incas would be deposited in the library of this same cathedral.

On his way to Peru, Cobo stopped for over a year in the West Indies. Continuing on through Panama, he reached Lima in 1599. The colonial town of Los Reyes, Lima, was a cultural center that boasted the best schools in Spanish America. Here young Bernabe received his secondary education before continuing on to advanced studies with the Jesuit Order.

Father Cobo traveled the Inca roads from Lima to Cuzco in the year 1609. Later, on several different trips, he walked on across most of central and southern Peru. He carefully examined the Inca

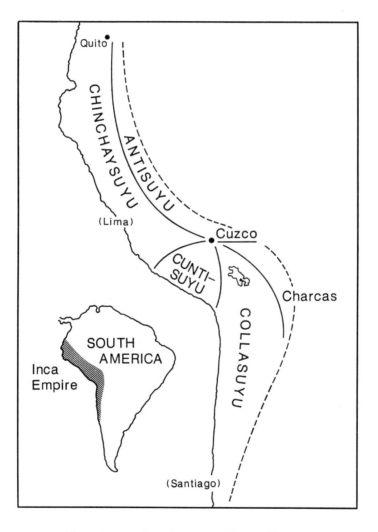

MAP I. *Tahuantinsuyu: Four Quarters of the World.*

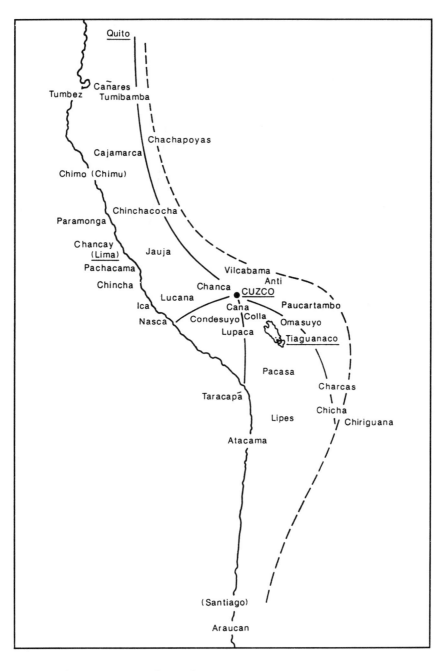

MAP 2. *The Inca empire: tribes and provinces.*

MAP 3.   *Peru and Tierra Firme in the early colonial period. The map at right shows modern national boundaries. Modified from* The Men of Cajamarca, *by James Lockhart (Austin: University of Texas Press, 1972).*

monuments in Cuzco and also conducted interviews with the descendants of the Incas.

Cobo visited the Lake Titicaca area at least twice, first in 1610 and again in 1615. He did missionary work here, getting to know the people and their languages, Quichua and Aymara. He also visited the ruins of Copacabana and Tiahuanaco.

During subsequent years, Father Cobo served as a Latin teacher in Arequipa and probably became director of a school in the coastal town of Pisco. After 1620, he spent most of his time in Lima, except for an extended trip to Mexico which lasted from 1629 to 1642. Devoting more and more time to his historical writings, he finally finished the *Historia del Nuevo Mundo* in 1653. He died in Lima in 1657.

Father Cobo explains in the prologue to his *Historia* that it contained forty-three books divided into three parts. The first deals with the natural history of the New World and the history and customs of the Incas; the second with the discovery and "pacification," as Cobo put it, of the West Indies and Peru, and with colonial institutions; the third deals mainly with New Spain. All that remains to us today is the first part, composed of fourteen books, and three books of the second part which tell of the foundation of Lima.

The manuscript for the section on the Incas, Books 11 through 14 of the first part, resides in the library of the cathedral of Seville, known as the Biblioteca Capitular Colombina. Until 1974, when I visited this library, the manuscript was considered to be a copy of a lost original. However, I wanted to identify Cobo's original writings for myself. Consequently I obtained a microfilm copy of the Colombina manuscript from the director. Next I went to the library of the University of Seville which houses the manuscript for Books 1 through 10, including the prologue, signed by Cobo. This manuscript is uniform in page size and binding with the Colombina manuscript; it is also clear that the two volumes were written in identical handwriting. Thus the prologue applies equally to both volumes. However, in order to make a positive identification of Cobo's handwriting, I needed another point of comparison. I knew there were letters written by Cobo from Mexico to Lima in 1630 and 1633. So the following year, I headed for Lima to inspect the originals held in the National Library. Careful comparison of the handwriting revealed that the manuscript at the Colombina Library in the cathedral was not a copy, but the original, executed in Cobo's own handwriting.

On the advice of the eminent Andean scholar Professor John H.

Rowe, I embarked on a project to translate the manuscript on the Incas. The first fruits of this labor resulted in the *History of the Inca Empire*, published in 1979 by the University of Texas Press. This is the only publication to date based on Cobo's original MS. This work comprised Books 11 and 12 of the original. Dealing with the physical features and customs of the Indians in general, it gives a detailed account of the origin and history of the Incas. The present translation of Books 13 and 14 of the original discusses Inca religion extensively and covers a wide variety of customs. All other books of Cobo's works published to date were based on imperfect copies of Cobo's originals. For more details, see my introductory materials for the *History of the Inca Empire.*

Book I of the present translation (Book 13 of the original) contains thirty-eight chapters on Inca religion. In it Father Cobo relates some fascinating origin myths, gives a careful explanation of many deities, and describes the major shrines in detail. He also tells about numerous rites and sacrifices, as well as the role of the priests, sorcerers, and doctors in Inca society.

Book II of this translation (Book 14 of the original) contains nineteen chapters on Inca customs. This book documents many topics of everyday life, such as clothing, weaving, building, food, drink, farming, marriage, and others.

Father Cobo's originality is that of any competent historian: the judicious use of primary sources in fashioning an overall view or thesis about a historical situation. His sources included interviews in Cuzco with descendants of the Incas, careful observation of the customs of the Indian peasants of the sierra, and the best written accounts by other chroniclers, some of which have since been lost.

His thesis was that the Inca believed a host of nature deities controlled their lives and needed to be appeased by careful attention to prescribed rituals and sacrifices. With respect to their customs, Cobo held that the Inca craftsmen achieved marvelous results with minimal equipment. For example, he points out that with simple tools the Inca's weavers made the most extraordinary cloth, the stonemasons constructed incredibly fine walls, and the farmers raised excellent crops.

While interviewing the Indians, Father Cobo soon realized that the peasants had forgotten all about the royal Inca political and religious institutions; therefore, he interviewed only descendants of the Inca on that subject. However, he collected much information on the customs of the common people. Many of these practices can still be observed today. For example, in the countryside near Cuzco, I have seen peasant houses with thatched roofs just as Cobo describes. Each house has a cooking fire inside and no chimney. The smoke rises through the thatch. (See Book II, Chapter 3.)

In other cases some changes have occurred. Father Cobo provides excellent descriptions of the monuments at Cuzco, especially the Temple of the Sun, Copacabana, Tiahuanaco, and Pachacama as he saw them in the early part of the seventeenth century. This information is very useful in determining how these monuments have been modified subsequently. For example, even my own casual observations at Tiahuanaco and Pachacama indicate that restoration has greatly altered these sites. Scholars need to do more studies using Cobo's material and that of others, as well as on-site research, if they are to continue the work of scholars like Max Uhle, who did an exemplary study back in 1896. (See Book I, Chapter 17, note 40.)

With respect to his written sources on the Incas, Cobo gives very general information. In the prologue to his *Historia* (not translated) he acknowledges having a manuscript copy of Pedro Pizarro's chronicle, *Relacion del descubrimiento y conquista de los reinos del Peru* . . . , dated 1571, first published in Madrid, 1844. Cobo also makes general reference to sources at the beginning of his account on the Incas (See *History of the Inca Empire*, Book II, Chapter 2.) Here Cobo indicates that he had manuscript copies of the account by the Licentiate Juan Polo de Ondegardo. In fact, he probably possessed the complete version of his treatise on Inca religion compiled in 1559, an extract of which was published in Lima in 1585 with the title *Errores y supersticiones de los indios*, as well as the work by Cristobal de Molina of Cuzco, *Relacion de las fabulas y ritos de los Incas*, written in 1575, published in Santiago, 1913. Additionally, he had a manuscript of a report done for the Viceroy Francisco de Toledo. This Toledo report, incidentally, has not been found by modern scholars.

In the same place mentioned above, Cobo also acknowledges his two most important published sources: the *Historia natural y moral de las Indias* (Seville, 1590), by the Jesuit scholar Jose de Acosta, and the *Comentarios reales . . . de los Yncas* (Lisbon, 1609), by the mestizo author Garcilaso de la Vega Inca.

Working within an overall framework of his own, Cobo turned to Acosta for the philosophical background of idolatry. Cobo drew on Polo de Ondegardo for the hierarchy of the gods, his insistence on the importance of sacrifice, including human sacrifice, and his

general ideas concerning the multitude of *huacas* or shrines and
other sacred objects. Cobo used Cristobal de Molina of Cuzco for
some legends, Inca rituals, and ceremonies as well as prayers. He
followed Pedro Pizarro for material such as the worship of the dead
(Book I, Chapter 10) and the shrine of Apurima (Book I, Chapter 20).

Although he used Garcilaso Inca's versions of some legends
and myths, Cobo, nevertheless, implicitly rejects the Garcilasan
interpretation of Inca religion as a kind of primitive Christianity.
For example, Garcilaso states that the Incas had no human sacrifice. Cobo explains in detail how Inca human sacrifices were performed, and for what reasons. Archaeological evidence corroborates
Cobo's explanation. Garcilaso stated that the Incas had only one
god, Pachacama. But Cobo, correctly, discusses hundreds of Inca deities, their powers, and the sacrifices made to them.

Father Cobo used some sources without acknowledging them
at all, a common practice at the time. For example, he based his
material about the shrine at Copacabana (Book I, Chapter 18) on
the work of the Augustinian Friar Alonso Ramos Gavilan, *Historia
del celebre santuario de Nuestra Señora de Copacabana . . .* Lima,
1621. Cobo also appears to have had an unidentified manuscript for
his account of the shrines of Cuzco (Book I, Chapter 13–16). New
research has discredited the theory that Cobo's source on the shrines
was written by either Polo de Ondegardo or Molina of Cuzco. (See
Book I, note 30). Whatever the sources may have been, it is clear
that Father Cobo has preserved invaluable material for the study of
the Incas.

Although Father Cobo did careful historical research, he still
retained the mentality of a seventeenth-century priest. He accepted
the authority of the Bible on all matters, historical or otherwise.
For example, on hearing a fable which included destruction by
water, he connects it with the Biblical Flood, thinking that the Indians had some knowledge of the Flood. He identifies the Inca gods
with the devil. Cobo did not think these deities were merely fig-
ments of the Indian's imagination. He truly believed they were
manifestations of the devil with certain supernatural powers. Hence
he felt compelled to condemn native beliefs.

Cobo believed the book of Genesis explained the creation of
the world and the beginnings of civilization. This influenced his
interpretation of the native myths. He considers most native myths
nonsense because they differ from the stories in Genesis. Nevertheless, Father Cobo was deeply interested in Inca religion, and he
compiled a very reliable and comprehensive study on the subject.

Father Cobo enlivens his account with interesting tales. He evidently told these stories as he got them in order to entertain the reader. But he always uses them to prove a point. For example, at one point he recounts a Spanish folk tale about the treasures buried at Tiahuanaco to teach a lesson about covetousness. This story indicates that the ancient rulers of Tiahuanaco were reputed to have had vast treasures (Book I, Chapter 19). He tells another fascinating story about a wondrous cure (Book II, Chapter 10), thus illustrating indigenous knowledge of medicinal plants. In order to show that at Tiahuanaco cut stones were found everywhere, he tells how the priest had his native sculptor dig just where they happened to be standing, and they found stones suitable for statues (Book I, Chapter 19). Professor John Rowe has investigated this matter, and he found that "the story is even better than Cobo thought. Those statues of San Pedro and San Pablo are still in front of the church, and they are genuine ancient statues, carved in the Pucara style. The Indian sculptor dug down and found two statues and palmed them off on the priest as his work" (personal communication).

Finally, I will say a word about the place Father Cobo's work occupies among the many sources on the Inca. There have been two periods of intense activity in Inca research: the second half of the sixteenth century up to the early seventeenth century and the twentieth century. During the first period, the novelty of initial contact and the desire to explain the new reality inspired the production of chronicles like those of Juan Polo de Ondegardo and Jose de Acosta.

During the second period, the development of scientific anthropology and archaeology resulted in much serious research on the Inca. Father Cobo comes at the end of the first period, and his method is that of a serious historian who has compiled and analyzed invaluable documents on the Inca. However, Cobo's manuscripts remained virtually unknown until the first publication in Spanish of the *Historia del Nuevo Mundo* came out in Seville between 1890 and 1893. This puts his work at the beginning of modern scientific research just before 1895, when another European working in Peru, the German archaeologist Max Uhle, started the field work and research with accounts by Cobo and others that greatly enlarged our understanding of the Inca Empire.

Through his training as a Jesuit and his keen observations gleaned from many parts of Peru, Father Cobo developed into an outstanding scholar. Carefully using original sources and personal experience, he prepared one of our most important and extensive sources on the Inca. Though earlier editions are based on imperfect copies, the present translation was based on the original. It completes the work initiated with the *History of the Inca Empire* and offers the reader an exciting new source in English on the religion and customs of the Incas.

A Note on the Translation In this rendering I have

followed the same procedures as with the *History of the Inca Empire*. Every effort was made to express the exact meaning set down by Cobo in his manuscript. In trying to achieve this I have consulted dictionaries, reference works, and chronicles which reflect seventeenth-century Spanish usage. However, in some cases I have found it necessary to add explanatory notes to maintain the continuity of the original text. These notes are intended only to clarify the text.

I have included almost all loan-words from American Indian languages as they appear in the original. In the few cases where there is an English equivalent (such as "hammock" for Spanish "hamaca") I have mentioned the original term in the glossary. In most cases the meaning of these loan words is clear in the text. However, since many of these words are new to most readers, all of them are defined in the glossary.

I have also included the three maps that appeared in the *History*. To these I have added a sketch map of the Cuzco area. Not all place names can be included on the maps because of problems of space. However, in any given passage, place names that do appear on the maps are found along with the ones that could not be included. Thus the reader can at least get the general idea of the area.

Many of the terms used by Cobo for measurements have no exact equivalent in modern English. Therefore, I have added a special explanation on measurements.

This translation was greatly enhanced by the advice of the eminent scholar John H. Rowe. He has discussed many problems with me, and he has given me permission to use his own translation of the section on the shrines of Cuzco, Book I, Chapters 13–16. (See Book I, note 30.) This model has been very helpful. I must also mention the valuable advice of two colleagues, Professors José Cerrudo and Dana Buchanan. Though I have sought and used the advice of experts, I made the final decisions.

R. H.

Measurements
The system of measures used by the Spaniards in the seventeenth century was different in several respects from what is commonly in use today. Therefore, I have made an explanation of the terms used in the Cobo manuscript. In doing this I have tried to be as precise as possible. Nevertheless, the reader should bear in mind that Father Cobo was usually giving very rough estimates in his measurements.

Each entry of the following list starts with the term or expression used in the English translation. The next item is the word or phrase in the Cobo manuscript. In some cases where an English equivalent is lacking, the word in the original remains. Finally there is a brief definition of each term. Sp refers to Spanish.

Length
finger width, *dedo*, Sp, the breadth of a finger, about ¾ inch
hand, *mano*, Sp, 4 finger widths, about 3 inches
geme, Sp, distance from the outstretched thumb to the tip of the forefinger, about 6 or 7 inches
span, *plamo*, Sp, distance from the tip of the outstretched thumb to the tip of the little finger, about 8 or 9 inches
tercia, ⅓ of a *vara*, or about 11 inches
cubit, *codo*, Sp, distance from the elbow to the end of the hand, 24 finger widths, about 16–19 inches
vara, Sp, Castilian yard, equals 4 spans or 3 Castilian feet, 2 cubits, about 33 to 34 inches
braza, Sp, fathom, the stretch of a man's arms, 2 *varas*, about 5 feet 6 inches, used for horizontal measurements
estado, Sp, the height of the average man, about 5 feet 6 inches, used for vertical measurements such as the height of a wall

Distance
foot, *pie*, Sp, the Castilian foot is about 11 inches, which is comparable to the *tercia*
pace, *paso*, Sp, approximately 3 feet
mile, *milla*, Sp, 1,000 paces
league, *legua*, Sp, approximately 3 miles or the distance a normal person can walk in an hour

Liquid
cuartillo, Sp, about 1 pint
azumbre, Sp, 2 quarts
arroba, Sp, 8 *azumbres*, 16 quarts, 4 gallons

Dry

almud, Sp, approximately 4 quarts

collo, Quichua term, equivalent to about 4 quarts

cesto, Sp for basket, used with reference to a package of coca leaves. The
    exact size is unclear, but a number of *cestos* were carried by a llama.

Area

hanegada, Sp, approximately 1.6 acres

topo, Quichua, area 50 *brazas* long and 25 wide

BOOK I
RELIGION

Chapter 1: Concerning the false religion that the Indians of Peru had and how devoted they were

to it   The Indians of Peru were so idolatrous that they worshiped as Gods almost every kind of thing created. Since they did not have supernatural insights, they fell into the same errors and folly as the other nations of pagans, and for the same reasons both the Peruvians and the other pagans were unable to find the true God. This is because they were immersed in such an abysmal array of vices and sins that they had become unfit and unworthy of receiving the pure light that accompanies a knowledge of their Creator. Moved by his arrogance and envy of our welfare, the common enemy of mankind, using malice and astuteness, succeeded in usurping from these blind people the adoration that they really owed to their true Creator, and he [the devil] kept them prisoners in harsh bondage, depriving them of the happiness which he himself did not deserve. Upon finding fertile ground in the simplemindedness and ignorance of these barbarians,[1] he reigned over them for many centuries until the power of the Cross started stripping him of his authority and ousting him from this land here as well as from the other regions of this New World.

This Peruvian region was very large and was inhabited by numerous Indian nations, so there were many different types of religion and idolatries, not only before the people were conquered and brought under one government, but afterward also. Although it is true that the Peruvian kings required all conquered persons to receive their Inca religion, they were not required to abandon entirely the religion that they had before. This was because the Incas only made the newly conquered subjects give up that part of their religion which seemed to contradict Inca religion. Therefore, not only did the conquered keep their former gods, but the Incas themselves accepted these gods and had them brought to Cuzco, where they were placed among the Incas' own gods. The Incas worshiped these new gods somewhat, but much less than they worshiped their native gods. It is remarkable how little the Incas cared for these new gods. When some province rebelled against them, the Incas ordered the protective native gods of the rebellious province to be brought out and put in public, where they were whipped ignominiously every day until such province was made to serve the Incas again. After the rebels were subdued, their gods were restored to their places and honored with sacrifices. At this time the Incas would say that the province had been subdued through the power of the rebels' gods, who wanted to avoid being insulted. And it is even said that the majority of the rebels surrendered just because they heard that their idols were exposed to public insults.

Since, as I have already stated, the peoples of this Peruvian Empire had so many different kinds of idolatries, if one were to write down the details about each one, the task would be endless. Therefore, I will write here only about the idolatry that was followed by the Inca nation, which had been adopted throughout the entire kingdom because the Inca kings imposed it on all of their vassals. These kings were so clever in imposing their idolatry that it was not only accepted by all of the Indians who were conquered, but it came to be so esteemed by them that it was an honor for them to profess it, and they heeded it more than their own idolatry. This the Incas achieved by emphasizing the importance of the special favor done for their vassals in allowing them to worship the Inca gods. Since their intention and desire was for the conquered to adopt their opinions about religion, they did not let them all enjoy this favor at first, nor did the Incas have celebrations with them. On the contrary, some things were reserved only for the Incas themselves and members of their families. In other cases, the conquered were not allowed to participate with the same solemnity and formality as was customary for the Incas. However, as time passed and services were rendered to the Incas, they would allow some provinces to do some of these things. Thus the vassals came to hold this as a great reward for their services. Since it was difficult to obtain this concession, it stimulated the Indians to be especially careful and diligent in observing the Inca celebrations. The fact that these ceremonies were not open to all and that those who did not have this privilege could not even be present increased the respect and devotion they had for these rites and superstitions. The foreign subjects esteemed these dispensations and privileges more than any other thing that the Incas could give them. They believed that with these dispensations and privileges they would be capable of achieving what they asked for to fulfill their needs and alleviate their tribulations. What is more, they felt that their needs were met when they were granted permission to practice the sacrifices and ceremonies of the Incas. The Incas themselves would guarantee them everything on granting them this favor. The Incas based all this on fantasies, dreams, revelations, and orders that they pretended to receive from their gods. The object was to make the common people think that only the Incas and whomever they selected would be permitted to worship Viracocha, who was their main god, and their other idols with the rites that were established for that purpose. All of this was a contrivance of the Incas to enhance the prestige of their religion, and by means of it to keep their subjects the more subdued and obedient.

It is true that from the beginning of their empire the Incas were not always steadfast in their religion, nor did they maintain the same opinions and worship the same gods. Actually, at various times they took on many new rites and ceremonies, and though they eliminated some, they always kept loading the people down with more of them. They were prompted to make such changes because they realized that in this way they improved their control over the kingdom and kept it more subservient. The entire basis for the Inca political government rested on an orderly mechanism for keeping their people subjugated and for ensuring that they give up any hope of rebelling against their rulers. The opinions that they formed on what pertains to religion were also aimed at the same objective. It was in the name of religion that they made their conquests, on the pretext that Viracocha, as the creator of the world, and the Sun, Thunder, and the rest of their gods must be honored and obeyed properly. The Incas considered that their gods were responsible for preserving all creation by means of the power that was given by the gods to the Incas for this purpose, especially the kinship they pretended to have with the Sun,[2] the special help they got from him personally in times of war, and other such fabrications. They were tyrant-lords, and time and experience taught them all the necessary means to sustain their tyranny and rule with more firmness. Moreover, since their many forms of worship and rites changed over the ages, it is appropriate to point out that the material gathered here is based only on what was observed at the time that the Spaniards came into this land and the Indians started to receive the doctrine of heaven. [Here are] the opinions which remained [from the previous forms of worship and rites] and which were the most widespread and uniform.

Although the Inca idolatry and false religion was the best organized and most reasonable compared with the nonsense and errors of the other nations of these Indies, in spite of all that, it was so full of fabrications, hoaxes, and absurdities that it is surprising to see how intelligent men could be persuaded to believe in it, how they could worship such an infinite number of things as gods, to the point of venerating the most vile and disgusting things on earth. It is also incredible what nonsense they attributed to their gods and how carefully they worshiped them and offered sacrifices to them, as will be shown in this book. This situation must not be construed as evidence that those who believed such things and abided by them were dumb animals. Anyone who knows about the vanities and foolishness of the most noble and wise nations of Europe and the other parts of the Old World such as the Egyptians, the Chaldeans, the Greeks, and the Romans, whose knowledge has been so highly valued throughout the ages, will find nothing new or strange in reading the fables and foolishness of these Indians. In fact, it will be seen that many of the ancient philosophers had some opinions that were more simpleminded and less reasonable than those of the Indians. Similarly, it does not follow logically to argue that the Indians were incompetent just because they worshiped idols and transitory things; on the contrary, it shows that though they lacked the true light of faith, they did have the ingenuity to look for something which they could respect and have confidence in. And it is no trifle that the Indians themselves took the trouble to look for the cause of each thing, like the pagans, and though the Indians were mistaken in their inquiry, not even the ancients, who were so given to scientific study and investigation into the nature of things, ever succeeded in finding the true Architect of all creation. Moreover, the ancients also worshiped sticks, stones, images of animals, and other man-made things such as these. In fact, the Indians achieved some things on the basis of natural reasoning which surpassed the practices of the other pagans. For example, the Indians had come to realize that there was only one true God and first cause, and though they were somewhat vague on the matter, they adored him as the Creator[3] of all things.

Not stopping here, the Indians set out to find explanations for the existence of each thing and causes for their origin. Thus they came to understand many of the second causes, which could be seen by their effects. Actually, they made a glaring mistake by believing that there was only one Universal Creator of all things, to whom they always made their supplications and sacrifices, while at the same time worshiping, with equal reverence and with the same ceremonial services and subservience, second causes such as the sun, water,earth, and many other things that they held to be divine. In each case they believed that these things had the power to make or preserve what was necessary for human life, and this was always their main interest. For this same reason the Indians felt obliged to worship the second causes the same as the Creator, and this gave origin to an infinite number of idolatries and superstitions. Nevertheless, the fact that they were willing to speculate is a good indication that they were intelligent people and less barbarian than the other peoples of this New World. Therefore, we find that the less religion a nation has, the more coarse and barbarian it will be. And it is important to realize that although the Peruvians were wrong, they certainly did seek out the first and second causes of things. If they were mistaken in worshiping the second causes, it was because of the power the Indians attributed to these second causes to take part in the preservation of the universe. What I think, as I carefully consider the rites and opinions of these Indians, is that in general they had the same customs and fabrications as the Romans, and this is no wonder because they both had the same master. This is borne out by the fact that after their victories the Incas sought to have all the people in their kingdom respect the authority of the city of Cuzco, and the principal gods were brought from all the provinces to be put at first in the Temple of the Sun. This is very reminiscent of the Romans, who had that magnificent building called the Pantheon.

The compliant nature of the Indians is the principal reason why they accepted so much nonsense and so many errors. After having accepted some error, the Indians would soon believe anything about the matter that the priests or Incas wanted to make up in order to substantiate their opinion. By taking advantage of this compliance, every day the priests and attendants would make up a thousand fictitious stories and mysteries of the visions and miracles that happened to their *guacas*.[4] They did this because they had a selfish interest in the offerings and sacrifices made by the people. The common people were made to believe these stories and mysteries so that as the reputation of the Inca gods grew, so also would the amount of offerings grow. Some firmly accepted things were so obviously unfounded that undoubtedly some people must have scrutinized them and realized how false and deceptive they were. Nevertheless, when something is well established, even though it is clearly bad, no one will contradict it, even though some understand its true nature. Certainly it is true that many philosophers realized that the multitude of gods was a mockery. Nevertheless, they did not dare talk about it because they did not want to contradict the multitudes of people. This is especially valid for these Indians, who had very little freedom, severe punishments, and many people who made their living by these [religious] occupations.

The devil had these blind people so thoroughly accustomed to his misguided sect, especially the Incas (the nation that was probably more given over to religion than any other in the world), that they performed his rites and sacrifices with so much determination and so often that practically all the products that they harvested and all the things they made, and even their own children, were consumed in them [sacrifices]. Actually they showed profound devotion, and each one was careful to worship and sacrifice what he was assigned. Their religion was so firmly established, universally received, and amazingly strict that they offered and sacrificed even their own children by killing them and their own property by burning it, as was their custom. Therefore, it cannot be presumed that their acts were empty gestures, because human nature would not allow them to kill their own children and jeopardize their property so happily if they did not expect some reward for what they were doing or if they did not believe that they were sending their children to a better place than the one they had here. And it is evident that for people to produce exterior signs of happiness in making these sacrifices, in their own minds they believed without any doubt that the sacrifices were not made in vain. Thus there is no question that these acts were conditioned by some hope. People who would kill their own children and destroy their own property would be acting more like animals than human beings, unless they felt that such acts were somehow useful.

Although all of the Indian nations of this Kingdom of Peru paid careful attention to their gods and shrines, none of them came anywhere near priding themselves on being as religious as the Incas. In fact the Incas were the most encumbered with ceremonies, superstitions, idols, and sacrifices, and they observed what was ordained with such care that their practices were inviolable laws and beliefs for them. Offenses committed against these laws or even carelessness in the stipulated forms of worship were severely punishable. Nevertheless, the Incas were so religious that they say very few were punished for noncompliance, even though great care was taken to keep track of religious observances. Certainly it was no easy matter to comply. Here is an example: For those selected to sacrifice their child, though this was an only child, it was a major offense to show any signs of sadness; on the contrary, they were obliged to do it with gestures of happiness and satisfaction, as if they were taking their children to bestow upon them a very important reward.

The most notable aspect of this religion is how they had noth-ing written down to learn and keep. They made up for this short-coming by memorizing everything so exactly that it seems as if these things were carved into the Indian's bones. For this purpose alone the Incas had more than a thousand men in the city of Cuzco who did nothing but remember these things. Along with these men others were raised from youth by them, and these youngsters were trained so that these things would not be forgotten. I certainly do not believe myself that such care in preserving their religion and remembering their opinions and shrines was taken by the ancient pagans nor any other people. Those responsible for this duty were normally old priests or attendants of temples, and they did this work with great care. Whenever one of them was questioned alone he would give an explanation and tell about the powers said to be possessed by the *guaca* that he was responsible for, the solemnities and words necessary to make sacrifices to it, and the offering that was to be given to it. He would promise high hopes for good for-tune, telling of other similar cases that he would make up in order to add to the reputation of his shrine. And since it is a fact that whatever does not follow the true path of God is weak and groundless, in many respects these Indians had their accounts more whitewashed to cover up the mistakes than the pagan philosophers and poets. Certainly it would not be possible to ask them for the full rationale for everything because they lacked sufficient insight. They did not even know the grounds on which they relied for their opinions. At the most, they considered the main cause to be the custom of their ancestors, which they held to be such an inviolable law for many things that some of them did not know how to give any other explanation, and if they did give any, though they were in agreement on the form, solemnity, and superstitions, they dis-agreed on the rationale. This is because they did not have any writ-ings, and thus the rationale and motives of their ancestors were lost. Later they accepted the views that they found about things pertaining to religion, and each one added whatever struck his fancy. The ones who concerned themselves with such matters were a small group of respected nobles. The common people did not take the trouble to sort out explanations for things; they generally fol-lowed the respected nobles, did as they were told, and did what they saw other people do. Thus even the very people who dedicated themselves entirely to their religion could not remember the begin-ning of most of their erroneous views. Without a doubt, the begin-ning must have been a very long time ago because so many things could not be invented in a short time and not all together. Moreover, the people could not assume such burdensome duties unless a long period of time was taken and a little bit was added during each succeeding age.

Apart from these people who were dedicated to their vain religious services and to maintaining their rites and ceremonies, very few of the other people had any idea about these things, nor did they know any of the rationale and motives for establishing them. The other people just did what was mandated and came to the *guacas* and shrines with sacrifices, without question. The most illustrious personages of the Inca lineage were the main exception because they achieved greater powers of reasoning in their views, and they expressed their ideas in a more orderly fashion than anyone else. Nevertheless, it was only possible to discuss this matter with a few of them.

These Indians used two names to designate their gods; one of the names was *vilca* and the other *guaca*. Both of them are used in the same way and mean not only any god or idol, but also all places of worship, such as temples, graves, and any other place that was venerated and where sacrifices were made. Therefore, I will use either word in this treatise, especially the word *guaca*, which was the most commonly used by the Indians, with the same variety of meanings used by them.

Chapter 2: Of the opinions and fables that these people had concerning their origin, the beginning of the world, and the Universal Flood, along with the guacas *that came to be as a result of these events*

The whole basis of any religion and divine worship hinges on a knowledge of the first cause, whether it be the true cause or some false or imaginary one, from which men believe that they originated and on which they depend for their preservation, and it also hinges on an understanding of the final state that awaits them after this life. For that reason, I decided to begin this treatise about the knowledge and belief, on which these Indians based their opinions, of those two things [first cause and afterlife] by putting down in this chapter the views that they had concerning the origins of man, and in the following one what they thought about life after death. All of the Indian nations of this Kingdom of Peru agreed that man's beginning was followed by a Universal Flood in which everyone perished except a very few who were saved by the Creator's divine providence in order for them to repopulate the world. On this point they are very confused because they do not distinguish the creation of the world from its restoration after the Flood had passed.[5] Some place Creation before the Flood, but the majority confuse Creation with the Flood and the restoration that came afterward. Thus they trace man's beginning to those who were saved from the waters of the Flood. With regard to who those people may have been and where they escaped from that great inundation, they tell a thousand absurd stories. Each nation claims for itself the honor of having been the first people and says that everyone else came from them.

There are three or four fables that are told by the people of several provinces. Since these are the most important and the ones most generally accepted on this matter, I will put them down here. Without mentioning the Flood, some say that there was a Creator of the Universe who created the sky and the earth with the diverse

nations of men that inhabit it. They say that after having put all
the things he created in order and making sure that each one had
its own proper place, he went from Tiaguanaco up to heaven. Others
deny that this happened at Tiaguanaco, and they say that the Creator stationed himself in a high place and from there he made man
and the other living creatures. However, there are as many opinions about where this place may be as there are provinces and nations in this kingdom. In fact each nation wished to place creation
somewhere within its own lands. The inhabitants of Collao are divided into two opposing views. Some hold that creation happened
in Tiaguanaco; others place it on the Island of Titicaca, which is
located on the great Lake Chucuito [Titicaca]. Actually, both places
fall within the Diocese of Chuquiabo.

The inhabitants of the coastal plains hold that creation took
place at Pachacama, a coastal town four leagues from the city of
Lima. The common people consider this to be more credible because of the etymology of the name Pachacama, which means creator of the world. This name is still used today, and in this town
there was a magnificent temple. Others believe that creation took
place on a high hill called Huanacauri, which is located near Cuzco.
The people from the provinces of Quito say that the Creator came
across the North Sea and passed through all this land creating men,
assigning provinces, and distributing languages. And many other
nations say so many other things in this vein that it would take too
long to tell about all of them. It is said that from one of the places
mentioned above or from some place referred to by other people,
the Creator started bringing forth all things. Some believe that
creation came forth from nothing, others hold that it came from
clay, and others that man was formed from stone and the animals
and birds from the leaves of trees. They go on to say that the Creator gave man the skills he needed to cultivate the land, and they
tell a thousand absurd stories about this Creator. For instance, it is
said that he did not have any joints in any part of his body, that he
was very swift, that he could break the earth with the end of a staff
and then the land would be cultivated and prepared for planting. It
was also said that his word alone could make maize or any other
vegetable grow, and they told an infinite number of other such
imaginary tales.

The other fables that they have on this subject place the origin
of man at about the time of the Flood. On the subject of the Flood
these Indians had ample information. However, the only explanation that they give for the Flood is that it was caused by the will of

Viracocha. In addition, they were convinced that since the world was brought to an end by water at that time, it would certainly come to an end again due to one of these three causes: hunger, pestilence, or fire. With respect to the Flood, there are considerable discrepancies about the exact place where the waters first receded and man began to populate and about who restored the human race. But since they are so much in the dark and deluded on this matter, lacking any other basis than the one they give for other matters pertaining to their religion, each one makes up whatever happens to suit his fancy. Some hold that when the waters started to recede, the first land that appeared was the Island of Titicaca. They state that the Sun hid there while the Flood lasted and that as the Flood got over, the Sun was seen there before it was seen any-place else. Other nations indicate that these things happened in other places, and each one imagines all sorts of foolishness. Almost all of them agree that all the people and all things created perished in the Flood because the water covered the highest peaks in the world. Therefore, nothing remained alive except one man and one woman who got into a drum that floated on the water without sinking. As the water decreased, the drum came down at Tiaguanaco.

Others say that after the Flood, in which everyone perished, in Tiaguanaco the Creator used clay to form all the nations that there are in this land; he painted each one with the clothing to be used by that nation, and he also gave each nation the language they were to speak, the songs they were to sing, as well as the foods, seeds, and vegetables with which they were to sustain themselves. This done, the Creator ordered them to go down beneath the earth, each nation by itself, so that they could emerge from there at the places where he ordered them to do so. Some of them were to come out of caves, others out of hills, springs, lakes, tree trunks, and others from still other different places. Thus each province started to worship their place [of origin] as a major *guaca* because their lineage had originated there. In addition, they held their earliest ancestors to be gods, and they put images of them in the places mentioned above. Thus each nation dressed in the clothing that they painted on their *guaca*. In addition, they say that after having begot their offspring, those same men in the same places as before changed into a variety of things, some into falcons, condors, and other birds and animals. For this reason, each nation's *guacas* and idols were shaped like different objects, birds, or animals.

Other nations believed that in the waters of the Flood everyone perished, except for some people who were able to escape by going into caves, up trees, or on top of hills. Only a few escaped, and they repopulated the world. Since they were saved in those places, each place was designated a shrine. Moreover, they put idols of stone, silver, and other metals there to commemorate those who escaped, and each idol was given the name of the one whom they boasted about being their ancestor. They adored these idols like their parents and protectors, and each nation offered sacrifices to them of the things they used.

The natives of the province of Cañaribamba, in the Diocese of Quito, say that two young brothers were saved from the Flood on a high mountain called Huacayñan located in their land, and after the Flood had passed and the provisions that they had gathered there were depleted, they went out into the surrounding area to look for something to eat. Meanwhile, their dwelling, which was a small hut that they had constructed so as to have a place to take shelter, was left unattended. During this time, they sustained themselves on roots and herbs, and for some time they suffered great privations and often went hungry. However, on returning to their hut one day, dead tired from searching for food, they found it well supplied with tasty foods and plenty of *chicha*. They had no idea either where it came from or who had bestowed such a notable gift on them. They were amazed at this, and they looked carefully to see if anyone would appear around there. They wanted to know who had aided them in such times of need, but since they did not find any trace of people, they sat down to eat, and for the time being they satisfied their hunger. Ten or twelve days passed in this same fashion, and they always found their shack as well supplied with food as it was the first day. At the end of this time, they were curious to find out who was treating them so well. Thus they agreed that one of them would remain hidden in the house. For their purpose, they made a hole in the darkest part of the shack. One of them hid in the hole, while the other went out to occupy himself in the countryside. During this time, the one who was keeping watch saw two *guacamayas* (birds similar to parrots)[6] enter through the door, and after they got inside, they were transformed into two beautiful *pallas*, which means noble woman of royal lineage. They were beautifully dressed in the manner of the Cañares women; they had long, well-kept hair, with beautiful bands wrapped around their foreheads. As soon as they had taken off their *llicllas*, which are their mantles, they started to prepare a meal with what they had brought. At this moment the young man came out from his hiding place; he greeted them courteously, and started to engage them in conversation. However, they became disturbed and bewildered because they had been seen. Without answering a single word, they hurriedly left the house. Changing into their original form of *guacamayas*, they flew off without leaving anything to eat that day. When the young man found himself alone and realized that his ruse had not turned out as he had hoped, he started to bemoan the outcome and curse his misfortune. While he was still feeling so distressed, the other brother arrived from his outing. When he found out what had happened, he scolded his brother angrily, accusing him of being a coward and a man without spirit or valor for having missed such an excellent opportunity. At last both decided to remain hidden at home in order to find out if the *guacamayas* would return. Three days later the *guacamayas* came back as they were accustomed to before, and on entering through the door, they changed into humans. Thus two beautiful ladies appeared, and they started to make the preparations for dinner. The young men, who were lying in wait, let them alone for a while so that they would feel secure. Then the men suddenly burst out, blocking the doorway, and with no further ado, they embraced the ladies, who became too bewildered to turn themselves into birds. The ladies started to scream angrily, and they struggled to break loose. But at last, by complimentary and loving words, the young men calmed them down. When they saw that the ladies were at ease, the young men pleaded earnestly with the ladies to tell about their family and explain why they had come to do that good deed for them. Since they were in a calm and sociable mood by now, the ladies answered that Ticciviracocha had ordered them to perform that task, coming to the aid of the young men in that dire situation so they would not die of hunger. In conclusion, the ladies stayed to become the wives of the young men, and it is said that their offspring populated the province of the Cañares. Thus for this nation, the hill named Huacayñan mentioned above was known as a *guaca* and a famous shrine, and the *guacamayas* were important gods. The feathers of these birds were used by them to adorn themselves for their festivities, and they worshiped idols made in the image of these birds. Not many years ago, in this city of Lima, I saw a small copper pillar with two *guacamayas* also made of copper perched on top. This piece had been brought from the province of Cañaribamba mentioned above where the Cañares Indians, in keeping with their paganism, worshiped these copper birds as gods in memory of the fable that has just been told.

The Indians of Ancasmarca, within the Cuzco district, had the following fable. They say that when the Flood was threatening to come, one month before, the llamas, or sheep of the land, became so sad that they stopped eating during the day and they spent the nights looking at the stars. This became so evident that one herder took special note of them, and he asked them why they were so sad. They answered by telling him to look at a certain group of stars that they pointed out to him. These stars were meeting together and discussing the fact that the world was going to be destroyed by water. Upon hearing this, the herder discussed the matter with his sons and daughters, who were six in number, and they decided to gather together as much food and livestock as possible. Having taken this precaution, they went up on top of a high hill called Ancasmarca. And it is said that as the waters kept rising and flooding the land, the hill mentioned here kept rising up in such a way that it was never covered by the waters. Later, as the waters were receding, the hill came back down until it remained in its original place. From the children of that herder, who escaped there, this province was repopulated.

Others say that before the beginning of the Flood, since the Creator had the intention of restoring the world, he arranged that three or four persons in each province would be warned about what was going to happen. Those were some of the very best and most important people. They were warned so that they could get into safe places and not perish. They believe that this was done and that the people that exist now came from those who were saved from the Flood.

In Chapter 3 of the preceding book,[7] I have already told the story the Incas had about their origin and lineage and how they escaped the Flood. The Incas worshiped the cave of Pacaritampu as an important shrine because in that place their ancestors had escaped from the destruction of the world. The Incas believed that the earth was repopulated by their ancestors and that all peoples in the world descended from them. However, they are not always in agreement because some say that the Incas who came out of that cave were created by God there; others disagree, saying that when the Flood came, the Incas went into the cave and covered the entrance well. In this way they escaped from the waters. Both the Incas and the other nations of this kingdom told these stories and other such nonsense. To avoid going into too much detail, I will not include any more here. The ones that have already been told are sufficient for my purpose here. The reason why these blind people accepted all this was because they never knew about the true God, and they gave a free reign to all sorts of vices. Another contributing factor was their lack of any kind of writing. If they had had a system of writing, they might not have made such dim-witted errors.

What I infer from these fabrications with respect to the present treatise is that many shrines and *guacas* originated from them, and each province has its own shrine, which was the place where they thought the originators of each nation were saved. These places were well known in each province, and they were worshiped with all kinds of sacrifices. The objective that they had in worshiping these places was the preservation and propagation of the people from that province. Likewise, originating from this same idea were the major gods and patrons of the provinces, who were the ones that escaped from the Flood in the places mentioned above. Although it is true that nowhere did the Indians have the bodies of these ancestors because the whole thing was imaginary, the devil found a way to deceive them also. He made them think that at the end of their lives, which they say were very long, their ancestors were changed into stones, and they worshiped these stones and offered sacrifices to them instead of worshiping their ancestor's bodies.

The reason why these nations of Peru came to believe so much nonsense about their origin was caused by the ambition of the Incas. They were the first ones to worship the cave of Pacaritampu as the beginning of their lineage. They claimed that all people came from there, and that for this reason all people were their vassals and obliged to serve them. The Incas made this claim in their conquests, and the result was this multitude of shrines and gods. Each province had its own shrine which was consecrated in the same way as the Incas had done with the one at Pacaritampu. Though the other nations did not deny the Flood, they explained it differently in order to avoid submitting to Inca rule. They defended themselves by saying that they did not have to recognize the Incas because they were not descended from them. After the Flood, new people appeared in every province, and these new people repopulated the land. The people were persuaded to adopt this explanation by their elders and sorcerers, and in order to lend veracity and substance to the explanation, they pointed out the places and told how their ancestors had been saved. Since the Incas paid their respects to the cave of Pacaritampu, the other nations also worshiped the place that was designated for the purpose mentioned. Nevertheless, none of the other nations paid their respects in such an orderly fashion as the Incas, nor did they offer such valuable sacrifices. Thus a shrine [similar to Pacaritampu] will be found in every province, and using their imagination, each nation told their story in a different way.

Chapter 3: Of the opinions that these Indians had with regard to the soul and the other life after this one

With regard to this matter, there were many differing opinions. However, there are two substantial things on which they all agreed with no discrepancies among them (so far as this can be determined). The first was knowing about the immortality of the soul and that man is composed of more than what meets the eye. The other thing was that good people would be given a heavenly reward and bad people would be punished after this life. The first thing was shown by the great care they took in preparing and adorning their graves. This included putting along with the deceased all of his property, women, servants, and an ample supply of food and drink. The second thing was shown by the teachings, exhortations, and reprimands which were given by their priests and teachers to the common people in order to deliver them from evil and persuade them to be good. Sometimes the priests threatened them with punishment, and other times they persuaded them by offering the reward of the other life. However, there was a lot of foolishness and many differences in the way they gave out these heavenly rewards and punishments. And without the light of faith, it was impossible for them to ascertain the truth.

Some believed that after the soul left the body, if the person had been good, that person would become a star, and in this way all the stars in the heavens were born, and there the good people enjoyed heavenly bliss. If a person had been bad, that person went to a certain place where he would suffer eternal punishment. There were also discrepancies about where and how the punishments were given, and each one made up whatever suited his fancy. Regarding this, nothing was fixed, established, or obligatory. Like unenlightened people, they were prone to vacillate and invent something new every day, which is in keeping with human frailty. Others held that the souls that left human bodies in some places came back to be born again in other places and that when these souls left this life for good (for they said that the world must come to an end), the souls would receive a reward or punishment, according to what they deserved. Other nations thought that the souls of the deceased remained in this world and that in some cases the souls were happy and in others afflicted. Thus they went wandering around alone, suffering from hunger, thirst, chills, heat, and fatigue. These souls or their apparitions would customarily visit the members of their family and other people as a sign that those visited were to die or that some evil was to befall them. They believed that the souls would get hungry and thirsty and have other needs. On the assumption that the deceased would avail themselves of these things, the people offered them food, drink, clothing, and other things at their graves. The belief in these needs is why they were so careful to celebrate the birthdays of the deceased.

The Incas state that the souls of those who have been good go to heaven and enjoy perpetual bliss. And they say that this means being with the Sun in places of great delight which were set aside for this purpose by Viracocha. Some believed that in heaven there would be no eating, drinking, sleeping, nor would there be women, for there would be no need for any of this. However, the majority held the opposite opinion, and they believed that those who went to heaven would eat and drink splendidly of the excellent foods that the Creator had ready for them and of the foods burned here by their relatives and friends as an offering in their honor. For this reason, they were so careful in offering food and drink to their deceased, especially to the embalmed bodies of their nobles. They would speak to these bodies as if they were alive, saying to them, "When you were alive you would always eat and drink of these tasty dishes and beverages. Let your soul receive them now and wherever it may be, let it partake of them." And they believed that this took place, that wherever the souls happened to be, they would eat the dishes that were offered to them, just as they had done before their death. And so that this error would be more ingrained in them, sometimes, when it was permitted by the will of God, the devil took the shape of some important man who had already died. Posing in the same dress and physique as when the man was alive, with his finery and retinue, the devil would appear before his relatives and acquaintances, explaining to them that the deceased was in some other kingdom and that he was happy and enjoying himself the way they saw him there. Owing to the devil's statement and illusions, the relatives believed those false appearances were really true. Thus they would become more careful in maintaining the service and comfort of the deceased. This would give the living high hopes of going to join the deceased where they would enjoy that bliss after this life, and it would temper the sadness that death brought them. Thus, when they were near death, they would entrust their homes and families to their relatives, asking them to comply with their requests and assuring them that they would see them again from heaven.

They were also convinced that the inferno exists for bad people and that demons tormented them there. These demons were described as very ugly and terrifying. The location of the inferno was said to be beneath the earth and was described as narrow and cramped. Moreover, those who go there suffer from hunger and thirst, and they are made to eat pieces of charcoal, snakes, toads, and other sickening vermin. They also had to drink muddy, foul-smelling water. The souls of the condemned had nothing else on which to sustain themselves, and it is said that their punishment was perpetual.

With regard to the merits that they needed to have in order to be admitted to heaven and the faults for which they would be condemned, they also disagree. Although they did agree that the bad people would be condemned and the good people would be saved, they were unable to distinguish the good people from the bad ones. The devil persuaded them that the nobility were always good, and even though their customs were depraved, it was impossible to condemn the nobles. The inferno was only for the common people who had no social rank, such as thieves and poor people, sorcerers who used herbs to kill, other people like them, and especially for those who disobeyed the laws of the king or spoke ill of the Sun or the *guacas*. However, these sins were not committed by the members of Inca lineage, who were all nobles. Moreover, they paid no attention to any other kinds of sins.

No nation was found among these Indians that mentioned the resurrection of the body, nor did they believe in any way that the body would ever become anything. This is not surprising because it is a point that cannot be understood by natural reason. Since they did not realize that there was anything other than heaven and hell [like purgatory], they did not make any sacrifices or intercessions for the souls of the deceased. They explained this by saying that if they were in heaven, they had no need of it, and if they were in the inferno, it would do them no good.

Chapter 4: Of the god Viracocha, who was held by these Indians to be the supreme lord and creator of all things

In the midst of their dense, dark ignorance, the light of reason did shine to some extent on these Indians. This is borne out by the fact that they came to believe in a universal creator god who was the sovereign lord and governor of all things. Nevertheless, their knowledge was so limited that they did not even have a proper noun to name this god. All the names that they gave him were metaphors, as I will explain later. For this reason, in the catechisms which are made to instruct the Indians in the Christian doctrine, our own term *Dios* [God] is used, and we always use it when we are speaking to them because there is no word in their language which corresponds exactly to our word *Dios*. And the Christian Indians themselves use the word *Dios* now as a part of their language, just as we use it ourselves. However, the Indians who do not know Spanish well alter the pronunciation somewhat. This is because they had no *d* in their language, and in place of it they used the letter *t*. Thus instead of saying *Dios*, they usually pronounce the word *Tios*.

Furthermore, this meager knowledge that they had of God was muddled with an infinite variety of illusions and errors. They imagined and attributed many things to him which are inappropriate and unworthy of his very noble nature. They also accepted along with the adoration of the Supreme Lord, that of innumerable other things, which they venerated with equal respect and reverence. Nevertheless, they did confess that the other gods were the Creator's servants and ministers, who acted as intercessors for him. Thus when they spoke with the Creator, they used different words, attributing to him power and authority over all things, while the other gods were considered to be lords over more limited domains. Each one had his own jurisdiction according to his specific title and patronage. The Indians gave the first cause names and titles of great excellence. The two most honorable and widely used were Viracocha and Pachayachachic, both figurative and most emphatic. Before or after the first one, they would usually place some other words, saying sometimes Ticci Viracocha, and other times Viracocha Yachachic. The title Ticci Viracocha was considered to be mysterious; translated, it signifies "divine origin." The name Pacha-yachachic means "Creator of the World," and Viracocha Yachachic has the same meaning.[8]

For as long as these Indians can remember, the account of Vira-cocha has been handed down from person to person, and this name was always greatly venerated. This is illustrated by the fact that the father of the Inca Yupanqui[9] took the name Viracocha Inca for him-self, and no other king before or after adopted this name, and (so they say) the fact that he had taken this name was not well received, even though he explained that his reason for doing so was that Viracocha himself had ordered it. Although this god Viracocha was much venerated before the time of the above-mentioned Inca and sacrifices were regularly made to him, Viracocha was not held to be superior to the Sun until the time of this Inca who adopted his name. What caused this king to order that the god Viracocha be preferred to all others and worshiped as universal god and supreme lord was the victory this Inca achieved over the Chancas,[10] as is explained in Chapter 5 of the previous book. The same thing was decreed later by his son Pachacutic, because it was ordered by his father and for other reasons which we mentioned in Chapter 6 of the book cited above.[11]

As a result of their decree, from the time of the two kings men-tioned above, Viracocha was held to be the universal god, and at all of the solemn festivals in which the statues of the gods were brought out in public, the statues of the Sun, the Moon, and the Stars made obeisance and did reverence to the statue of Viracocha. From then on the image of Viracocha which was located in the Temple of the Sun was put in the highest and most prominent place, and special sacrifices were made to it. Moreover, it was worthy of note that although Pachacutic, ninth king of the Incas, set aside *chacaras* [fields] and livestock for the Sun, the Thunder, and the rest of the *guacas*, he did not assign any lands to Viracocha. And the follow-ing explanation is given. Since Viracocha was the universal lord of all things, there was no need to set anything aside for him. Goods were distributed to the other gods so that from them sacrifices could be made to the Creator, and the other gods could act as inter-cessors and mediators between the Creator and man.

In the city of Cuzco there was a temple called Quishuarcancha, dedicated to the god Viracocha. The temple was built for him by Pachacutic, and on his orders a statue of Viracocha was put in this temple. The statue was in human form, about the size of a ten-year-old boy, and it was made entirely of solid gold of very high quality. In addition to this one, in the temple called Coricancha, which was dedicated to the Sun, among the statues of the other gods there was another statue of Viracocha, and this one was made of mantles. During the major festivals, this statue was brought out in public along with the other idols. The Indians were profoundly devoted to Viracocha, and the reason why this devotion became so deeply rooted was that the Inca had told them before the battle with the Chancas that Viracocha promised them victory as a sign of his power. Since it turned out as promised, and the Inca had been almost alone when Viracocha made the promise, it struck them as a matter of great mystery. Thus this incident, along with the many sacrifices and veneration that the Incas started to offer Viracocha, was the reason why he came to be held in such high esteem.[12]

Chapter 5: Of their practice of Sun worship

The Indians assumed that Viracocha was the universal god, and they believed that Viracocha had designated for each thing created a secondary cause that would look after the growth and preservation of each species. As a result of this opinion there originated not only as many gods as there are things which are necessary to sustain human life, but also gods for all things that could be harmful. The devil was not satisfied merely to make them worship the universal causes, whose operations we experience clearly in each created thing. He influenced them to such an extent in this respect that he made them subservient to as many specific things as there are that bring any benefit or danger to them. For instance, [they worshiped] the spring that gave them water to drink and to irrigate their fields; the sea which provided them with fish; they even venerated wild beasts and vermin so that these creatures would not do them any harm.

With the exception of Viracocha, the god that was most highly respected by them was the Sun, which stood out among all other things. Sun worship grew much because of the Incas' diligence. Since they boasted of being children of the Sun, the Incas made every effort to legitimize and enhance Sun worship with more brilliant services, a larger number of priests, and more frequent offerings and sacrifices. Little effort was necessary to establish the Sun's reputation among these people. They were highly respectful of these secondary causes because of the good they received from them. In the case of the Sun, the effects that this planet produces are so obviously beneficial for mankind that the people themselves already held it in high esteem. The authority and example of the Incas only served to make the exterior demonstrations of veneration more elaborate and costly. They believed that Pachayachachic had given the Sun the power to raise all foods together with the earth. Thus the Sun was the most important *guaca* of all, except for Viracocha. This is why the Sun was called Apu Inti, which means "Lord Sun." They visualized the Sun in their imagination as if it were a man, and consequently they said that the Moon was his wife and the stars were the daughters of them both.

The Sun was so venerated throughout this entire Inca Empire that I doubt that there has ever been any place where idolatry was so widespread, respected, and served. This is clearly illustrated by the fact that there was no other god to whom so many and such magnificent temples were dedicated. There was no major town that did not have a Sun temple with ample service of priests and *mama-conas*[13] and a large income to sustain them. Above all, the Sun temple was always the most sumptuous. And the most magnificent temple of all was the one called Coricancha that the Incas had built at their court. This temple housed their most important and highly venerated image. It was a solid piece, called Punchau, which means "the day," and it was entirely made of the finest gold with an exquisite display of jewels. It was shaped like a human face surrounded by sunrays, as we always depict the sun ourselves. The image was placed in such a way as to face toward the east, and as the sun rose it would strike the image. Since it was a sheet of the finest metal, the sunrays reflected off it, shining with such brightness that it looked like the sun. The Indians said that along with its light the sun transmitted its power.[14] And that beautiful sheet of gold was a soldier's share of the plunder that the Spaniards took from that luxurious temple, the Coricancha. In those days, the play was for high stakes, and the soldier lost the gold image in a single night of gambling. This event was the origin of a proverb which in Peru is said of big gamblers, and this is what they say: "He plays away the sun before it rises." That soldier's name was Manso Serra. He was one of the prominent citizens of Cuzco, where I met one of his sons named Juan Serra.

Within the temple of the Coricancha itself they had another statue of the Sun which was full of ground-up gold mixed with ashes and dust of the hearts of the Inca kings. For this idol there was a chair also of gold, and it weighed more than the idol. Manco Inca took this idol with him when he withdrew to Bilcabamba [Vilcabamba], and the idol was found by the Spaniards when they conquered that province and took Tupa Amaro Inca prisoner.

Moreover, there were three other statues of the Sun in the same temple. These statues were made from thick, closely woven mantles in such a way that they would stand up with no special device to hold them. Each one had a *llauto* band around its head. These bands were made of thick wool braids in the form of a mitre, except that they were wrapped tightly all around the head. The statues also had very large earplugs like the ones worn by the Incas. Some say that these three figures were made because at one time three suns were seen in the sky. Others say that one of them was for the Sun itself, the other for the day, and the third for the power to grow things. There were also some among them who were of the opinion that the most important statue represented the Sun, and the others were his guards. Each one had its own name. The first was called Apu Inti, the second one Churi Inti, and the third Inti Guauqui. They had special attendants for each one, and many people participated in making special sacrifices for each one. During the festivals and general sacrifices, all their statues were brought out by their priests and placed in the square along with the image of Viracocha. The statue of the Sun was brought out by a priest with a long tunic worn over his ordinary garments; the tunic reached down to his ankles, and it had decorative tassles all the way around the edge forming a fringe about the width of one hand. Each of the other statues had in its hand a shaft larger than a halberd, and axe heads of gold were mounted on the shafts to form a kind of cudgel. These shafts were covered with a full sheath, like a sleeve. More-over, these shafts were adorned all around with gold bands, and the Indians said that the shafts were the Sun's weapons. The statue of the Sun was seated in the center of the square on a small bench which was completely covered with mantles made of fine, colorful feather cloth. The other two statues were stationed on each side with their shafts held up.

They felt that the eclipse of the Sun was a grave matter, and when an eclipse occurred, they consulted with their diviners about its significance. Once they were certain of the effects implied by the eclipse, they made large and expensive sacrifices, including in them several images of gold and silver. In addition they would kill much livestock and many boys and girls. Normally, the sorcerers would pretend that the eclipse foretold the death of some prince and indicated that the Sun went into mourning because he had nothing to do in the world. When this happened, all of the women dedicated to the Sun would go on long fasts, wear clothing that showed their sadness, and offer frequent sacrifices. The Inca would withdraw to a secret place, and there, removed from all conversation, he would fast for many days. During the time of the Inca's fasting, no fires would be lit in the city.

Fourteen universally worshiped shrines came about as a conse-quence of their Sun worship. These were the markers or pillars called Sucanca that indicated the months of the year. These pillars were considered very important, and sacrifices were offered to them at the same time as they were made for the other *guacas* and in places designated for this purpose. These sacrifices were made in the fol-lowing way. After the sacrifices were taken to the other *guacas* in the order in which they were located along the *ceques*,[15] as will be explained in the proper place,[16] what was left over was offered to these markers. This was because the markers were not located in the same order as the other shrines but were distributed according to the course of the Sun, and each one came with a sacrifice to the marker-shrine located nearest to his *ceque*.

Chapter 6: How they considered the Moon and the Stars to be deities and the way they worshiped them

After the Sun, the Moon and the Stars follow, according to their natural order, and not the order that the Indians had in worshiping them because if we were to go by their worship, this place must be reserved for the Thunder. In authority and honor the Thunder ranked second after the Sun, as we will soon see. The Moon was considered to be a deity for the same reasons that led them to respect the Sun—that is, owing to the Moon's admirable beauty and the great benefits that she bestows on the world. They imagined that the Moon looked like a woman, and the statue of the Moon that they had in the Temple of the Sun was in the form of a woman. This statue was cared for by women who held the rank of priestess, and when the statue was taken outside, these women themselves carried it on their shoulders. They had as many foolish ideas about the eclipse of the Moon as they did about that of the Sun. They said that when there was an eclipse of the Moon a [mountain] lion or a serpent was attacking in order to tear her apart, and for that reason they shouted at the top of their voices and whipped their dogs so that they would bark and howl. The men made ready for war by blowing their trumpets, beating their drums, and yelling as loud as they could. They hurled arrows and spears at the Moon, and they made menacing gestures with their spears, as if they were going to wound the lion and the serpent. They said that this was done to frighten the lion and the serpent so that they would not tear the Moon apart.

This they did because they understood that if the lion accomplished his aim, the world would be left in darkness. This custom was so ingrained in their minds that even though they have been Christians for many years and always heard sermons against this custom, they have not forsaken it entirely. In fact they still shout loudly when there is an eclipse of the moon. However, today they do it only because it is such an ancient custom among them, not because of the fantasy upon which it was originally based. In order to encourage them to forsake this custom, some of their priests would generally forewarn them of the coming of the eclipses, notifying them beforehand so that they would be persuaded that it was a natural phenomenon and not a supernatural mystery as they believed. And this measure has produced very fruitful results. In addition, the Spaniards have acquired the reputation of being very wise because the Indians are extremely impressed by the fact that we are capable of predicting the eclipses with such precision that we let them know not only the night that one will occur but even the exact time that it will begin, the amount of the moon that will be darkened, and how long it will last. Since they do not understand the causes of such an admirable phenomenon, they are struck dumb when they see that we can predict an eclipse.

The worship of the stars was the result of their opinion that the creator had designated a second cause which was to look after the preservation of each kind of thing. In accordance with this belief, they thought that there was a patron in heaven for each of the animals and birds that provided for their preservation and increase. This function was attributed to several constellations of stars. And they thought that all of these patrons came from that group of small stars commonly known as the Pleiades, which these Indians called Collca, and the power that conserved the animals and birds flowed from this group of stars. For this reason it was called "mother," and it was universally considered to be a major *guaca* by all of the *ayllos*[17] and families. They were all familiar with it, and those Indians who were informed about such matters kept better track of its course all year long than that of any of the other stars. However, they did not make use of it for anything else, nor did they mention that it had any other powers. Nevertheless, all the provinces offered great sacrifices to it. The rest of the stars were worshiped only by those who considered that they had need of them, according to the functions that they attributed to them, and they were the only ones who were familiar with them, kept track of them, and made offerings to them. The others did not do any of these things, nor did they feel any obligation to do so. The worship of each star was carried out in the following way.

All herders respected and made sacrifices to the constellation called Lira by the astronomers and known to the Indians as Urcuchillay. They said it was a parti-colored ram that took care of their livestock. Two other small stars that are below it, forming the letter T, were said to be the animal's feet and head. The herders also worshiped another one called Catachillay which is found nearby and is also rather large and yet another smaller one close to it. They pretended that these stars were a llama with its lamb which both came from Urcuchillay.

Those Indians who lived in the forests and *yunca* lands worshiped and made sacrifices to another star that they call Chuquichinchay, which they say is a tiger [jaguar] and was thought to watch over tigers, bears, and lions. As sacrifices were offered to it, they requested that these wild animals do them no harm. Those who needed to travel through dense woodlands also entrusted themselves to this star for the same reason as those who lived there.

They took great care in worshiping another star called Machacuay. They thought that this star watched over snakes, serpents, and vipers. This is because it looks like a snake when lightning flashes. In addition to this, the Incas had snakes for weapons, and they even raised them and kept them here for *guacas*, especially the people in the province of Chinchaysuyu. In the district of Cuzco, three snakes made of thin strips of metal were found, all wound together around a pole. These snakes had their own temple, *chacara*, and attendants to watch over them and take care of the sacrifice, which was an ordinary one. They say that people suffering from snake bite came there. The origin of this is a long fable that they tell. Nevertheless, it was a highly esteemed shrine. Finally, they worshiped this star for the same reason as the others: so that serpents and vipers would do them no harm. They also respected another star which they called Ancochinchay. They said it looked after the welfare of other animals.

In short, they identified a star in the sky for every species of animal, and for this reason they worshiped many stars, had names for them, and made sacrifices to them. Here are the names of some of the other stars: Topatoraca, Chacana, Mirco, Mamana, Miquiquiray, Quiantopa, and others. In fact, they had names for all the stars of the first magnitude, the morning and evening star [Venus], and the most noteworthy signs and planets. Although I have not mentioned the general causes, for every one of these things the unfortunate Indians told fables and happenings that were invented by those who were in charge of these sacrifices. Since these attendants ate and sustained themselves from these sacrifices, they found it necessary to make up miraculous things which were handed down by them from person to person, in order to maintain the people's devotion [to their shrines].

Chapter 7: Of their worship of the Thunder, the Sea, and the Earth

In accordance with the assumption stated above, the Indians searched for the second cause of the water that falls from the heavens, and as a result they came to share the opinion that it was the Thunder and that he was in charge of providing them with water whenever he saw fit. After Viracocha and the Sun, this god was ranked in third place, with respect to their worship. They imagined that he was a man who lived in the sky and that he was made up of stars, with a war club in his left hand and a sling in his right hand. He dressed in shining garments which gave off the flashes of lightning when he whirled his sling, and the crack of this sling made the thunder, and he cracked his sling when he wanted it to rain. Moreover, they say that he passed across a very large river in the middle of the sky. They indicated that this river was the white band that we see down here called the Milky Way. Regarding this matter, they made up a great deal of foolishness that would be too detailed to include here. Anyway, they believed that from this river the Thunder drew the water that he would let fall down upon the earth. Since the Thunder was credited with the power to make it rain or hail, along with all the other things associated with the clouds and the realm of the sky where these imperfectly mixed bodies are formed, under the name of the Thunder or as his adherents, they worshiped thunderbolts, lightning, rainbows, rain, hail, and even storms and whirlwinds.

The Thunder had three names: the first and most important was Chuqui Illa, which means the radiance of gold; the second was Catu Illa, and the third Inti Illapa. They made a statue of mantles in the same manner as those of the Sun. It was said that the Thunder had a son and a brother, and this was explained by each one in any way he saw fit. These statues were placed in the Temple of the Sun, and each one was on its own altar. During the major festivals, all three were placed near Viracocha, right by the statues of the Sun.

Each statue was given a *chacara* of its own and the service of *mamaconas*, attendants, and priests. They made sacrifices to Viracocha in the name of the Thunder when such sacrifices were made for the Sun and the Inca. The Thunder also had a separate temple in the Totocache district. Inside the temple there was a gold statue of the Thunder placed on a litter of the same metal. This statue was made by the Inca Pachacuti in honor of the Thunder, and he called the statue Inti Illapa. Pachacuti took this statue as a brother, and during his lifetime he carried it with him whenever he went to war. This idol was greatly venerated, and it was served in a very stately and ceremonious fashion.

Since there was general recognition of this god, he was represented by images, *guacas*, and shrines everywhere, and when it started to rain in one place before it did anywhere else, it was felt that the *guaca* of that town had gained greater approval. When there was a water shortage or when it started to freeze sooner than usual, the sorcerers cast lots, and once they determined the kind of sacrifice that they needed to make to the Thunder, all the people contributed, each one doing his part, in accordance with the amount that was assigned. Once everything was turned over to his priests and attendants, they divided it among themselves, and each one of them went separately up to the puna wasteland, to the highest place that they could find. There they made the sacrifice, saying certain words according to what they hoped to achieve. Once this was done, they returned and told the people how the Thunder had answered them, both regarding the decision he had made and how he would act on what they had asked of him, as well as the reason why he was angry and if he was pleased with that sacrifice or if he wanted them to offer more. Complete credence was given to this, and action was taken on it immediately. During the time of the sacrifices, they did a great deal of drinking and dancing, in addition to performing other ceremonies and superstitious acts. It was their custom whenever a woman gave birth in the country on a day when it was thundering, to offer the child that was born to the Thunder, and after the child grew up, he would dedicate himself to the priesthood of the Thunder. Many *guacas* and shrines originated from this idolatry because whenever any object, such as a stone or a piece of metal, differing from the others of its kind, was found to hold water when it rained, it was held as a proven fact that the Thunder had sent it as an object of worship.

The Sea was called Mamacocha, which is as if we were to say "mother of lakes and water." She was widely worshiped, especially by the inhabitants of the coastal plains, who were mostly fishermen. They asked the Sea not to become rough and to give them an abundance of fish. And when the highland Indians came down to the coast, as soon as they saw the sea, even though it was a long way off, they would make a reverent gesture to it.

They all worshiped the Earth also, and they called her Pacha-mama, which means "earth mother." And it was their custom to put a long stone in the middle of their fields or *chacaras* as an altar in honor of this goddess. They would pray to her before this altar-stone, call upon her, and ask her to protect their *chacaras* and make them fertile. The more fertile a field was, the more they respected her.

Chapter 8: Of the gods called

pururaucas

Descending in the order that we are following here to the things that are in the closest and most familiar to us, such as those that are made up of the elements that we call perfectly mixed, both animate and inanimate, the fact is that these Indians had specific gods for every kind of creature or thing within this whole category or list of perfectly mixed things—from the noblest of these creatures, which is man, to the lowest of them all.[18] Starting with man, I can tell you that these people believed that those who were saved from the Flood were gods, and they were respected as such. Besides them, this honor and title was given to almost innumerable other people; some of them actually did live in this world, while others were purely imaginary. The *pururaucas* belong to this second group, and I will discuss this topic only in this chapter. This name, *pururaucas*, means "hidden traitors," and the origin of the expression has already been explained in Chapter 5 of the previous book because the expression was made up by the Inca Viracocha.[19] There were a great many of these gods because of the story which the Inca used to introduce them. The Inca made his people believe that in spite of the fact that these gods had turned into stones after the war of the Chanca Indians, in all of the wars that he waged from then on these *pururaucas* reverted back to their own human form, and armed as he had seen them for the first time, they accompanied him and were the ones who would throw the enemy into confusion. This illusion had such an effect on the Indians that they all started to become fearful of the Incas. Thus it happened that from then on the fear inspired by the *pururaucas* was more effective than the fighting of the Inca's troops in all of their successful encounters because often the enemy would flee almost without putting up a fight.

There is no doubt that this opinion had a similar effect on the Inca's people; it made them take heart to know that there was someone to help them. Thus, when the Incas found themselves in a tight spot, their captains would call upon these gods, and they say the people were greatly encouraged by this. These pururaucas were deified, and their worship was introduced in the following way. When the Inca Viracocha saw the effects produced by this nonsense, in order to make it more convincing he explained to his people that in his dreams the *pururaucas* had complained, saying

that although they had done so much for him, very little attention
was paid to them. Even though they had turned into stones after
the Battle of the Chancas was over, they emerged from there to help
the Inca's people when it was necessary. They were badly treated out
in the fields and along the roads, and it was unfair that this should
take place. After all, it was very important for the Incas to appease
the *pururaucas* for their undertakings. Everyone agreed with the
Inca, and he ordered that a large and elaborate retinue be assembled. The Inca had himself carried on a litter along with his retinue
out through the countryside. He said that he knew the stones that
had been converted into the *pururaucas*; so he went around point-
ing out the ones that struck his fancy, which were at some distance
apart, and he named each one. Then he had them brought to Cuzco
with great dignity, where some of them were placed in the Temple
of the Sun, while others were placed in other places designated by
the Inca. He gave all of the stones people to serve them and oversee
their sacrifices. From then on these stones were worshiped as idols.
Whenever strangers came to Cuzco, they would be shown these
stones and told about their exploits. Then the strangers would be
persuaded to worship the stones. And the Incas had people delegated exclusively for this purpose. The stones were offered a great
number of sacrifices, especially when the Inca went to war or returned from one, during the coronations of the kings, and for other
major festivals that they celebrated. Although this name *pururaucas* was applied to all of these idols together, each one had its own
special name, and many of their names will appear ahead in the
account of the *guacas* and shrines of the city of Cuzco.[20]

Chapter 9: Of the statues and idols called guauques

During their lifetimes, all of the kings and lords of the Inca class were in the habit of each making a statue that depicted its owner, and with a certain solemnity and ceremonies they would take the statue for their brother, calling it *guauque*, which means brother. Some made the statue large; others made it small; still others made it the same size and shape as themselves. Some of the statues were made of gold, others of silver, wood, stone, or other materials. The kings gave their *guauques* a house and servants. They also assigned some farmland to support those who were in charge of each statue. From the day that they made their *guauques* their brothers, the Inca kings would order the people, especially those of their lineage and family unit, to treat the *guauques* with the same reverence as the king himself. These idols were greatly venerated during the lifetime of the lords whom they represented. After the death of the lords, the idols were kept with their bodies, and both the bodies and the idols were always respected and served equally. The idols were kept very well dressed, and during the less solemn festivals, when the occasion did not warrant bringing out the bodies of the lords, their *guauques* or images were brought out. This custom was so ancient that if it was not a fabrication of theirs, it must date from the time of their earliest recollections. Although initially it was only the practice of the kings and great lords, as time passed the custom was extended so much that any important man might have a *guauque*. During his lifetime he would have a statue made or designate a stone or idol, made of whatever material struck his fancy, and he would take it for his *guauque*. He would order the members of his family to treat the *guauque* as if it were him during his lifetime, and after his death his family was to continue to venerate the *guauque* in the same way. As a result, before long there were a great number of these idols in Cuzco and the surrounding area. And there would have been many more if it had not been for the custom of the majority to forsake the less important ones; the people would forget these after a time. However, the *guauques* of the Inca kings lasted up to the arrival of the Spaniards, and at that time the *guauques* were venerated as much as when this practice started. This veneration was so great that in all their times of need, the descendants of the deceased's family unit would entrust themselves to these *guauques*, and these idols were carried

by the armies with all of the authority that they could muster because they thought that this was a great help to them in their victories and that it made the enemies fearful. At least, there is no
doubt that the warriors felt very confident about their success with
the patronage of the *guauques,* and according to what the elders
say, this patronage fired the imagination of the warriors. The sacrifices made to these statues of the *guauques* were noteworthy and
extensive, and the people thought that as long as these *guauques*
endured, they had the same powers as the bodies of their owners
when they were still alive. During the time when they had them in
the city the *guauques* were placed in the company of the bodies,
and whenever the kinship units and families carried them, they
honored the *guauques* as much as when their owner was alive.
Thus they contributed offerings to the people who looked after the
guauques.

Chapter 10: Of the idolatry that these Indians had for their deceased

Although these Indians gave some justification for their other idolatries and errors, none could be given for the beastly act of venerating the bodies of the dead as much as they did. However, since it was such an important matter to them, and for converting them, being the most prejudicial of their heathen customs, a special account must be given.

This strange practice of theirs is so reprehensible because they worshiped the bodies of the dead in spite of believing, as they did, that these bodies would never live again nor serve any useful purpose. It seems that if they were to consider this matter and let themselves be guided only by what they saw and held to be certain, they would stop worshiping the dead on purely reasonable grounds alone; they would realize that the service and care that they took in paying tribute to the dead was useless. But it is impossible to go into this matter among them without giving offense. It is not even possible to pressure them into making an analysis of the rationale upon which this practice is based. Therefore, we will proceed no further with the problem of convincing the Indians, but instead we will discuss the facts of what they did with these dead bodies.

In the first place, it is necessary to explain a strange and barbarous notion that these people had. No matter how important and esteemed a person may have been while his manly vigor and strength lasted, when he grew old, they paid very little attention to him for the rest of his life. However, when he died, they took great care in respecting his dead body, so much so that they worshiped it like a god, and as such they made sacrifices to it. For this purpose, as soon as the soul had left the body, the members of the deceased's *ayllo* and family unit would take the dead body, and if the deceased was a king or a great lord, the body would be embalmed with great skill. As a result, it would be preserved intact for many years, and it would not deteriorate or give off a foul odor. Some of the bodies lasted this way for two hundred years. All of their personal property would also be taken, including dishes of gold and silver. None of this was given to the heirs. Part of it was placed with the deceased, and part of it was buried in places where the deceased customarily spent his leisure time when he was alive.

The relatives of the deceased would look after these dead

bodies, and they kept them adorned and carefully preserved. The
bodies were wrapped in a large amount of cotton with the face covered. The bodies were not brought out except for major festivals.
No ordinary people saw the bodies except for those responsible for
dressing them, watching over them, and caring for their preservation. These attendants sustained themselves on the farmland that
the descendants of the deceased had designated for this purpose.
The embalmed bodies were greatly venerated, and sacrifices were
made to each one according to their resources. Some kept the bodies
of their relatives in their own houses, but the bodies of the Inca
kings were placed at first in the Temple of the Sun, each one in
its own chapel with its own altar. Later it was determined that in
order to preserve these bodies with more decorum, the members of
their family unit should be put in charge of them, and so it was
done. Each body was placed along with its *guauque* in a house of
its own with an adequate number of attendants and servants, befitting the rank of the deceased. However, the lords and chiefs of their
family units always looked after them, and the whole family devoted itself to paying tribute to their deceased. The bodies were
brought out with a large retinue for all solemn festivals, and for
less solemn occasions, in place of the bodies, their *guauques* were
brought out. In the square they were seated in a row according to
their seniority, and there the servants and guardians ate and drank.
A flame was kindled before the deceased of a certain firewood that
was carved and cut all the same length. The food set before the
dead bodies for them to eat was burned in this flame. Also placed
before these bodies were large tumblers made of gold and silver like
pitchers, which were called *vilques*. Into these tumblers they put
the *chicha* with which they would drink a toast to their deceased,
but before drinking, they would show it to the deceased. The deceased would toast each other; the deceased would toast the living,
and vice versa. The toast of the dead bodies was done in their name
by the attendants. With these *vilques* full, the *chicha* was poured
over a round stone idol located in the center of the square. There
was a small reservoir made around the stone where the *chicha* fil-
tered through certain hidden drains. Normally, this stone was covered with a sheet of gold that fit entirely over it, and in addition
there was a kind of round *buhío* or hut made of woven fibers; it
was used to cover the stone at night.

There was an important Indian man and woman assigned to each
one of these bodies, and whatever these men and women wanted was
said to be the will of the deceased. Whenever the men and women

felt the desire to eat or drink, they said that the deceased was making a request. And they would say the same thing if they felt like going out to enjoy themselves at the homes of some of the other deceased, since it was customary for the dead to visit each other, and these visits included extensive dancing and drinking. Sometimes the dead would visit the homes of the living, and sometimes the living would visit the dead. A great many people, both men and women, devoted themselves to the service of these dead bodies. Moreover, they were usually the most prominent people of the land, since they were free to live dissolutely and indulge in banquets and drinking bouts. So many nobles were involved in serving these dead bodies, and their lives were so licentious, that one day Huascar Inca became angry with them, and he said that there should be an order to have all the dead bodies buried and to take all their riches away from them. He went on to say that the dead should not be a part of his court, only the living, because the dead had taken over the best of everything in his kingdom.

Apart from the income used for the preservation of these bodies and the sustenance of their servants and attendants, the descendants of the deceased made large offerings to them. These offerings included not only the frequent sacrifices they made to the deceased of all the things that they offered to their gods, but also included offerings of ordinary foods to sustain the bodies and for their souls to eat. In spite of this, it is an established fact that none of those charged with teaching the rationale for their opinions believed that dead bodies such as these could either eat or drink or feel any passion whatsoever after the souls had departed from the bodies. Regarding this matter, the only thing that should be taken seriously is what was said by those individuals charged with teaching. No faith should be placed in what was said by the common people who lived by guarding and serving these bodies. Since these people sustained themselves on the offerings and provisions given to the bodies, there is no doubt that they fabricated a great deal of nonsense so that the offerings would not be cut off or reduced. For instance, whenever the customary treatment was not forthcoming, they would pretend that the bodies complained. Rather than trying to have them punished for these fabrications, the heirs were pleased and would thank them. Thus, although all of the relatives provided these bodies with food and other things, it was not because they believed the bodies ever got hungry or had any need of food. Actually they laughed at those who made such statements. Therefore, in providing food for their dead, their only consideration was to sustain those who took care of the dead. However, the simple-minded among them believed those stories.

But it must be pointed out that not all of the living generally worshiped all of the dead bodies. Not even all of their relatives worshiped them. The dead were worshiped only by those who were descended from them in a direct line. Therefore, they took great care to worship their father, grandfather, and great-grandfather, and so on as far back as their information reached. But they were not concerned with the brother of their father, nor with the brother of their grandfather, nor with anyone who had died without leaving descendants. In searching for the fundamental cause of this custom, I find that they took into account in this case the second cause, the same as in all other things. Therefore, they worshiped all those who had been the cause of their being, and they used the following line of reasoning. If it were not for that person, I would not have been born. In this way they determined the distribution, lines, and order for worshiping the deceased, which was enough of a burden to keep them occupied whenever they had nothing else to do.

Although it is true that this was their ideal, still the worshiping lasted only for the lords. For everyone else it discontinued when the deceased's children or grandchildren died, and after that the deceased was forgotten. Since it was such a heavy burden, worshiping the other lords would have been discontinued also if it had not been for the farmlands assigned to them for their preservation. This ensured that there was always someone who benefited from looking after them. Moreover, in accordance with their customs, the Incas were under the same obligation. For this reason they took great care to worship the dead bodies of the lords, especially their own ancestors, whom they saw as the cause of their birth. Everyone else worshiped these lords in order to please the Incas. To this was added their opinion (and it is the second reason why they worshiped them) that by preserving and respecting these bodies their progeny would multiply. Thus this custom had continued up to our times, and only a few years ago I saw one of these bodies that had been taken away from certain idolaters. This body was so well preserved and adorned that it looked as if it was alive. The face was so full, with such a natural skin complexion that it did not seem to be dead, though it had been for many years. The face was preserved in that way because there was a calabash rind placed under the skin of each cheek. As the flesh dried out, the skin had remained tight and had taken on a nice gloss. The artificial eyes were open, and this gave the impression that it was looking at those who were present.

The bodies of the kings and lords were the only ones that were venerated by the rest of the people, in addition to their own descendants. This is because they were convinced that God made certain people superior and bestowed good fortune upon them in this life. Without any doubt these superior people would go to heaven, and in that place their souls would be in a good position to help and protect those on earth in times of need. Therefore, they entrusted themselves to these souls when they went to war, and the young men did the same when they became *orejones*[21] and were knighted.

Another harmful kind of worship resulted from their practice of venerating these bodies. They held that certain graves and some places were shrines. The graves were those of the lords, and the places were those where these lords most commonly sat or that they frequented during their lives. For this reason the number of shrines and *guacas* greatly increased. Moreover, in addition to worshiping all of these places, they normally cast offerings to them.

Chapter 11: Of the rest of the things that these Indians of Peru

worshiped The things that these Indians worshiped were countless, and therefore it is not easy to determine the total number of them. Nevertheless, they can be divided into two categories. The works of nature unaltered by human contrivance can be put in the first category, and in the second, all of the objects and idols that did not represent anything other than the material from which they were produced and the form given to them by the craftsman who made them. In order to explain the first ones, it must be pointed out that these people customarily worshiped and offered sacrifices to any natural things that were found to differ somewhat from others of the same kind because of some oddity or extraordinary quality found in them. Thus the Indians were moved to believe that there was a mystery in God's creation of all those things that differed somewhat from the rest, for it was not by chance that God marked these things and set them apart from the ordinary. On the basis of this idea, any man whose birth was unusual would be considered a *guaca*.[22] An example would be when two or three were born together from the same womb or when someone was born with some mark or peculiarity. Great care was taken with these individuals in order to show them due respect and support. They were provided with whatever they needed or with some occupation by which they could earn their living without needing to work.

They said that these special individuals were marked by nature through some sort of mystery. This was a figment of their imaginations, and they let themselves be deceived very easily. For instance, if a woman declared that she had become pregnant through the action of the Thunder[23] without any man having touched her, they believed her. The child she gave birth to was held in great veneration, and from an early age it was consecrated to the cult of their gods. Anything out of the ordinary that happened to these people or to their possessions was attributed to this mystery. Especially if they found some stone or shell or anything unusual, it was considered to be more notable than if anyone else found it.

Moreover, they worshiped exceptionally large trees, roots, and other things that come from the land. At harvest time, on seeing the *papas* [potatoes] called *llallahuas,* which are of a peculiar shape, ears of maize or vegetables whose form was different from the rest, they would worship these things by kissing them, drinking, dancing, and performing other special ceremonies in their honor. They also worshiped springs, rivers, lakes, and hills which were different in shape or substance from those nearby, being formed of earth or sand, where the rest were rocky, or vice versa. Also included was the snow-capped mountain range and any other sierra or high peak which had snow on it, boulders or large rocks, cliffs and deep gorges, as well as the high places and hilltops called *apachitas*.[24] They worshiped these places, saying that when they had finished climbing uphill and had reached the top, they rested there after the climb. They had made large piles of stones at these *apachitas*, as well as at level places and crossings along the roads. They also did reverence to these places and made offerings. Those who went to the mines worshiped the hills where they worked and the mines themselves, which they call *coya*.[25] They asked the mines for their metals, and in order to obtain what they asked for, they stayed up at night drinking and dancing as a sign of reverence to the hills. They also worshiped the metals which they call *mama* and the rocks called *corpa* which contain these metals.[26] They would kiss these rocks and perform other ceremonies with them. The same is true of the metal they call *soroche*,[27] silver itself, and the *guayras* or braziers where it is melted. They also worshiped gold nuggets, grains of gold, gold dust, and vermilion, which they call *llimpi;* it was much prized for a variety of superstitions. In conclusion, they worshiped any thing from nature that they perceived to be notable or different from the rest, and they recognized some special divinity in these things. This they did even with bright and colorful pebbles, and they thought very highly of them. The inhabitants of wooded lands and tropical forests also worshiped many animals, such as [mountain] lions, bears, tigers [jaguars], and serpents, so that they might suffer no harm from them.

In the second category there are an infinite variety of images and statues. All of these idols were worshiped for their own sake, and these simple people never thought to search or use their imaginations in order to find what such idols represented. Some of these idols were painted, and others were carved from different materials into various forms and sizes. Some were made of silver, others of gold, wood, clay, and other things. Some of them had a human form, and others had the form of various animals, fish, birds, and vegetables. There were idols shaped like sheep, serpents, toads, *guacamayas* [macaws]; some were like an ear of maize or other grains and vegetables. Each thing was very well imitated. Those made in the form of animals were nearly all smaller than life size, inasmuch as they had statues of men that were no taller than the length of a finger. Within this diversity of idols, I have noticed one thing in particular, and it is that the ones that had the form of animals and vegetables normally were more perfectly carved and looked more like their real-life models. On the other hand, the idols shaped like humans normally had such hideous expressions that they clearly showed by their evil countenances in whose honor they were made, and it was the devil. Certainly he must have liked having himself worshiped through these unpleasant-looking figures. Actually, the devil always gave answers through the wildest and most frightening ones.

Chapter 12: Of the temples and shrines of Peru; a special description is included of the major temple of the city of Cuzco

It has already been pointed out that the Peruvian Indians used the term *guaca* for all of the sacred places designated for prayers and sacrifices, as well as for all of the gods and idols that were worshiped in these places. There were so many of these *guacas* and so many different kinds of them that it is impossible to write about all of them. Apart from the major shrines that belonged to each nation and province, there were many others of lesser importance in each town. In addition to these, every kinship unit and family had its own personal *guacas*. Although the principal shrines common to the major towns and provincial capitals were not as numerous as those in Cuzco, they were arranged in the same order and dedicated to the same gods. (This was ascertained later by the Spaniards, and it was verified in more than one hundred towns, some far away [from Cuzco].) I will include here all of the shrines of the city of Cuzco, explaining what each one was used for, the offerings that were made to it, and the reason why the sacrifices were made. And these will only be the major shrines, because the personal idols and shrines that were possessed by every individual were countless, as I have said before. Moreover, I will only mention the shrines that belonged to the city of Cuzco. Since that city was the universal sanctuary of the entire kingdom, in addition to the local *guacas*, there were many provincial ones there, which were the major *guacas* from all of the provinces that obeyed the Inca. The Inca had them brought to Cuzco on the assumption that no one would be able to rebel against him without being severely punished by their gods. Since the Inca had all of his vassals' gods in his possession, the vassals were obliged to aid and defend him. These gods were very numerous, and they were kept individually by the members of the family and *ayllo* of the king who conquered the province of each one. Each family was in charge of the safekeeping of these gods, and they received the sacrifices sent by the natives of the god's province. These foreign *guacas* will not be included in this account, which will cover only the *guacas* of Cuzco. However, anyone who is familiar with the *guacas* of Cuzco will easily understand what the Indians had in other places. Everywhere the arrangement of the *guacas* was the same as in Cuzco. In addition to these native Cuzco *guacas*, I will describe two or three from other parts of the kingdom. These were rich, magnificent temples, and like sanctuaries that were widely venerated; people went to them on pilgrimages from every part of Peru, much in the same way that Christians customarily visit the Holy Sepulcher of our Savior, the temple of the Apostles Saint Peter and Saint Paul, and the famous sanctuary of Santiago in Galicia.

These temples and shrines, including those of Cuzco as well as those from other parts of the kingdom, were located in numerous places. Some were in towns, others in the countryside, in rugged woodlands and sierras, some along roads, and others in the punas and deserts and anywhere at all. Moreover, there were so many temples and shrines that we hardly ever make a day's journey on foot anywhere without coming across traces and ruins of them. Not all of the shrines were temples and houses with living quarters. The ones that were hills, ravines, cliffs, springs, and other things of this sort had no house or building; at the most there might have been a *buhio* or hut where the attendants and guards of the *guacas* lived. But all were endowed with sufficient income and services. The most elaborate and widely venerated temples especially had incomparable riches in gold and silver; all of the tumblers and pieces of the service for the temples were made of these metals, along with all the adornments for celebrating their festivals. Normally a great many priests and attendants resided permanently in these temples, and they were sustained on the income of the temples themselves. In order to dedicate any of these temples over again, they had great festivals and ceremonies. At the end of these ceremonies, they used an aspergillum made of green branches to sprinkle the temples with the blood of a lamb that had been solemnly sacrificed that day.

The most important and most sumptuous temple of this kingdom was the one located in the city of Cuzco; this temple was held to be the chief center or capital of their false religion and the most venerated sanctuary that these Indians had, and for this reason, it was visited by all of the people of the Inca Empire, who came to it out of devotion on pilgrimages. This temple was called Coricancha, which means "house of gold," because of the incomparable wealth of this metal which was embedded in the temple's chapels and walls, its ceiling and altars. Although this temple was dedicated to the Sun, statues of Viracocha, the Thunder, the Moon, and other important idols were placed there. In this respect, it was similar to the Pantheon at Rome, and at one time all of the major gods of the provinces that fell within the dominions of the Inca kings were in this temple. However, later these provincial gods were placed in separate temples so that they could be given better care, and the natives of the provinces mentioned above came to worship their gods and make sacrifices to them.

The edifice of this great temple was of the best stonework to be found in these Indies. Both inside and outside, the whole structure was made of carefully hewn ashlar stones that were skillfully set in place without mortar, and the job was done so well that the stones could not have been fit together more perfectly. However, it has often been said that in place of mortar, thin sheets of silver were placed in the joints between the stones. Today the Monastery of Santo Domingo is built on the same site. Now forty years have passed since I was in that city. At that time, many walls of this edifice were still standing, and on one corner that was still intact part of a thin sheet of silver could be seen in the joint between two stones. I saw it myself on numerous occasions. From this it can be inferred that the ashlar stones of some of the walls may have been set on the sheets of silver. The site of the temple was the most level part of the city, beyond the hillside slopes upon which most of the city was built and at the edge of the city where the valley begins. Moreover, the site is next to the stream that runs through that part of the city.²⁸ The plan of the edifice was as follows. A square enclosure of high, attractive stone walls was constructed on this site. One section of the enclosure followed the path of the stream, another was adjacent to the square where the festivals and sacrifices for the Sun were celebrated,²⁹ the third section was facing along the valley, and the other faced the Pomachupa district. Most of the wall was still standing when I saw it, and it was possible to estimate the size and workmanship of the structure. In addition to the exterior walls, other parts of the ancient edifice of the Coricancha still remained outside the monastery. Each side or section of the enclosure measured about four hundred to five hundred feet in length. Thus the entire edifice was about two thousand feet square. The walls were made of solid, dark grey stones which were straight and exactly perpendicular. The ashlar stones were large and attractive. Moreover, there were some hollow places made like niches at ground level. Although many buildings were found within

these walls, the most important ones were four large, skillfully
built structures placed to form a square. These structures were like
chapels for Viracocha, the Sun, the Moon, the Thunder, and the
rest of the principal gods. One of the structures was a retreat for
the *mamaconas* who served in the temple, and the largest building
was used as a dwelling for the many priests and servants who resided there. The main structure, or (as we would describe it) the
main chapel, which housed the altar of the Sun and of the other
major gods, contained incredible riches. In place of tapestries, the
entire inside, including both the ceiling and walls, was embellished
with sheets of gold. Judging from this, it is possible to appreciate
the enormous wealth of this temple, which was greater than that
of any other temple which has been found in all of this New World.
Apart from many images and statues of gold and silver, there were
countless other valuables, including the service and pieces of these
precious metals, as well as the large quantity of fine clothing that
the Inca kings had stored in it and used in worshiping the Sun.
From this temple Atauhualpa had most of the ransom taken which
he offered in exchange for his freedom to the Marquis Francisco
Pizarro at Cajamarca.

On the other side of the façade wall of this temple, in place of
a cornice, there was a band made of sheets of gold about eleven
inches wide which were inserted between the stones. The only
door was located on the same side, and it led to a small patio where
the statue of the Sun was placed during the day, unless it was taken
to the square. At night this statue was put in its chapel. Many
mamaconas slept with the Sun. These women were the daughters
of lords, and they were said to be the Sun's wives. Moreover, the
Sun was even supposed to have intercourse with them. In front of
this chapel there was a garden, and on the days when a festival of
the Sun was held, maize stalks complete with leaves and ears made
of the finest gold were fixed in place there. These pieces were stored
for this purpose.

Chapter 13: The shrines and guacas on the Road to Chinchaysuyu

From the Temple of the Sun, as from the center, there went out certain lines which the Indians call *ceques*; they formed four parts corresponding to the four royal roads which went out from Cuzco. On each one of those *ceques* were arranged in order the *guacas* and shrines which there were in Cuzco and its region like stations of holy places, the veneration of which was common to all. Each *ceque* was the responsibility of the kinship units and families of the city of Cuzco, from within which came the attendants and servants who cared for the *guacas* of their *ceque* and saw to offering the established sacrifices at the proper times.[30]

Beginning, then, with the Road of Chinchaysuyu, which leaves the city through the district of Carmenga, there were in [the part corresponding to] it nine *ceques* on which were included eighty-five *guacas*, in this order:

[Ch-1:0] The first *ceque* was called Cayao; it was the responsibility of the kinship unit and *ayllo* of Goacaytaqui and had the following five *guacas*.

[Ch-1:1] The first was named Michosamaro; it was located up against the slope of Totocache, and they said it was one of those who they fancied had emerged with the first Inca Manco Capac from the cave of Pacaritampu.[31] They relate that one of the women who came out of the cave with them killed him because of an act of disrespect toward her which he committed. He turned to stone, and his spirit appeared in this same place and ordered that they make sacrifices to him there. Thus the sacrifice at this *guaca* was very ancient. It always consisted of gold, clothing, seashells, and other things, and it used to be made for good rains.

[Ch-1:2] The second *guaca* of the *ceque* was called Patallacta. It was a house which Inca Yupanqui designated for his sacrifices, and he died in it. The Incas who succeeded him thereafter made ordinary sacrifice here. In general, all the things which they consumed in sacrifice were offered for the health and prosperity of the Inca.

[Ch-1:3] The third *guaca* was named Pilcopuquio. It is a fountain next to the house just mentioned from which an irrigation ditch issues. The Indians relate that when Inca Yupanqui had made

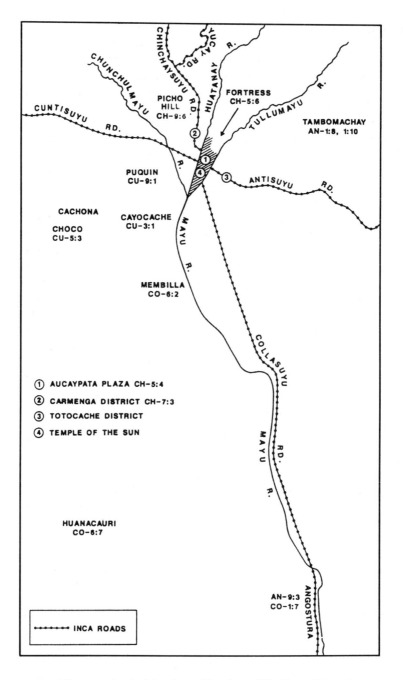

MAP 4. *Cuzco region in Inca times. Sketch modified from* Cuzco, la traza urbana de la ciudad inca, *by Santiago Agurto Calvo (Cuzco: INC, 1980).*

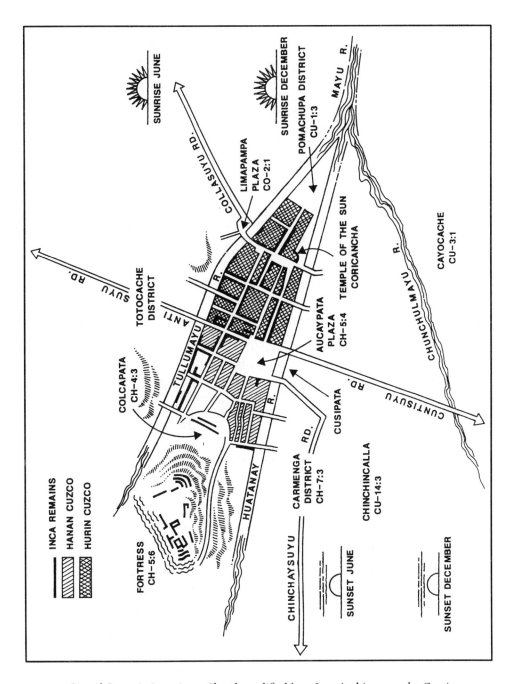

MAP 5. *City of Cuzco in Inca times. Sketch modified from* Inca Architecture, *by Graziano Gasparini and Luise Margolies, translated by Patricia J. Lyon (Bloomington: Indiana University Press, 1980).*

that house for the sacrifices, he ordered that water to emerge there and afterward decreed that ordinary sacrifice should be made to it.

[Ch-1 : 4] The fourth *guaca* was called Cirocaya. It is a cave of stone from which they believed the hail issued. Hence, at the season when they were afraid of it, all went to sacrifice in the cave so that hail should not come out and destroy their crops.

[Ch-1 : 5] The fifth and last *guaca* of this *ceque* had the name Sonconancay. It is a hill where it was a very ancient custom to offer sacrifices for the health of the Inca.

[Ch-2 : 0] The second *ceque* of this same Road of Chinchaysuyu was called Payan; on it were eight *guacas* of the *ayllo* and family of Vicaquirao.

[Ch-2 : 1] The first *guaca* was called Guaracince, which was in the square of the Temple of the Sun; this square was called Chuquipampa (it means "plain of gold"). It was a bit of flat ground which was there, where they said that the earthquake was formed. At it they made sacrifices so that it would not quake, and they were very solemn ones, because when the earth quaked children were killed, and ordinarily sheep and clothing were burned and gold and silver were buried.

[Ch-2 : 2] The second *guaca* was named Racramirpay; this one was a stone which they had set in a window a little way below where the monastery of San Agustín is now; they relate the story of it in this way. In a certain battle which Inca Yupanqui fought against his enemies, an Indian appeared to him in the air and helped him to conquer them. After the victory had been won, he came to Cuzco with the said Inca, sat down in this window, and turned to stone. From that time on they worshiped it and made ordinary sacrifice to it. Particularly solemn sacrifice was made to it when the Inca went to war personally, asking it to aid the king as it had aided Inca Yupanqui in the former war.

[Ch-2 : 3] The third *guaca* was an idol of solid gold named Inti Illapa, which means "Thunder of the Sun," which was set on a rich litter of gold. Inca Yupanqui made it and took it for his *guauque* or brother. It had a house in the district of Totocache, and they did it great veneration. In the same house or temple was the body of the said Inca Yupanqui. To this idol they very commonly made sacrifices of children and of everything else, asking it that the strength of the Inca be preserved and his dominion not decrease.

[Ch-2 : 4] The fourth *guaca* was called Viroypacha; it is a conduit of fairly good water which was declared a *guaca* by Inca Yupanqui. It was prayed to for the tranquillity of the Inca.

[Ch-2 : 5] The fifth *guaca* was a flat place called Chuquibamba, which is next to the fortress;[32] they sacrificed to it as to the others.

[Ch-2 : 6] The sixth *guaca* was called Macasayba. It was a large stone which Inca Yupanqui set next to the flat place of Chuquibamba, and he ordered that veneration and sacrifices for the health of the king be made to it.

[Ch-2 : 7] The seventh *guaca* was a quarry named Guayrangallay, which is above the fortress. In it they made sacrifices for various reasons.

[Ch-2 : 8] The eighth and last *guaca* of this *ceque* was called Guayllaurcaja. It is a little pass formed in the middle of a hill, where Viracocha Inca many times sat down to rest climbing the said hill, and from that time on, by his command, it was considered a shrine.

[Ch-3 : 0] The third *ceque* of this road was called Collana; it had ten *guacas*.

[Ch-3 : 1] The first was named Nina, which was a brazier made of a stone where the fire for sacrifices was lit, and they could not take it from anywhere else. It was next to the Temple of the Sun; it was held in great veneration, and solemn sacrifices were made to it.

[Ch-3 : 2] The second *guaca* was called Canchapacha. It was a fountain which was in the street of Diego Maldonado, to which they made sacrifice on account of certain stories that the Indians tell.

[Ch-3 : 3] The third *guaca* was another fountain named Ticicocha, which is inside the house that belonged to the said Diego Maldonado. This fountain belonged to the *coya* or queen, Mama Ocllo. In it were made very great and ordinary sacrifices, especially when they wanted to ask something of the said Mama Ocllo, who was the most venerated woman there was among these Indians.

[Ch-3 : 4] The fourth *guaca* was called Condorcancha and was the house in which Inca Yupanqui lived.

[Ch-3 : 5] The fifth *guaca* was another house called Pomacorco, and they give no other reason for sacrificing in it, except that it had belonged to Guayna Capac.

[Ch-3 : 6] The sixth *guaca* was named Mollaguanca; it was a certain stone which was in the middle of a flat place which they called Calispuquiu. Inca Yupanqui ordered it to be placed there and considered a shrine.

[Ch-3 : 7] The seventh *guaca* was the house which formerly belonged to the king, Tupa Inca, named Calispuquio Guaci, in which sacrifices were offered to the said Tupa Inca.

[Ch-3 : 8] The eighth *guaca* was a fountain which was called Calispuquio, which was below the said house of Tupa Inca. All those who were made *orejones* in the festival of Raymi³³ went to wash in it. The water for the Inca was brought from this fountain with many songs made for this one purpose, and the girls who carried it were maidens.

[Ch-3 : 9] The ninth *guaca* was named Cugiguaman. It was a stone shaped like a falcon which Inca Yupanqui said had appeared to him in a quarry, and he ordered that it be placed on this *ceque* and that sacrifices be made to it.

[Ch-3 : 10] The tenth *guaca* of this *ceque* was a small fountain called Quinoapuquiu which Inca Yupanqui designated as a shrine. Sacrifices for the health of the Inca were made to it.

[Ch-4 : 0] The fourth *ceque* they named Payao [*sic*]; it had eight *guacas*.

[Ch-4 : 1] The first of these was called Araytampu. It was a large stone with four other small ones which were next to the house which belonged to Benito de la Peña, and they were *pururaucas*.

[Ch-4 : 2] The second *guaca* was named Puñui; it was in a small flat place next to the house of Diego Maldonado. It was a very solemn shrine because it was held to be the cause of sleep; they offered every kind of sacrifice to it. They went to it with two petitions, one to pray for those who were unable to sleep, and the other that they might not die in their sleep.

[Ch-4 : 3] The third *guaca* was named Curiocllo. It was a house of Curiollo [*sic;* for Curi Ocllo], who had been the wife of Amaro Topa Inca, which was in Colcapata; and they worshiped also a fountain which was next to it.

[Ch-4 : 4] The fourth *guaca* was named Colcapata and was the house of Paullu Inca, where there was a stone serving as an idol which the *ayllo* of Andasaya worshiped. Its origin was that Pachacutic Inca had ordered it worshiped, because he said that a certain lord had been transformed into the said stone.

[Ch-4 : 5] The fifth *guaca* was called Guamancancha and was near the fortress on a small hill of this name. It was an enclosure inside of which there were two small *buhios*³⁴ designated for fasting when *orejones* were made.

[Ch-4 : 6] The sixth *guaca* was a large stone named Collaconcho which was in the fortress. They declared that, bringing it for that structure, it fell three times and killed some Indians. The sorcerers said that it had replied to questions they put to it that, if they persisted in wanting to put it in the structure, all would have a bad end, apart from the fact that they would not be able to do it. From that time on it was considered a general *guaca* to which they made offerings for the strength of the Inca.

[Ch-4 : 7] The seventh *guaca* was called Chachacomacaja; it consisted of certain trees set out by hand next to which was a stone to which they made sacrifice so that the Inca would not be wrathful.

[Ch-4 : 8] The eighth and last *guaca* of this *ceque* was a high hill named Chuquipalta, which is next to the fortress, on which were placed three stones in representation of the Pachayachachic, Inti Illapa, and Punchau [i.e., the Creator, the Thunder, and the Sun]. On this hill, universal sacrifice was made of boys and girls and figurines of the same made of gold; and clothing and sheep were burned, because this was considered to be a very solemn shrine.

[Ch-5 : 0] The fifth *ceque* of this same road and direction of Chinchaysuyu was called Cayao [*sic*]; it included ten *guacas*.

[Ch-5 : 1] The first, named Cusicancha, was the place where Inca Yupanqui was born, opposite the temple of Coricancha; for this reason the members of the *ayllo* Inacapanaca sacrificed there.

[Ch-5 : 2] The second *guaca* was a temple named Pucamarca, which was in the houses which belonged to the Licentiate [Antonio] de la Gama; in it was an idol of the Thunder called Chucuylla.

[Ch-5 : 3] The third *guaca* was called Cuzcocalla. It was on the street which leads to the square following this line or *ceque,* and it consisted of a fair quantity of stones which they said were all *puruaucas.*

[Ch-5 : 4] The fourth *guaca* was the main square, named Aucaypata, which is also the main square at the present time. In it was made the universal sacrifice for the Sun and the rest of the *guacas,* and the sacrifice was divided and taken to the other parts of the kingdom. It was a very venerated place.

[Ch-5 : 5] The fifth *guaca* was a *buhio* named Coracora, in which Inca Yupanqui used to sleep, which is where the *cabildo* [municipal council] houses are now. This said Inca ordered worship of that place and burning of clothing and sheep[35] in it, and so it was done.

[Ch-5 : 6] The sixth *guaca* was named Sabacurinca; it was a well-carved seat where the Incas sat. It was very venerated, and solemn sacrifices were made to it. On account of this seat, the whole fortress was worshiped; for the seat must have been inside or next to the fortress.

[Ch-5 : 7] The seventh *guaca* was named Chacaguanacauri. It is a small hill which is on the way to Yucay, where the young men who were preparing themselves to be *orejones* went for a certain grass which they carried on their lances.

[Ch-5 : 8] The eighth *guaca* was a small tomb named Guamanguachanca, the tomb of a brother of Guayna Capac, which was on the other side of the fortress. They made a shrine of it because the Inca's brother had died as a small child, and they said that because of the veneration they paid to it, no more children of that age would die.

[Ch-5 : 9] The ninth *guaca* was a hill which is on the way to the valley of Yucay named Cinca, on which was a stone which the Indians of Ayamarca worshiped, holding the opinion that they originated from it.

[Ch-5 : 10] The tenth *guaca* was a *puquio*, or spring, named Corcorpuquiu at which children were offered and everything else.

[Ch-6 : 0] The sixth *ceque* was called Collana, like the third, and it had eleven *guacas*.

[Ch-6 : 1] The first was called Catonge and was a stone of the *pururaucas*, which was in a window next to the Temple of the Sun.

[Ch-6 : 2] The second *guaca* was named Pucamarca [*sic*; probably for Quishuarcancha]; it was a house or temple designated for the sacrifices of the Pachayachachic [Creator] in which children were sacrificed and everything else.

[Ch-6 : 3] The third *guaca* was called Ñan, which means "road." It was in the square where one took the road for Chinchaysuyu. Universal sacrifice was made at it for travelers, and so that the road in question would always be intact and not cave in and fall.

[Ch-6 : 4] The fourth *guaca* had the name of Guayra and was in the doorway of Cajana. At it sacrifice was made to the wind so that it would not do damage, and a pit had been made there in which the sacrifices were buried.

[Ch-6 : 5] The fifth *guaca* was the palace of Guayna Capac named Cajana, within which was a lake named Ticcicocha which was an important shrine and at which great sacrifices were made.

[Ch-6 : 6] The sixth *guaca* was a fountain named Capipacchan [*sic*; for Çapi Pacchan], which was in Capi [Çapi], in which the Inca used to bathe. Sacrifices were made at it, and they prayed that the water might not carry away his strength or do him harm.

[Ch-6 : 7] The seventh *guaca* was called Capi [Çapi], which means "root." It was a very large *quinua* [tree] root which the sorcerers said was the root from which Cuzco issued and by means of which it was preserved. They made sacrifices to it for the preservation of the said city.

[Ch-6 : 8] The eighth was named Quisco; it was on top of the hill of Capi [Çapi], where universal sacrifice was made for the same reason as to the above-mentioned root.

[Ch-6 : 9] The ninth *guaca* was a hill named Quiangalla, which is on the Yucay Road. On it were two markers or pillars which they thought denoted the beginning of summer when the sun reached there.

[Ch-6 : 10] The tenth was a small fountain which was called Guarguaillapuquiu, and it is next to this hill. In it they threw the dust which was left over from the sacrifices of the *guacas* of this *ceque*.

[Ch-6 : 11] The eleventh and last *guaca* was called Illacamarca; it was in a fortress built on a steep rock on the way to Yucay, and at it the *guacas* of this *ceque* ended.

[Ch-7 : 0] The seventh *ceque* was called Cayao and was [the responsibility] of the *ayllo* of Capac Ayllu; it had the following eight *guacas*.

[Ch-7 : 1] The first was named Omanamaro and was a long stone which they said was one of the *pururaucas* and which was in the doorway of the house which belonged to [Juan de] Figueroa. Universal sacrifice was made there for the health of the Inca.

[Ch-7 : 2] The second *guaca* was two small *buhios*, one named Sanca Cahcha and the other Hurin Sanca, where they had a quantity of [mountain] lions, tigers [jaguars], serpents, and all the other evil vermin that were available. In these *buhios* they thrust the prisoners they brought back from war. Whoever died that night, the said wild beasts ate; whoever remained alive, they took out. They took this [survival] as a sign that the prisoner had a good heart and intended to serve the Inca.

[Ch-7 : 3] The third *guaca* was called Marcatampu. It consisted of some round stones which were in Carmenga, where the parish of Santa Ana is now, which [stones] Inca Yupanqui designated as an important shrine. Children were offered to it for the health and preservation of the Inca.

[Ch-7 : 4] The fourth was named Taxanamaro; it consisted of five round stones which Viracocha Inca ordered placed on the hill of Toxan [*sic*], which is above Carmenga. The offering they gave it was only of cut shells. This *guaca* was prayed to for the victory of the Inca.

[Ch-7 : 5] The fifth *guaca* of this *ceque* they named Urcoslla

Amaro; it consisted of many stones placed together on a small hill above Carmenga. Sacrifices were made to it for the health of the Inca.

[Ch-7:6] The sixth was called Callancapuquiu; it is the spring of Ticutica [*sic*; for Ticatica] to which they offered shells so that it would always flow.

[Ch-7:7] The seventh *guaca* was called Churuncana; it is a round hill above Carmenga where the royal road of Chinchero leaves that of Yucay. From this hill the sacrifices to Ticci Viracocha were made, asking him that the Inca be victorious throughout the land to the limits of the sea. They offered him all kinds of things, especially children.

[Ch-7:8] The eighth and last *guaca* of this *ceque* was a fountain named Muchayllapuquiu which is near Guarguaylla. They offered it cut shells for certain purposes.

[Ch-8:0] The eighth *ceque* of this road was called Payan, like the second, and there were thirteen *guacas* on it.

[Ch-8:1] The first was a small house next to the Temple of the Sun named Illanguarque in which were kept certain weapons which they said the Sun had given to Inca Yupanqui; with them he conquered his enemies. Universal sacrifice was made to this *guaca*.

[Ch-8:2] The second was called Mancochuqui. It was a *chacara* of Huanacauri,[36] and what was harvested from it was sacrificed to him.

[Ch-8:3] The third *guaca* was a fountain named Aucaypata [Paccha], which was next to where the house of the municipal council is now. In it the priests of Chucuilla said that the Thunder bathed, and they made up a thousand other absurdities.

[Ch-8:4] The fourth *guaca* was called Cugitalis; it was a flat place where the house of Garcilaso was built. The origin they tell was that Guayna Capac slept there and dreamed that a certain war was coming. Because it afterward came to pass, he ordered that that place be venerated.

[Ch-8:5] The fifth *guaca* was a *chacara* named Chacuaytapara, which was in Carmenga and belonged to Amaro Tupa Inca. They offered it only shells, and they were not supposed to stop to sacrifice but make their offerings as they passed by.

[Ch-8:6] The sixth was a spring named Orocotopuquiu, which was in Carmenga, to which were given ground-up shells.

[Ch-8:7] The seventh was called Sucanca. It was a hill by way of which the water channel from Chinchero comes. On it there were two markers which indicated that when the sun arrived there they had to begin to plant the maize. The sacrifice which was made there was directed to the Sun, asking him to arrive there at the time which would be appropriate for planting, and they sacrificed to him sheep, clothing, and miniature lambs of gold and silver.

[Ch-8:8] The eighth *guaca* was a house called Mamararoy in which were venerated certain stones which they said were wives of Ticci Viracocha, and that, walking at night, they had turned to stone. Finding them in that place, they made that temple for them.

[Ch-8:9] The ninth *guaca* was called Urcoscalla. It was the place where those who traveled to Chinchaysuyu lost sight of the city of Cuzco.

[Ch-8:10] The tenth *guaca* was called Catachillay. It is a fountain which is in the first flat place that descends to the Road of Chinchaysuyu.

[Ch-8:11] The eleventh was another fountain, next to the one above, which is called Aspadquiri, to which Inca Yupanqui ordered sacrifices made because he said that its water took away fatigue.

[Ch-8:12] The twelfth was another fountain named Poroypuquiu which is next to the mill which belonged to Juan Julio [de Hojeda]. They offered it finely ground shells.

[Ch-8:13] The last *guaca* of this *ceque* was called Collanasayba; it was a marker on a hill at the beginning of Sicllabamba, marking the end and limit of the *guacas* of this *ceque*.

[Ch-9:0] The ninth and last *ceque* of this said Road of Chinchaysuyu was named Capac and had twelve *guacas*.

[Ch-9:1] The first was a fountain called Aypanospacha, which was on the street of Pedro Alonso Carrasco.

[Ch-9:2] The second was a small house which was in Piccho, a farm which now belongs to the Society of Jesus, in which Guayna Capac ordered that they make sacrifice, because his mother, Mama Ocllo, used to sleep there.

[Ch-9:3] The third was a hill named Quinoacalla, which is in Carmenga, where it was ordained that the *orejones* should rest in the festival of Raymi.

[Ch-9:4] The fourth *guaca* was a fountain named Pomacucho, which was somewhat separated from this *ceque*. They offered shells to it.

[Ch-9:5] The fifth *guaca* was called Vicaribi; it was a well-wrought tomb, which was in Piccho, of an important lord so named of the *ayllo* of Maras.

[Ch-9:6] The sixth *guaca* was a stone named Apuyauira, which was on the hill of Picho [Piccho]. They believed that it was one of those who emerged from the earth with Huanacauri, and that after having lived for a long time he climbed up there and turned to stone. All the *ayllos* went to worship at it in the festival of Raymi.

[Ch-9 : 7] The seventh was a flat place called Cutirsaspampa, where the Inca won a certain victory, and for this reason alone the place was made a shrine.

[Ch-9 : 8] The eighth was another flat place near this one named Queachili, which is between two hills like a gateway; in it the said victory was completed, and for that reason it was venerated.

[Ch-9 : 9] The ninth *guaca* was called Quishuarpuquiu; it was a spring at which they said the Inca's men had drunk when the above battle was finished.

[Ch-9 : 10] The tenth was named Yuyotuyro; it consisted of five stones together which were next to the hill mentioned above.

[Ch-9 : 11] The eleventh was a stone called Pillolliri, which the Indians relate had jumped from another hill to that which is so named, and for this flight of fancy which they had, they worshiped it.

[Ch-9 : 12] The twelfth and last *guaca* of this *ceque* was a fountain named Totorgoaylla; here ended the *guacas* of the nine *ceques* of the Road of Chinchaysuyu, which came to eighty-five.

Chapter 14: The shrines and guacas on the Road to Antisuyu

The Road of Antisuyu had nine *ceques* and on them seventy-eight *guacas*, in this order.

[An-1:0] The first *ceque* was named Collana and was under the care of the *ayllo* of Cubcu [Çubçu] Pañaca Ayllu.

[An-1:1] The first *guaca* of it was called Chiquinapampa. It was an enclosure next to the Temple of the Sun in which the sacrifice for the universal health of the Indians was made.

[An-1:2] The second *guaca* was called Turuca. It was an almost round stone, which was next to the said Temple of the Sun in a window; this stone was said to be the *guauque* of Ticci Viracocha. Universal sacrifice was made to it for all the needs that arose.

[An-1:3] The third *guaca* was a large stone named Chiripacha which was at the beginning of the Road of Collasuyu. All those who traveled by the said road made offerings to it, so that the journey would turn out well for them.

[An-1:4] The fourth was called Autviturco. It was a large cave which is down the ravine from Patallacta; they held the view that the Indians of the town of Goalla had been born there. The sacrifice was to sprinkle it with the blood of llamas, which are the sheep of the land.

[An-1:5] The fifth was a fountain named Pacha, which is in the ravine of Patallacta, in which the Inca washed himself a certain time.

[An-1:6] The sixth was another fountain called Corcorchaca, which is in the same ravine as the one mentioned above; they offered it finely ground shells.

[An-1:7] The seventh *guaca* was called Amaromarcaguaci; this was a house of Amaro Tupa Inca, which was on the road of the Andes [i.e., the *montaña*].

[An-1:8] The eighth *guaca* was named Tipcpuquiu [*sic*; for Tinpuc Puquiu]; it was a fountain which is near Tambo Machay. It is so called because it wells up in such a way that the water boils.

[An-1:9] The ninth was named Tambomachay; it was a house of Inca Yupanqui where he lodged when he went hunting. It was set on a hill near the road of the Andes. They sacrificed all kinds of things to it except children.

[An-1 : 10] The tenth *guaca* was called Quinoapuquiu; it was a fountain near Tambo Machay which consists of two springs. Universal sacrifice was made to it, except children.

[An-1 : 11] The last *guaca* of this *ceque* was called Quiscourco; it was a round stone, not very big, which served as the limit and marker of these *guacas*.

[An-2 : 0] The second *ceque* of the said Road of Antisuyu was called Payan and had ten *guacas*.

[An-2 : 1] The first was a place called Vilcacona, where the house which belonged to Juan de Salas was built. To this shrine they brought at a certain time of the year all the *guacas* and idols of the city of Cuzco, and they sacrificed to them there, all together, and then they returned them to their places. It was a very solemn *guaca*; they offered it very small *cestos*[37] of coca.

[An-2 : 2] The second *guaca* of this *ceque* was named Pachatosa; it was a large stone which was next to [Diego] Cayo's house. The sacrifice was burned on top of it, and they said that the stone ate it.

[An-2 : 3] The third *guaca* was called Chusacachi; it is a large hill on the way to the Andes on top of which were certain stones that were worshiped.

[An-2 : 4] The fourth was named Curovilca; it was a quarry from which they extracted stone. They sacrificed to it so that it might not give out, and so that the buildings built of stone from it might not fall.

[An-2 : 5] The fifth *guaca* was named Sunchupuquiu; it was a shrine which was next to the slope of a hill so named. They offered it sheep and clothing.

[An-2 : 6] The sixth was a spring called Aucapapirqui, which is on a flat place near the said road.

[An-2 : 7] The seventh was named Caynaconga; it was a resting place of the Inca on a flat place near Tambo Machay.

[An-2 : 8] The eighth *guaca* was called Puquiu; it was a fountain which is at the end of Tambo Machay. They offered it sheep, clothing, and shells.

[An-2 : 9] The ninth was named Cascasayba; it consisted of certain stones which were on the hill of Quisco. It was an important *guaca* and had a certain long origin story which the Indians tell. They offered it all kinds of things and children as well.

[An-2 : 10] The tenth was named Macaycalla. It is a flat place between two hills where what is on this side is lost to sight and the other side is revealed, and for this reason alone they worshiped it.

[An-3 : 0] The third *ceque* was named Cayao, and it had ten *guacas.*

[An-3 : 1] The first was a bridge called Guarupuncu, which passed from the Temple of the Sun to a square which they named [the Plaza de] Peces [i.e., Francisco Peces]. They sacrificed to it for many reasons, and especially because the sacrifices which were offered at the king's coronation passed over it.

[An-3 : 2] The second *guaca* was a wall next to the *chacara* of [Hernando] Bachicao, which had an outward bulge in it, the origin of which, they said, was that when the Inca passed that way the wall had gone out to do reverence to him, and from that time on they worshiped it, offering it colored shells.

[An-3 : 3] The third was a fountain named Ayacho, which is in the same *chacara.* They offered it shells of all colors, not very well ground.

[An-3 : 4] The fourth was called Chuquimarca; it was a temple of the Sun on the hill of Mantocalla, in which they said that the Sun descended many times to sleep. For this reason, in addition to everything else, they offered it children.

[An-3 : 5] The fifth *guaca* was called Mantocallaspa; it was a fountain of good water which is on the above-mentioned hill where the Indians bathed.

[An-3 : 6] The sixth was called Mantocallas [*sic*], which was a hill held in great veneration on which, at the time of shelling maize, they made certain sacrifices. For these [sacrifices], they placed on the said hill many bundles of carved firewood dressed as men and women and a great quantity of maize ears made of wood. After great drunken feasts, they burned many sheep with the said firewood and killed some children.

[An-3 : 7] The seventh *guaca* was named Caripuquiu; it was a fountain which is on the slope of the said hill. They offered shells to it.

[An-3 : 8] The eighth was called Yuncaypampa; it was a flat place which is on the road to the Andes, and it has a small fountain.

[An-3 : 9] The ninth *guaca* was named Yancaycalla [*sic;* probably for Yuncaycalla]; it is a sort of gateway where the plain of Chita is seen and Cuzco is lost to sight. Guards were placed there so that no one would carry off anything stolen. Sacrifice was made by the merchants each time they passed, and they prayed that things would go well for them on the journey. Coca was the usual sacrifice.

[An-3 : 10] The last *guaca* of this *ceque* was a fountain called Urcomilpo, which is in the great plain of Chita; they offered it only sheep.

[An-4 : 0] The fourth *ceque* of this road was called Collana; it was the responsibility of the *ayllo* and family of Aucailli Panaca and had seven *guacas*.

[An-4 : 1] The first was named Cariurco, and it was a hill which is near Mantocalla, on top of which there were certain stones which were venerated, and they offered them clothing and spotted sheep.

[An-4 : 2] The second *guaca* was named Chuquiquirao Puquiu; it was a fountain which has its source in a ravine on the slope of the above-mentioned hill; the sacrifice was of sheep and clothing.

[An-4 : 3] The third *guaca* was called Callachaca; it consisted of certain stones placed on the said hill.

[An-4 : 4] The fourth was a quarry which is near there named Viracocha. In it there was a stone which resembled a person. They say that when they were cutting stone from there for a house of the Inca, it came out so, and the Inca ordered that it should be a *guaca*.

[An-4 : 5] The fifth was named Aucanpuquiu; it was a fountain which is near the ravine of Yancacalla [*sic*; see above, ninth *guaca*, An-3 : 9].

[An-4 : 6] The sixth *guaca* was called Illansayba; it was a certain hill on top of which were some stones to which they sacrificed for the health of those who entered the province of the Andes.

[An-4 : 7] The last *guaca* of this *ceque* was a stone named Maychaguanacauri, shaped like the hill of Huanacauri, which was ordered placed on this Road of Antisuyu, and they offered all kinds of things to it.

[An-5 : 0] The fifth *ceque* had the name Payan, and there were ten *guacas* on it.

[An-5 : 1] The first was a stone named Usno, which was in the square of Hurin Aucaypata; this was the first *guaca* to which those who were being made *orejones* made offerings.

[An-5 : 2] The second *guaca* was the spring named Cachipuquiu, which is in Las Salinas. Much salt of very fine quality is made from it. They offered it all kinds of things except children.

[An-5 : 3] The third was called Subaraura. It was a round stone which was in the town of Yaconora and was a very ancient shrine.

[An-5 : 4] The fourth was a fountain called Pachayaconora, which was in the said town of Yaconora. They offered it only shells, some whole and others cut in pieces.

[An-5 : 5] The fifth *guaca* was called Oyaraypuquiu; it was a small fountain which is somewhat higher up. They offered it shells of all colors, according to the times.

[An-5 : 6] The sixth was another fountain named Arosayapu-quiu, which is in Callachaca; they offered it only shells.

[An-5 : 7] The seventh was called Aquarsayba. It was a greatly venerated *guaca*, and they had the opinion that whatever they offered to it all the *guacas* received.

[An-5 : 8] The eighth was a spring named Susumarca, which is in Callachaca, and they offered it the usual things.

[An-5 : 9] The ninth was called Rondoya; it consisted of three stones which were on the hill so named. The Inca Pachacutic placed them there and ordered them to be worshiped.

[An-5 : 10] The tenth and last *guaca* of this *ceque* was another stone named Poma Urco, which was set as the end and limit of the *guacas* of this *ceque*.

[An-6 : 0] The sixth *ceque* was named Cayao, and on it there were seven *guacas*.

[An-6 : 1] The first was called Auriauca; it was a sort of portico or arbor which was next to the Temple of the Sun, where the Inca and the lords took their places.

[An-6 : 2] The second *guaca* was a curved stone named Como-vilca which was near Callachaca; they offered it only shells.

[An-6 : 3] The third was named Chuquicancha; it is a well-known hill which they held to be a house of the Sun. On it they made very solemn sacrifice to gladden the Sun.

[An-6 : 4] The fourth was a small stone called Sanotuiron which was on a little hill. They made offerings to it for the health of the prince who was supposed to inherit the kingdom, and when they made him an *orejon* they offered a solemn sacrifice to this *guaca*.

[An-6 : 5] The fifth was called Viracochapuquiu; it was a fountain which is in a flat place on the way to Chita.

[An-6 : 6] The sixth was a house called Pomamarca which was on the said flat place. In it was kept the body of the wife of Inca Yupanqui, and children were offered there along with all the other things.

[An-6 : 7] The seventh was called Curauacaja; it is a knoll on the way to Chita where sight of the city is lost, and it was designated as the end and marker of the *guacas* of the *ceque*. They had a dead [mountain] lion there, and they told a story of its origin, which is long.

[An-7 : 0] On the seventh *ceque*, named Yacanora [*sic*], there were another seven *guacas*.

[An-7 : 1] The first was called Ayllipampa; it was a flat place where the *chacara* is which belonged to [Alonso de] Mesa. They said it was the goddess Earth named Pachamama, and they offered her small women's garments.

[An-7 : 2] The second *guaca* was a small fountain next to this field named Guamantanta; the usual things were offered to it.

[An-7 : 3] The third was another fountain named Pacaypuquiu, which is a little below the one mentioned above. They offered it ground-up shells.

[An-7 : 4] The fourth was a large square named Colcapampa, where the parish of the Martyrs was made, at the end of which there was a stone which was an important idol, to whom children were offered, along with other things.

[An-7 : 5] The fifth *guaca* was called Cuillorpuquiu; it was a small spring which is further down. They offered it only shells.

[An-7 : 6] The sixth was named Unugualpa; this was a stone which was at Chuquicancha. They relate that when they were taking out stone they found it resembled a human figure, and from then on they worshiped it as a remarkable thing.

[An-7 : 7] The seventh and last was a fountain named Cucacache, where some small salt pans are made.

[An-8 : 0] The eighth *ceque* was called Ayarmaca; it had eleven *guacas*.

[An-8 : 1] The first was a spring called Sacasaylla Puquiu, which is next to the mill of Pedro Alonso [Carrasco]. They offered it only shells.

[An-8 : 2] The second *guaca* was another spring named Pirquipuquiu, which is in a ravine lower down. They offered it small miniature lambs made of silver.

[An-8 : 3] The third was named Cuipanamaro; it consisted of some stones next to this spring, which were regarded as an important *guaca*. They offered it small garments and little lambs made of shell.

[An-8 : 4] The fourth was a spring called Auacospuquiu. They offered it only shells.

[An-8 : 5] The fifth was called Sabaraura; it consisted of three stones which were in the town of Larapa.

[An-8 : 6] The sixth was named Urcopuquiu and was a squared stone which was in a corner of the said town. They considered it a *guaca* of authority and offered it small women's garments and little pieces of gold.

[An-8 : 7] The seventh was a fountain called Pilcopuquiu, which was near the town of Corcora. Shells and small women's garments were offered to it.

[An-8 : 8] The eighth was named Cuipan; it consisted of six stones which were together on the hill so named. They offered to this *guaca* only red shells for the king's health.

[An-8 : 9] The ninth was a spring which they named Chora, which was near Andamacha. They offered it ground-up shells and little bits of gold.

[An-8 : 10] The tenth was called Picas. It was a little pebble which was on a hill above Larapa, which they held to be an advocate against the hail. They offered it, in addition to the usual things, little round bits of gold.

[An-8 : 11] The eleventh and last *guaca* of this *ceque* was named Pilcourco; it was another stone to which they did great reverence, which was on a big hill near Larapa. When there was a new Inca, in addition to the usual things they sacrificed to it a girl twelve years old or less.

[An-9 : 0] The last *ceque* of this Road of Antisuyu was called Cayao. It was the responsibility of the *ayllu* and kinship unit of Cari and had the following five *guacas*.

[An-9 : 1] The first was called Lampapuquiu; it was a fountain which was in Undamacha [*sic*; for Andamacha]. They sacrificed to it shells of two colors, yellow and red.

[An-9 : 2] The second *guaca* was another fountain named Suramapuquiu, which was in a ravine in Acoyapuncu. They offered it only shells.

[An-9 : 3] The third was called Corcorpuquiu; it was another spring which is in the puna above the Angostura [narrows; Spanish name of Acoyapuncu].

[An-9 : 4] The fourth *guaca* consisted of some stones named Churucana, which were on top of a hill further down.

[An-9 : 5] The fifth and last [*guaca*] of this *ceque* and road was called Ataguanacauri; it consisted of certain stones placed next to a hill. It was an ancient shrine, and the usual things were offered to it.

Chapter 15: The ceques and guacas of the Road of Collasuyu

There were in [the part corresponding to] this third road nine *ceques* and on them eighty-five shrines or *guacas*.

[Co-1:0] The first *ceque* was called Cayao, and the family of Aguini Ayllu took care of it; it included nine *guacas*.

[Co-1:1] The first was named Pururauca. It was where the house of Manso Serra [sic; Mancio Serra de Leguizamo] was later. This [guaca] was a window which opened into the street, and in it was a stone of the *pururaucas*. They offered the usual things to it, except children.

[Co-1:2] The second was called Mudcapuquiu. It was a small fountain which comes out below the houses which belonged to Anton Ruiz. They offered it only shells.

[Co-1:3] The third *guaca* was called Churucana. It is a small and round hill, which is next to San Lázaro, on top of which were three stones regarded as idols. The usual things were offered to it, and children as well, so that the Sun might not lose its strength.

[Co-1:4] The fourth was a flat place called Caribamba, which is in the town of Cacra. Children were usually sacrificed to it.

[Co-1:5] The fifth was called Micaya Puquiu. It is a fountain which is on the slope of the hill of Guanacauri.

[Co-1:6] The sixth was named Atpitan. It consisted of certain stones which were in a ravine, where one loses sight of Guanacauri. They relate that these stones were men [who were] sons of that hill, and that in a certain misfortune which befell them they turned into stones.

[Co-1:7] The seventh, Guamansaui, was a large stone which was on top of a hill next to the Angostura. To this *guaca* all the families sacrificed for the Inca's strength, and they offered it small garments, gold and silver.

[Co-1:8] The eighth, Guayra, is a ravine of the Angostura where they related that the wind went in. They made sacrifice to it when strong winds blew.

[Co-1:9] The ninth and last [guaca] of this *ceque* was called Mayu. It is a river which runs through the Angostura. They made sacrifices to it at certain times of the year to give thanks because it came through the city of Cuzco.

[Co-2:0] The second *ceque* of this road was named Payan. It was the responsibility of the *ayllu* of Haguayni and had eight *guacas*.

[Co-2:1] The first was a flat place called Limapampa where the *chacara* of Diego Gil was made; there they held the festival when they harvested the maize so that it would last and not rot.

[Co-2:2] The second *guaca* was called Raquiancalla. It is a small hill which is in the *chacara*, on which there are many idols of all four *suyus*. Here a celebrated festival was held which lasted ten days, and the usual things were offered.

[Co-2:3] The third was named Sausero. It is a *chacara* of the descendants of Paullu Inca to which, at sowing time, the king himself went and plowed a little. What was harvested from it was for sacrifices of the Sun. The day when the Inca went to do this was a solemn festival of all the lords of Cuzco. They made great sacrifices to this flat place, especially of silver, gold, and children.

[Co-2:4] The fourth was a *chacara* which was called Omatalispacha, which afterward belonged to Francisco Moreno. They worshiped a fountain which is in the middle of it.

[Co-2:5] The fifth was a flat place called Oscollo, which belonged to Garcilaso. They offered it the usual things.

[Co-2:6] The sixth was named Tuino Urco. It consisted of three stones which were in a corner of the town of Cacra.

[Co-2:7] The seventh was a spring, Palpancay Puquiu by name, which is on a hill next to Cacra, and they only offered it finely ground shells.

[Co-2:8] The eighth and last *guaca* of this *ceque* was called Collocalla. It is a ravine where there was a marker beside the road, for the offerings.

[Co-3:0] The third *ceque* had the name of Collana, and on it there were nine *guacas*.

[Co-3:1] The first was named Tampucancha. It was part of the house of Manso Sierra [*sic*; Mancio Serra de Leguizamo] in which there were three stones worshiped as idols.

[Co-3:2] The second *guaca* was a stone named Pampasona which was next to the house mentioned above. They offered it only ground-up shells.

[Co-3:3] The third was a fountain named Pirpoyopacha which is in the *chacara* of Diego Maldonado, in which the Incas washed themselves on certain days.

[Co-3:4] The fourth was named Guanipata. It was a *chacara* farther down where there was a big wall which they said the Sun had made there. They sacrificed children to it and everything else.

[Co-3 : 5] The fifth was named Anaypampa. It was a *chacara* of the *coya* Mama Ocllo.

[Co-3 : 6] The sixth was called Suriguaylla. It was a fountain which had its source in a flat place so named. They offered it ground-up shells.

[Co-3 : 7] The seventh, Sinopampa [*sic;* for Sañopampa], consisted of three round stones which were on a flat place in the middle of the town of Sano [Saño]. They sacrificed children to it.

[Co-3 : 8] The eighth, Sanopuquiu [Sañopuquiu] was a certain fountain which was in a ravine of the said town. They offered it sheep and shells.

[Co-3 : 9] The ninth and last *guaca* of this *ceque* was a small hill named Llulpacturo, which is opposite the Angostura. It was designated as a place where offerings were made to the Ticci Viracocha. A greater quantity of children was sacrificed here than anywhere else. They also offered it children made of gold and silver, and small garments, and it was a usual sacrifice of the Incas.

[Co-4 : 0] The fourth *ceque* of this said road was called Cayao and was the responsibility of the *ayllu* of Apu Mayta; it had ten *guacas*.

[Co-4 : 1] The first they named Pomapacha. It was a fountain where the Incas bathed, with a house next to it into which they retired when they came out of the bath. It was where the houses of [Cristóbal de] Sotelo were afterward.

[Co-4 : 2] The second *guaca* was named Taucaray. It was a tomb which was in the *chacara* of Diego Maldonado, where they believed that at a certain time all the dead assembled.

[Co-4 : 3] The third was a fountain called Quispiquilla, which is in the said farm of Diego Maldonado.

[Co-4 : 4] The fourth was a hill, Cuipan by name, which is on the other side of Guanacauri. On top of it there were five stones which were regarded as *guacas*. They sacrificed all things to them, especially children.

[Co-4 : 5] The fifth was called Ayavillay. It was a tomb where the lords of the *ayllu* of this name were buried.

[Co-4 : 6] The sixth was called by the same name as the one above. It consisted of certain stones together placed on a hill which is opposite Cacra.

[Co-4 : 7] The seventh was called Raurao Quiran. It is a large hill which they worshiped for its great size and because it was designated [as a *guaca*].

[Co-4:8] The eighth, Guancarcalla, is a ravine like a gateway which is next to the hill mentioned above. It was dedicated to the Sun, and they offered it children in the festivals which they held there.

[Co-4:9] The ninth *guaca* is a large hill named Sinayba which is at the far end of Quispicanche.

[Co-4:10] The tenth and last was called Sumeurco. It is a hill which they had set as the limit of the *guacas* of this *ceque*. It is next to the one above, and they offered it shells.

[Co-5:0] The fifth *ceque* was named Payan, and it had ten *guacas*.

[Co-5:1] The first they named Catonge. It was a stone which was by the house of Juan Sona. They worshiped it as an important *guaca* and offered it all kinds of things, especially small figures of men and women of gold and silver.

[Co-5:2] The second was a fountain named Membilla Puquiu from which those of the town of Membilla drank. They offered it only cut shells.

[Co-5:3] The third was called Quintiamaro. It consisted of certain round stones which were in the town of Quijalla.

[Co-5:4] The fourth was called Cicacalla. It consisted of two stones which were in the same town mentioned above. Small shells and burned garments were offered to it.

[Co-5:5] The fifth *guaca* was named Ancasamaro. It consisted of five stones which were in the same town.

[Co-5:6] The sixth, Tocacaray, was a hill which is facing Quijalla. There were three venerated stones on it; they sacrificed children to them.

[Co-5:7] The seventh was a fountain called Mascaguaylla, which is on the Guanacauri road.

[Co-5:8] The eighth was named Intipampa. It was a flat place next to Cacra, in the middle of which there were three stones. It was an important shrine at which children were sacrificed.

[Co-5:9] The ninth was another flat place called Rondao, which is next to the royal road of Collasuyu, facing Cacra.

[Co-5:10] The tenth and last [*guaca*] was a small hill named Onotourco, which is opposite Quispicanche in the puna or paramo.[38] On top of it were three stones to which they offered sacrifices.

[Co-6:0] The sixth *ceque* they named Collana and there were ten *guacas* on it.

[Co-6 : 1] The first was a *buhio*[39] called Tampucancha, which was on the site of the house of Manso Sierra [*sic*; Mancio Serra de Leguizamo] and which was a residence of Manco Capac Inca. They offered it the usual things, except children.

[Co-6 : 2] The second *guaca* was named Mamacolca. It consisted of certain stones which were in the town of Membilla.

[Co-6 : 3] The third was a house called Acoyguaci, which was in Membilla, in which the body of the Inca Cinchi Roca was kept.

[Co-6 : 4] The fourth was called Quiracoma. It was a large stone with four small ones which was in the flat place of Quicalla [Quiçalla].

[Co-6 : 5] The fifth was named Viracochacancha. It consisted of five stones which were in the town of Quijalla.

[Co-6 : 6] The sixth was called Cuipan and consisted of three stones placed in the flat place of Quicalla [Quiçalla].

[Co-6 : 7] The seventh was named Huanacauri; it was among the most important shrines of the whole kingdom, the oldest which the Incas had after the window [cave] of Pacaritampu, and where the most sacrifices were made. This is a hill which is about two and a half leagues distant from Cuzco by this Road of Collasuyu we are following. On it they say that one of the brothers of the first Inca turned to stone, for reasons which they give. They had the said stone hidden. It was of moderate size, without representational shape, and somewhat tapering. It was on top of the said hill until the coming of the Spanish, and the Incas held many festivals for it. After the Spanish arrived, they removed a great quantity of gold and silver from this shrine but paid no attention to the idol, because it was, as I have said, a rough stone. This situation gave the Indians an opportunity to hide it until Paullu Inca, on his return from Chile, built a house for it next to his own. From that time on, the festival of the Raymi was held there until the Christians found out about the stone and took it away from him. With it was found a quantity of offerings, small garments for little idols, and an abundance of earspools for the young men who are knighted. They very commonly took this idol to war with them, particularly when the king went in person. Guayna Capac took it to Quito, whence they brought it back again with his body. The Incas, indeed, were convinced that it had been largely responsible for their victories. For the festival of the Raymi, they placed it on the hill of Huanacauri, dressed richly and adorned with many feathers.

[Co-6 : 8] The eighth *guaca* was a fountain named Micaypuquiu on the road to Tambo.

[Co-6 : 9] The ninth was called Quiquijana. It is a very small hill where there were three stones. They offered them only shells and small garments.

[Co-6 : 10] The last *guaca* of this *ceque* was a small fountain named Quizquipuquiu which was on a flat place near Cacra.

[Co-7 : 0] The seventh *ceque* had the name Cayao, and there were on it eight *guacas*, which were the responsibility of the *ayllo* Usca Mayta.

[Co-7 : 1] The first was named Santocollo. It was a flat place down from the *chacara* of Francisco Moreno. They offered it very fine painted garments.

[Co-7 : 2] The second *guaca* was a stone called Cotacalla, which was on the royal road near the town of Quicalla [Quiçalla]; it was one of the *pururaucas*.

[Co-7 : 3] The third was another stone named Chachaquiray, which was not far from the one above.

[Co-7 : 4] The fourth was a flat place which they named Vircaypay, where afterward the Chachapoyas Indians settled.

[Co-7 : 5] The fifth was called Matoro. It is a slope near Guanacauri where there were some ancient buildings, which they relate was where those who went out from Guanacauri after the flood slept at the end of the first day's journey. In this connection they allude to other absurdities.

[Co-7 : 6] The sixth is a fountain named Vilcaraypuquiu, which is near the said slope, where they say that those who left Guanacauri drank.

[Co-7 : 7] The seventh is a great flat place near Guanacauri named Uspa.

[Co-7 : 8] The eighth and last [*guaca*] of this *ceque* was a fountain named Guamancapuquiu, which is in a ravine.

[Co-8 : 0] The eighth *ceque* was called Payan, and it had eight *guacas*.

[Co-8 : 1] The first was a prison named Sancacancha, which Mayta Capac made; it was on the house lot which belonged to [Juan de] Figueroa.

[Co-8 : 2] The second *guaca* was a *chacara* called Guanchapacha, which afterward belonged to Diego Maldonado. All sorts of things were offered to it, except children.

[Co-8 : 3] The third was called Mudca. It was a stone pillar which was on a small hill near Membilla. They offered it only ground-up shells.

[Co-8 : 4] The fourth was a small hill named Chuquimarca,

which is next to Guanacauri. They offered it ground-up shells.

[Co-8 : 5] The fifth was called Cuicosa. It consisted of three round stones which were on a hill so named, next to Guanacauri.

[Co-8 : 6] The sixth was a certain fountain named Coapapu- quiu, which is next to the same hill of Guanacauri.

[Co-8 : 7] The seventh was another fountain called Puquin [*sic;* possibly should read Puquiu], next to the one mentioned above.

[Co-8 : 8] The last *guaca* of this *ceque* was a ravine which is next to Guanacauri. Everything which was left over after the other [*guacas*] of this said *ceque* had been taken care of was offered to it.

[Co-9 : 0] The ninth and last *ceque* of this road we are following was named Collana, and it had thirteen *guacas.*

[Co-9 : 1] The first was a seat named Tampucancha, where they said that Mayta Capac used to sit, and that while he was sitting here he arranged to give battle to the Acabicas [*sic;* Alcabiças]. Be- cause he defeated them in the battle, they regarded the said seat as a place to be venerated. It was next to the Temple of the Sun.

[Co-9 : 2] The second *guaca* was called Tancarvilca. It was a small round stone which was in the house lot which belonged to Don Antonio [Pereira]; they said that it was one of the *pururaucas.*

[Co-9 : 3] The third was a flat place called Pactaguañui which belonged to Alonso de Toro. It was a much venerated place; they sacrificed to it to be preserved from sudden death.

[Co-9 : 4] The fifth [*sic;* fourth] was called Quicapuquiu. It is a spring which is this side of Membilla. They offered it ground-up shells.

[Co-9 : 5] The fifth was named Tampuvilca. It was a round hill which is next to Membilla, on top of which were five stones which they relate had appeared there, and for that reason they venerated them. They offered them the usual, especially burned *cestos* of coca.

[Co-9 : 6] The sixth was named Chacapa. It is a flat place on that end of Membilla. They offered it ground-up shells.

[Co-9 : 7] The seventh was called Chinchaypuquiu. It is a foun- tain which was in a town of this name.

[Co-9 : 8] The eighth, Guarmichaca Puquiu, is another fountain which is farther up in a ravine next to Guanacauri.

[Co-9 : 9] The ninth, Cupaychangiri Puquiu, was another foun- tain next to the one above, and they offered it only shells.

[Co-9 : 10] The tenth, Quillo, consisted of five stones placed on top of a hill of this name near Guanacauri.

[Co-9 : 11] The eleventh *guaca* was called Cachaocachiri. It consisted of three stones which were on another small hill so named;

it was an ancient shrine in which, and in the one above, children were sacrificed.

[Co-9 : 12] The twelfth was a large stone named Quiropiray, which was on top of the hill of this name; they said it was one of the *pururaucas.*

[Co-9 : 13] The last *guaca* of this road was a hill named Puncu, where they offered what was left over from the *guacas* of this *ceque.*

Chapter 16: The ceques and guacas of the Road of Cuntisuyu

The Road of Cuntisuyu, which we call Condesuyo, had fourteen *ceques* and eighty *guacas*, as they are here set forth.

[Cu-1:0] The first *ceque* they named Anaguarque, and it had fifteen *guacas*.

[Cu-1:1] The first was a stone called Sabaraura, which was where the belvedere of Santo Domingo is now; they believed that it was an officer of the *pururaucas*.

[Cu-1:2] The second *guaca* was another stone like this one, named Quingil, which was in a wall next to Coricancha.

[Cu-1:3] The third was called Poma Chupa (it means "lion's [i.e., puma's] tail"). It was a flat place in the district so named, and from there offerings were made to the two small rivers which flow through there.

[Cu-1:4] The fourth was named Uxi. It was the road which goes to Tampu. Sacrifices were made at the beginning of it for certain reasons which the Indians give.

[Cu-1:5] The fifth, Guaman, is a ravine where there was a small round stone which was an idol.

[Cu-1:6] The sixth, Curipoxapuquiu, was another ravine next to the one above, on the Membilla road; they offered it the usual and children on certain days.

[Cu-1:7] The seventh, Anaguarque, was a big hill which is next to Guanacauri, where there were many idols, each of which had its origin story and history. Children were usually sacrificed.

[Cu-1:8] The eighth, Chataguarque, was a certain small stone which was on a little hill next to that other one.

[Cu-1:9] The ninth, Achatarque Puquiu, was a fountain next to the hill above; they offered it only clothing and shells.

[Cu-1:10] The tenth, Anahuarque Guaman, was a stone which was on a hill next to the one above; they offered it children.

[Cu-1:11] The eleventh *guaca* was a fountain named Yamarpuquiu, which was in a ravine on the slope of the above hill.

[Cu-1:12] The twelfth was another fountain called Chicapuquiu, which comes out near the one above.

[Cu-1:13] The thirteenth was called Incaroca. It was a cave which was farther along than the fountains named above and was an important shrine. They offered it children.

[Cu-1 : 14] The fourteenth was a certain stone named Puntuguanca, which was on top of a hill of the same name near the hill of Anaguarque.

[Cu-1 : 15] The last *guaca* was called Quiguan. It consisted of three stones which were in a small gap on the way to Pomacancha.

[Cu-2 : 0] The second *ceque* of this Road of Cuntisuyu was the responsibility of the *ayllo* of Quisco. It was named Cayao and had four *guacas.*

[Cu-2 : 1] The first was a great flat place called Cotocari, which afterwards was a *chacara* of [Antonio] Altamirano.

[Cu-2 : 2] The second was called Pillo Lluri. It was a ravine on the way to Tambo in which there was a long stone of medium size held in veneration.

[Cu-2 : 3] The third, Paylla Llanto, was a certain cave into which they believed that a lady of this name, mother of a great lord, Apu Curimaya by name, entered and never again appeared.

[Cu-2 : 4] The fourth was called Rauaraya. It is a small hill where the Indians finished running on the feast of the Raymi, and here a certain punishment was given to those who had not run well.

[Cu-3 : 0] The third *ceque* was called Payan and had another four *guacas.*

[Cu-3 : 1] The first was a fountain named Chuquimatero from which the Indians of Cayocache drink.

[Cu-3 : 2] The second was called Caquia Sabaraura. It is a hill opposite Cayocache on top of which were five stones regarded as idols.

[Cu-3 : 3] The third, Cayascas Guaman, was a long stone which was in the town of Cayascas.

[Cu-3 : 4] The fourth, Chucuracay Puquiu, is a ravine on the way to Tambo where the valley of Cuzco is lost to sight.

[Cu-4 : 0] The fourth *ceque* they named Collana, and it had five *guacas.*

[Cu-4 : 1] The first was called Pururauca. It was one of those stones into which they said that the *pururaucas* had changed, and it was on a stone bench next to the Temple of the Sun.

[Cu-4 : 2] The second was called Amarocti. It consisted of three stones which were in a small town named Aytocari.

[Cu-4 : 3] The third, Cayaopuquiu, was a fountain which was opposite Cayocache, on the slope of the river.

[Cu-4 : 4] The fourth, Churucana, was a certain large stone which was on a hill next to that of Anaguarque; they offered children to it.

[Cu-4 : 5] The fifth was named Cuipancalla. It is a ravine which is on the way to Tambo, where they cast what was left over of the offerings of this *ceque.*

[Cu-5:0] The fifth *ceque* was called Cayao. It was the responsibility of the *ayllu* of Chima Panaca, and it had the same number of *guacas* as the preceding one.

[Cu-5:1] The first they named Caritampucancha. It was a small square which is now inside the monastery of Santo Domingo, which they held to be the first place where Manco Capac settled on the site of Cuzco when he came out of Tampu. Children were offered to it along with everything else.

[Cu-5:2] The second *guaca* was called Tiucalla. It consisted of ten stones of the *pururaucas* which were in Cayocache.

[Cu-5:3] The third, Cayallacta, consisted of certain stones which were on a hill near Choco, a town which belonged to Hernando Pizarro.

[Cu-5:4] The fourth, Churupuquiu, is a fountain which is above the said town of Choco.

[Cu-5:5] The fifth was called Cumpu Guanacauri. It is a hill in line with Choco, on top of which there were ten stones which they believed that the hill of Guanacauri had sent there.

[Cu-6:0] The sixth *ceque* of this same road was named Payan, and it had five *guacas.*

[Cu-6:1] The name of the first was Apian. It was a round stone of the *pururaucas* which was on the site which Santo Domingo has today.

[Cu-6:2] The second *guaca* was called Guaman. It was a stone which was in Cayocache.

[Cu-6:3] The third, Ocropacla, consisted of some stones of the *pururaucas* which were in Cayocache.

[Cu-6:4] The fourth, Pachapuquiu, was a fountain which is toward Pomapampa.

[Cu-6:5] The fifth was called Intirpucancha. It was a *buhio* in the middle of the town of Choco and had belonged to its first lord.

[Cu-7:0] The seventh *ceque* was named Collana, and it had another five *guacas.*

[Cu-7:1] The first was a small house called Inticancha, in which they held the opinion that the sisters of the first Inca, who came out of the window [cave] of Pacaritampu with him, dwelt. They sacrificed children to it.

[Cu-7:2] The second *guaca* was named Rocromuca. It was a large stone which was next to the Temple of the Sun.

[Cu-7:3] The third, Caruinca Cancha, was a small house which was in Cayocache, which had belonged to a great lord.

[Cu-7:4] The fourth, Sutirmarca; this is a hill from which they say that an Indian came out, and that he reentered it again without having any children.

[Cu-7:5] The fifth, Cotacotabamba, was a flat place between Choco and Cachona where a festival was held on certain days of the year in which they stoned one another.

[Cu-8:0] Half of the eighth *ceque* was named Cayao and the other half Collana; the whole of it had fifteen *guacas*.

[Cu-8:1] The first they named Tanancuricota [*sic*; for Chañan Curi Coca]. It was a stone into which they said that a woman who came with the *pururaucas* turned.

[Cu-8:2] The second was a tomb of a principal lord; it was named Cutimanco. They sacrificed children to it.

[Cu-8:3] The third was called Cauas. It was another tomb which was in Cachona.

[Cu-8:4] The fourth was named E Con Con Puquiu. It was a fountain which is in Cachona.

[Cu-8:5] The fifth, Chinchay Puquiu, was another fountain which is on a slope of the puna.

[Cu-8:6] The sixth, Mascata Urco, is a hill where one loses sight of Cuzco on this *ceque*.

[Cu-8:7] The seventh, Cachicalla, is a ravine between two hills like a gateway; they did not offer anything to it except the coca which passers-by cast from the mouth.

[Cu-8:8] The eighth, Quiacas Amaro, consisted of certain stones which were on top of a hill beyond Cayocache.

[Cu-8:9] The ninth, Managuanunca Guaci [Managuañunca Guaci], was a house of one of the *coyas* or queens, which was on the site which the monastery of La Merced now has.

[Cu-8:10] The tenth, Cicui, was a tomb which was on the slope of Cachona.

[Cu-8:11] The eleventh, Cumpi, is a large hill which is on the way to Cachona, on top of which there were ten stones regarded as idols.

[Cu-8:12] The twelfth, Pachachiri, is a fountain which is in the puna of Cachona.

[Cu-8:13] The thirteenth, Pitopuquiu, is another small fountain which was next to the one mentioned above.

[Cu-8:14] The fourteenth, Cauadcalla, was a sort of gateway between two hills, which is toward Guacachaca.

[Cu-8:15] The last *guaca* of this *ceque* was called Lluquiriui.

It is a big hill next to the above ravine.

[Cu-9:0] The ninth *ceque* had the name Cayao and included three *guacas*.

[Cu-9:1] The first was called Colquemachacuay (it means "silver serpent"). It is a fountain of good water, very well known, which is on the slope of the hill of Puquin, next to the city of Cuzco.

[Cu-9:2] The second was named Micayurco. It is a large hill which is above Puquin.

[Cu-9:3] The third, Chaquira, is a hill which is near the Alca road, on top of which there were ten stones held to be idols.

[Cu-10:0] The tenth *ceque* they named Payan, and it had four *guacas*.

[Cu-10:1] The first was a fountain called Pilcopuquiu, which is in the garden of Santo Domingo.

[Cu-10:2] The second was called Puquincancha. It was a house of the Sun which was above Cayocache. They sacrificed children to it.

[Cu-10:3] The third had the name Cancha. It was the enclosure wall of the above house, where they also made offerings.

[Cu-10:4] The fourth, Viracochaurco, is a hill which is above Puquin.

[Cu-11:0] The eleventh *ceque* was named Collana, and on it there were four *guacas*.

[Cu-11:1] The first was a fountain called Matarapacha, which is on the way to Cayocache.

[Cu-11:2] The second was named Cuchiguayla. It is a small flat place which is located below the said fountain.

[Cu-11:3] The third, Puquinpuquiu, is a fountain which is on the slope of the hill of Puquin.

[Cu-11:4] The fourth, Tampu Urco, is another hill which is to one side of the one of Puquin.

[Cu-12:0] The twelfth *ceque* was named Cayao, and it had three *guacas*.

[Cu-12:1] To the first, they gave the name Cunturpata. It was a seat on which the Inca rested when he went to the festival of the Raymi.

[Cu-12:2] The second was called Quilca. It was a very ancient tomb of a lord who was so named.

[Cu-12:3] The third, Llipiquiliscacho, was another tomb which was behind Choco.

[Cu-13:0] The thirteenth *ceque* was named Cayao [*sic*; Payan], and it had four *guacas*.

[Cu-13:1] The first was a *puquiu* or fountain named Chilquichaca.

[Cu-13:2] The second was called Colcapuquiu. It was another fountain which is in a ravine which descends from Chilquichaca.

[Cu-13:3] The third, Chinchincalla, is a large hill where there were two markers; when the sun reached them, it was time to plant.

[Cu-13:4] The fourth, Pomaguaci, is a small hill at the end of this *ceque* which was [there] as the end and limit of its *guacas*.

[Cu-14:0] The last *ceque* of this Road of Contisuyu was called Collana, and it had four *guacas*.

[Cu-14:1] The first was a stone of no great size named Oznuro, which was in the *chacara* of the Gualparocas.

[Cu-14:2] The second *guaca* of this *ceque* was called Otcuropuquiu. It was a fountain near Picho, a farm of the Society of Jesus.

[Cu-14:3] The third was named Rauaypampa. It was a terrace where the Inca lodged which was on the slope of the hill of Chinchincalla.

[Cu-14:4] The fourth, Pantanaya, is a large hill cleft in the middle which divides the Roads of Chincha [Chinchaysuyu] and Condesuyo, or Cuntisuyu.

The four following *guacas* belong to various *ceques* but they were not set down in the order that the rest were, when the investigation was made.

[Ch-Ex:1] The first was called Mamacocha. It is a small lake up above the fortress.

[Ch-Ex:2] The second is a fountain called Tocoripuquiu, from which issues a stream which passes through the city.

[Ch-Ex:3] The third was named Chinchacuay. It is a hill which is opposite the fortress.

[Ch-Ex:4] The fourth and last of all was called Ququijana. It is another hill which is behind the one above.

These were the *guacas* and general shrines which there were in Cuzco and its vicinity within four leagues; together with the Temple of Coricancha and the last four, which are not listed on the *ceques*, they come to a total of three hundred thirty-three, distributed in forty *ceques*. Adding to them the pillars or markers which indicated the months, the total reaches the number of three hundred fifty at least. In addition, there were many other private *guacas*, not worshiped by everyone, but by those to whom they belonged, such as those of the provinces subject to the Inca, which were shrines only of their natives, and the dead bodies of each lineage, which were revered only by their descendants. Both kinds had their guardians and attendants who, at the proper times, offered the sacrifices which were established. For all of them these Indians had their stories and fables of how and for what reasons they were instituted, what sacrifices were made to them, with what rites and ceremonies, when and for what purposes, so that if it were necessary to give a detailed account of everything, it would be prolix and tedious. Indeed, I very nearly refrained from listing, even in this brief fashion, the *guacas* named in these four chapters, and I would have done so, except that I judged it necessary to enumerate them to explain more clearly the gullibility of these people and how the devil took advantage of it to inflict on them such a harsh servitude, of so many and such foolish errors with which he had taken possession of them.

Chapter 17: Of the famous temple of Pachacama

In magnitude, devotion, authority, and richness, the Temple of Pachacama[40] was second only to the magnificent [Cuzco] Temple of the Sun. Since it was a universal sanctuary, people came to the Temple of Pachacama on pilgrimages from all over the Inca Empire, and there they made their votive offerings. This famous temple was located four leagues from this city of Los Reyes [Lima] in a pleasant and fertile valley by the sea. During the reign of the Incas, there was an impressive town in the valley which was a provincial capital. The temple building was next to the town, but set back from the sea, which lies five hundred paces west of it. The river that waters this valley lies three hundred feet to the north. Next to the temple was a small lake which seems to have been connected to the sea long ago. The temple site is a tiny hill, but since the valley is very flat, the hill dominates it. The hill seems to be artificial, built by hand as the groundwork for this structure, which is in the form of a square, somewhat longer than it is wide. It is composed of six parts progressively smaller toward the top, stacked up like a truncated pyramid; all of the parts are solid, of adobes and earth. The temple and many lodgings were constructed on top. Thus, this large mound seems to have been built to provide the magnitude [necessary] for the foundations of the temple.

At the present time all that remains standing of this construction are the ruins and some walls of the temple and lodgings. Furthermore, the six parts of the mound are still intact, except for some pieces which were chipped off and some sections with hollowed-out places made by the Spaniards looking for treasure. Moreover, by looking at the site and thinking about it carefully, I was able to determine the design and magnitude of the whole edifice very well, including the measurements and layout of all its parts, which are as follows.

The first part of the mound is six hundred feet long from corner to corner and five hundred and sixteen feet wide. Therefore, the distance around the four sections comes to two thousand two hundred thirty-two feet. In height it does not rise up more than one *estado*[41] above the small, flat-topped hill on which it was erected. This first part seems to have been made to serve as the base of the whole construction and to provide a level place for the arrangement of the complex. On top of it there is a ridge or terrace forty feet wide, like a large street forming a circle around the second part, which rises out of the first. This second part is as much smaller than the first as the space occupied by the above-mentioned terrace. Thus the face of the second part is five hundred twenty feet long, four hundred thirty-six feet wide, and twenty-four feet high. Between the wall of this second part and that of the third there is another ridge or landing thirty-two feet wide which is a street or flat terrace like the first one forming a circle around the third part, which is twelve feet high and rises out of the second level. On top of this third part there is another ridge twenty-six feet wide. The fourth part is fifteen feet high, and the top of it forms a ridge which cuts twenty-four feet into the structure. The fifth part seems to be only a buttress for the top level; its ridge is only ten feet wide, and it rises no more than five feet above the fourth level. The sixth and final part of this great mound rises twelve feet above the fifth level. Therefore, the structure is seventy-four feet high from the ground level up to the flat roof or plaza forming the top of the final part, and this plaza is very large. It is three hundred thirty-six feet long and two hundred fifty feet wide. On each side of it, there were two sections of buildings which are in ruins today, although in some places the walls are still standing at the original height and in the same condition as before.

Each section of these buildings was lined up along the sides of the above-mentioned plaza or patio. This was set up in such a way that the length of the buildings made the plaza wider. There was a street sixteen feet wide behind the above-mentioned building, and this was the space between the rear wall of this building and the wall of the top part of the mound. On the side facing the sea there was a fifty-six foot space between the wall of the same building and the upper level of the [six] solid parts; on the inland side there was another space thirty feet wide. Each section of the above-mentioned buildings was one hundred sixty feet long and seventy-five feet wide. One section was in front of the other, at an equal distance and with equal dimensions; the back parts as well as the sides of each section were the same distance away from the edge of the mound. The plaza or patio between the two sections was one hundred sixty feet wide. On the other sides, the whole width of the top part was visible, and as has already been stated, it was two hundred fifty feet wide. The fresh sea breeze which always blows along this coast bathed the sides of the plaza, and from it one enjoyed a broad and magnificent view. From one point, many leagues of sea could be seen, and from the others, the whole valley was visible. All year

around this valley is green and pleasant. The Indians went up to
this large plaza to make offerings and celebrate their festivals, dances,
and drinking bouts.

These two sections of buildings that stood up on the upper
level of the solid parts were twenty-four feet high; the walls were
of adobe, the same as the walls of the six solid parts of the mound.
The buildings had many window spaces all around, similar to the
other magnificent edifices of the Peruvian Indians. Each window
was no more than a space as deep as the thickness of the wall; this
space was covered up by a thin wall on the inside. From the outside it looks like a cupboard or niche. These window spaces were
placed in an orderly fashion along the sections of each of the above-
mentioned buildings, and between each one there was no more
space than the width of each window. In these buildings there were
many rooms, chambers, and cells, which were like chapels where
the idols were kept and where the priests and attendants lived.
Both the walls of these lodgings and the walls of the terraces, as
well as the walls of the rest of the edifice that made up this complex, were plastered with earth and paint of several colors, including many fine works for their style, though these works seemed
crude to us. There were diverse figures of animals, though they
were poorly formed like everything else these Indians painted.

Apart from the edifice mentioned above which was on the
plaza of the mound, there were many other lodgings around the
solid parts of this construction, especially on the second, third, and
fourth parts of it. Some of the lodgings were incorporated into the
solid parts themselves, and some were next to them on the ridges,
and since these ridges were so wide and ample, there was plenty of
room. But the place where they had done the most building was
the side by the sea from the fourth solid part up to the upper level,
and this appears to be the face or front of the whole complex. First
of all, there was a narrow room like a passageway that ran the whole
length of the structure; on both sides the walls were covered on the
inside with door spaces, in the same style as the windows described
above. In front of this room there was a corridor or gallery twelve
feet wide; its wall had a series of door spaces that looked like cupboards, with a group of crudely made adobe pillars in front. The
roof of this room or gallery was a flat terrace which reached up to
the same level as the floor of the patio. Thus, when someone walked
on the above-mentioned patio or plaza, they would not notice this
structure until they stepped on its roof, at which time they would
realize there was a hollow place beneath; this differed from the rest

of the above-mentioned plaza, which had a solid floor. The leveled-off part which was just below this gallery also had a series of window spaces. And this was the most beautiful and decorated style of construction that these Indians used for the façade of their buildings, just as we use columns, cornices, and various moldings and other decorative trimmings. All of these rooms were the lodgings for priests, attendants, and guards of the temple, and the *mamaconas* had a separate house next to it. Somewhat farther away, some ruins of many large houses can be seen, and they say that these houses were the hostelry for the many pilgrims who frequented this sanctuary.

Although many doorways covered with a variety of paintings can be seen along the exterior walls of this temple, there was only one way to go up to it. This was a long stairway made of rough stones without mortar; the steps were so low that even though the stairway was quite long, going up was no work. The entrance was located on the inland side, which is to the east, and the stairway made ten or twelve turns; there were landings and doorways decorated with paintings at each turn. Since most of this stairway is in ruins now, it is impossible to make an accurate count of the number of steps it had; nevertheless, one section is intact, and I counted twenty steps there. On the basis of this one part, and taking into consideration the height and proportions of the structure, it seems to me that the whole stairway must have had at least one hundred fifty steps or more.

This great temple was not constructed by the Inca kings. Actually it was much more ancient, as the Indians say. This can be seen in the form and quality of its construction, which is different from the others done by the Incas because these were almost all made from hewn stone. And if this one [Pachacama] were of stone, it would compete with the most magnificent buildings in the world. It is called Pachacama, the name of the idol or false god to which it is dedicated. Pachacama means "maker of the world." The idol was carved from wood into a fierce and frightening figure. Nevertheless, it was highly venerated because the devil spoke through it and gave its answers and oracles to the priests. In this way the devil deceived the credulous people, for he made them think that the idol had control over all things. The attendants and sorcerers made sacrifices to the idol before the multitude of the people. At the moment they were to consult the idol, they backed up toward it with their eyes cast down, full of worry and fear; they made gestures of humbleness and assumed an indecent, ugly posture while awaiting the oracle. The sacrifices they made to it included a great many animals, silver, gold, and the rest of the valuable things that they had, and they also made some sacrifices of human blood.

It was the custom of the Incas to compel all the nations that they subjugated to adopt their gods, rites, and the cult of their false religion. However, after they conquered the Valley of Pachacama, they saw the grandeur, antiquity, and veneration of this temple and the way the neighboring provinces were so devoted to it. And they decided that it would not be easy to change this because the authority which the place commanded over everyone was so extraordinary. It is said that the Incas conferred with the local *caciques* and lords of this valley and with the priests of this god or devil. Thus the Incas decided that the temple would remain with the majesty and service that it had before, on the condition that another building or chapel be built there and that a statue of the Sun be placed in this chapel and worshiped. This was carried out as the Incas ordered, and at the time, the convent of the *mamaconas* located next to the temple was constructed. This arrangement did not displease the devil; in fact it is said that from then on he showed he was very pleased by his answers. Actually, this did not hamper his standing; in fact with both things he increased his sway over these wretched people, whose souls remained trapped in his clutches. From that time on the authority of this temple grew much more because of the fact that the Incas esteemed it very much, and they enhanced the temple with such rich decorations that it came to be the temple most celebrated and worshiped of their whole empire except for the Coricancha of Cuzco. The amount of gold and silver that had been gathered there was incredible. Besides the fact that the walls and ceiling of the chapel of the Pachacama idol were covered with sheets of these metals, all of the tumblers and other articles of the service of the temple were also of gold and silver. Moreover, there were many animal figures made from these rich metals on the walls, which came as votive offerings from these blind people, and along both the high and the low terraces there was a large amount of gold and silver buried.

The first Spanish captain to enter this temple was Hernando Pizarro. He took a great deal of wealth from it, in spite of the fact that the Indians found out about his arrival and hid many loads of silver and gold. To this day it has not turned up, nor does anyone know where it is located. This captain knocked down idols and broke the main idol to pieces; this was the one through whom the devil spoke. On seeing the audacious way in which the Spaniards offended the gods whom they respected so much, the Indians' astonishment was so great that they were beside themselves. By virtue of the Holy Cross which was erected in this temple and by preaching the Holy Gospel, the devil was silenced, and he gave no more answers in public. However, the Indians say that he continued to speak in secret places with the old sorcerers because he saw that he was losing credibility and authority. On seeing through his errors, many of those who used to serve him had forsaken him to embrace the truth of our holy faith. Thus he endeavored to keep others from receiving the holy waters of baptism with new trickery. He sought to persuade them by saying that he and the God the Christians preached about were the same. However, his crafty attempts to keep the worship of this great temple from ending completely were to no avail. The ruins of the temple are deserted today and have been turned into the abode of vermin. Moreover, the few Indians who are still native to this Valley of Pachacama are so far from paying any attention to this shrine of their ancestors that it is hard to find one living now who even remembers what it was.

Chapter 18: Of the famous temple of Copacabana

On the basis of its reputation and authority, this sanctuary was the third most important one for these Peruvian Indians. (Notice that for our purposes here we are treating it as if it were a single entity.) Actually, it comprised two magnificent temples, which were located on two separate islands of Lake Chucuito [Titicaca]. And since both islands are close to the town of Copacabana, we use this name to make reference to the sanctuary. One of these islands was called Titicaca, and the other Coata [*sic;* for Coati]. The former was dedicated to the Sun, and the latter to the Moon. Both of them, along with the mainland adjacent to them, which is a boundary of Copacabana, fall within the province of Omasuyu, Diocese of Chuquiabo. The aforementioned town of Copacabana is located on a promontory projecting out from the mainland up to the Straits of Tiquina. This promontory extends out one league, and serving as its entrance is the town of Yunguyo, where the two beaches that surround this headland come so close together that it is actually an isthmus, more or less one mile wide. The town of Copacabana is located by the shore of two pleasant inlets of the lake which are in view. The inlets are between two high steep hills. On one of the hills, the place for torture where the Inca punished rebels can be seen. The distance from the aforementioned town of Copacabana to the Island of Titicaca is one league.[42] Formerly, the inhabitants of this island were the Colla Indians, and the natives of Copacabana were from the same nation. The Island of Coata, which was dedicated to the Moon, is located one and a half leagues east of the Island of Titicaca. The Island of Coata is smaller than the other one, and the weather is the same, but Coata has no water except that of the lake which surrounds it. For this reason, before being dedicated to the Moon, it was a wasteland, uninhabited by either man or beast.

The shrine of the Sun, which was on the Island of Titicaca, was a large solid crag. The reason it was consecrated to the Sun and worshiped can be traced to a ridiculous story. It is said that in this province the people of ancient times tell of being without light from the heavens for many days, and all of the local inhabitants were astonished, confused, and frightened to have total darkness for such a long time. Finally, the people of the Island of Titicaca saw the Sun come up one morning out of that crag with extraordinary radiance. For this reason they believed that the true dwelling place of the Sun was that crag, or at least that crag was the most delightful thing in the world for the Sun. Thus a magnificent temple, for those times, was constructed there and dedicated to the Sun, although it was not so magnificent as it was after the Incas enlarged it and enhanced its fame.

Others tell this fable differently, saying that this crag was dedicated to the Sun because the Sun remained safely hidden under it during the whole time that the waters of the Flood lasted, and after the Flood, the Sun came out from there and began to illuminate the world from that place. Therefore, that crag was the first thing to be favored with light. Whatever the origin of this shrine may have been, it was very ancient and highly venerated by the people of the Collao before they were subjugated by the Inca kings.

But after the Incas took possession of these provinces surrounding the lake and its islands and took charge of enhancing this shrine, those who had the shrine before became more devoted to it and its influence spread to all the provinces of the kingdom. The way the Inca found out about this shrine and how it became so famous is as follows. At the time that the Incas had made themselves the lords over all this land, their authority and power was increasing more and more each day. They had inspired so much respect and fear in the Indians that those who had defended their property with arms had so freely surrendered their arms to these kings that they judged a man to be a traitor who concealed anything from the Inca kings that they might find important or enjoyable. Since this island (in the opinion of these people) was worthy of the highest esteem because of the great sanctuary located there, one of the old men who had served as an attendant there since boyhood headed for Cuzco, the court where the Inca kings resided. He was moved to do this by his fervent desire that with the new leadership of the Incas the worship of this shrine would not wane, but be augmented, and that the shrine would be exalted. And also by this means the old man wanted to earn the favor of the Inca Tupa Yupanqui, the tenth king of this land, who was in power at the time. Upon reaching the court and presenting himself with the customary ceremonies and submissiveness, he gave the Inca a long account of the origin and worship of this sanctuary, of which the Inca had heard nothing until then. The old man told the Inca how the Colla Indians had possession of the sanctuary unjustly, and he explained to the Inca how worthy the sanctuary was, and for his highness to take it under his protection. In this way the sanctuary's authority would grow among the Inca's vassals, and they would become more devoted to it. The Inca was inclined to believe him, and the Inca soon left to pay a visit to the provinces of the Collao because he wished to see what this temple and shrine were like. He entered the Island of Titicaca, and found the altar and temple which were dedicated to his gods. The Inca found out about how much the local people worshiped that sacred place; he thought over the arrangement of the site and the fact that it was a shrine dedicated to the Sun for the reasons mentioned. He also took into consideration how much the Incas boasted of being descendants of the Sun. Thus, he was pleased to have found a place so appropriate to further increase the worship and reverence of the Sun among his subjects.

Since he was very favorably impressed with the sanctuary, the Inca decided to employ all of his power and solicitude in endeavoring to extol it with all sincerity, and he took it as an undertaking worthy of his own grandeur and majesty. In conclusion, he took the matter of enhancing the importance of this shrine so seriously that he did everything in his power to sustain it, enlarge it, and make it more illustrious. Before anything else, in order to make a display of his devotion and add to the reputation of this pilgrimage, the Inca fasted here for many days, abstaining from salt, meat, and *aji* [chile pepper], as was their custom. And on the many occasions when the Inca came to this sanctuary afterward, he became accustomed to removing his sandals two hundred steps before reaching it. Since the Indians considered this to be an act of exemplary devotion, they made a gateway in the same place which was called Inti-puncu, and this means gateway of the Sun. Besides this, this Inca had many buildings constructed in order to enlarge and lend more authority to this shrine. The former temple was augmented with new and impressive buildings. In addition, it was ordered that other buildings be constructed for other purposes; these included a convent for *mamaconas* which was placed here, many magnificent lodgings and rooms to serve as a dwelling place for the priests and attendants, and one quarter of a league before one reaches the temple, there was an impressive *tambo* or inn for the pilgrims to stay in. In order to keep them supplied, the Inca had large storehouses built near Copacabana for provisions of food, clothing, and other supplies. The ruins of these storehouses remain to this day, and I have seen them myself. And even in these ruins the magnificence of the work can be seen, as well as the zeal for promoting public welfare of the one who exhibited the foresight to take such measures by means of which the people never went hungry in this land. This certainly is admirable, especially taking into consideration the multitude of people who came here and how barren the land was.

Since the area starting from the straits or isthmus which I mentioned above between Yunguyo and Copacabana was considered to be a sacred place, the Inca had this entrance closed off with a wall which he had made from one beach to the other. He had gates put along the wall with watchmen and guards to look over the people who came to the sanctuary on pilgrimages. According to what the Indians say, it was the Inca's will that the land be opened up so that the water from either side of the area would encircle or enclose the promontory; in this way the water would serve as a wall. And since the town of Copacabana was the most appropriate, accessible, and calm place (as far as the water was concerned) for an entrance to the island with the sanctuary, the Inca populated it with *mitimaes*⁴³ selected from all the provinces of his kingdom, as well as with a large number of Inca nobles, and it was much enlarged both in the number of residents and the number of buildings. Therefore, in this place, the same as in the other towns within his jurisdiction that were provincial capitals, the Inca had a temple built for the Sun and for the other major gods. The inhabitants of the Island of Titicaca were natives of Yunguyo, and it was to this island that the Inca sent his people, reserving for some old men the task of informing those who were recently ordered to populate the area about the secrets of the island. Instead of sending those people who had been dispossessed [of their lands], he sent other people who were brought in from Cuzco, in whom he could put the trust that the gravity of the case required. He made a moderate-sized town one league from the temple, and the majority of the inhabitants were *mitimaes* of Inca blood and lineage. And he had a dwelling built there for them to live in.

Since it seemed to the Inca that the only thing lacking which could enhance the grandeur of this temple and shrine was the plant called *coca*, which was among the most highly esteemed offerings that they had, he decided to plant it on the island itself. In order to compensate for the plant's aversion to this highland location, he made up his mind to have such a deep place dug on the island that it would be warmer there. But carrying out such a difficult undertaking was impossible. Since the island is small and completely surrounded by water, moisture soon seeped in and stopped the work before a very deep hole could be dug. In spite of all that, they made such a large hollow that the coca was planted and it started to grow, though this was accomplished with great difficulty. But because of the barren land and the cold climate, the coca grew very poorly and with inferior leaves. And it certainly was a great feat to put this plant in such a place, since it requires a very warm climate. However, since the project was so unnatural, it did not last. Besides the fact that the climate was so adverse, the high part of the gully caved in, burying the coca and along with it many of the Indians who were in charge of cultivating it. Therefore, the Inca rescinded his order because it was too difficult to carry out.

But the Inca was not content with what had been done to decorate and enhance this sanctuary. He felt that he still had not entirely fulfilled his obligation and that he was not responding with prudence to the service of the Sun if he did not designate a woman or even women for the use and service of the Sun. Therefore, he decided to do it, and while he had this on his mind, he found a convenient way to carry it out. It was the Island of Coata, which he dedicated to the Moon, giving it the name Coata or Coyata, which means 'of the Coya,' that is to say queen, and he constructed a magnificent temple on it. In the temple he placed a statue of a woman; this statue was gold from the waist up and silver from the waist down. The statue was the size of a woman, and it appeared to be an image of the Moon. Thus, along with the living women who were dedicated to the service of the Sun on the Island of Titicaca, there was this idol; it was a representation of the Moon and had the name of the Inca's wife. Nevertheless, some hold that this statue was called Titicaca, and they say that it represented the mother of the Incas. Be that as it may, the statue was carried to the city of Cuzco on the orders of the Marques Francisco Pizarro, who sent three Spaniards for it.

Finally, the Inca enhanced this sanctuary whenever it was possible. He added expensive buildings to it, designated a large number of people to serve there, put priests and confessors there according to their customs, and increased the sacrifices of animals and human blood, along with the rest of the valuable things that they normally offered to their false gods. He enriched it greatly with tumblers of gold and silver, and among other things, he gave it a piece worthy of his royal glory; this was a very large brazier made of pure gold with lions to support it; two of the lions were silver, and the other two gold. In addition to the priests and attendants who were always present for the services at this sanctuary, the Inca put two thousand Indians in it who were exempt from paying any tribute. Their only obligation was to clean up and maintain in good repair the two temples of the two islands and of Copacabana. For these Indians and for the priests and *mamaconas,* the Inca had designated sufficient income to sustain them so that they would never shirk their duties. By taking these measures, the Inca achieved his aspiration of introducing the veneration of this ancient shrine throughout his entire kingdom. This veneration was so widespread that people came to this place on pilgrimages from everywhere. And there was always a large gathering of people there from far away. Thus this place became so famous that its memory will live on among the Indians as long as they last.

As has already been stated, there were guards stationed at the gates of the wall between Yunguyo and Copacabana. They inspected the travelers, and once they found out that the travelers were just coming on a pilgrimage with no other motive, the guards handed the travelers over to the confessors who were there for that purpose. In accordance with the gravity of the offences that were confessed, the penitence was imposed upon them. It started with some blows on the back with a stone, after which the rest consisted of abstaining from salt, meat, and *agi* [chile pepper]. Once this ceremony was completed, the travelers went on to the town of Copacabana, where they made another confession so as to enter with more purity into the Island of Titicaca, and the only ones to set foot on the island were those who came on a pilgrimage and those who came from the mainland to care for some fields that were sown there on the island. But no one was permitted to come empty-handed up close enough to see the sacred crag, much less anyone who had not been fully approved of by the confessors who were stationed at the above-mentioned places for this purpose. Moreover, they did not get close to the crag; they were only allowed to view it from the gateway called Intipuncu, and there they handed over their offerings to the attendants who resided there. Upon finishing their prayers and offerings at this sanctuary of Titicaca, they continued on to Coata Island, which was considered to be the second station. And since a visit to these sanctuaries was sold to them at such a high price, the result was that such visits were held in higher esteem.

The size, form, and location of the sanctuary of Titicaca, after the Inca enlarged and enhanced it, was as follows. The crag that was so venerated was out in the open, and the temple was next to it, located in such a way that this crag was about where the cemetery would be, or to put it more properly, within the main chapel, even though it was out in the open; actually it was the most sacred place. The front of it faces north, and the back faces south; there is not much to the concave part of it, which is what they worshiped. The altar of the Sun was inside. The convex part is the living stone, whose slopes reach out as far as the water, where there is a cove made by the lake. The adornment was a covering over the convex part, a curtain of *cumbi,* which was the finest and most delicate piece [of this cloth] that has ever been seen. And the entire concave part of it was covered with sheets of gold, and they threw the offerings into some holes that can still be seen now. Ahead of this crag and altar a round stone can be seen which is like a basin, admirably wrought, about as large as a medium-sized millstone, with its orifice; the stone is used at the foot of a cross now. The *chicha*[44] for the Sun to drink was tossed into this orifice.

The temple was located to the east, about forty paces from the crag. In it the image of the Sun was worshiped, and along with it the images of the Thunder and the other gods that the Indians worshiped. And in the windows, cupboards, or niches along the walls, many idols were placed. Some of the idols were in human form, others were shaped like sheep [llamas], and others were of birds, and other animals. All of the idols were made of copper, silver, and gold. Some of them were large, and others small. Near the temple the ruins of a storehouse of the Sun can be seen, and the chambers of this place look like the labyrinth of Crete. The skillful workmanship that characterized the construction of this superstitious shrine can be seen in the large walls and other traces of it that remain standing today. In addition, the outline of a garden with its walk lined with alder trees[45] is visible, and under the shadows of these trees there were some very well made baths of stone that were constructed on the Inca's orders. The Inca said that these baths were constructed so that the Sun could bathe there.

Apart from these, there are other constructions in ruins, but no one can remember what these were used for. The entrance to all of these constructions was through that gate called Intipuncu, located two hundred paces from the crag. A living stone was located between this gate and the constructions mentioned, and the road that leads to the sanctuary passes through this stone. On it are what appear to be the traces of certain enormous footprints left by Indian sandals. The old Indians thought that these were miraculous footprints that remained there from the extremely obscure times of their heathendom. However, they are really watermarks on the stone itself. To one side of the entrance mentioned above, certain old buildings can be seen which, according to what the Indians say, were lodgings for the attendants and servants of the temple, and on the other side there are signs of a large building which was the retreat of the *mamaconas*, women dedicated to the Sun. These women served in making the beverages and finely woven cloth that were used in the services for the shrine. This house for the *mamaconas* was in the best location of the island. The old Indians say that this sanctuary was guarded by a serpent or large snake, and the devil could have deceived them in that way to entice them more in the main thing he was doing. However, what I think is that by saying that a serpent encircled the whole island they meant, and it should mean, the water of this island, and on clear days the rays of the sun shimmer on the water in such a way that from the beach the waves seem like painted snakes of various different colors.

There was constant communication between the priests and attendants of this shrine [on the Island of Titicaca] and those of Coata, and there were frequent missions from one island to the other with large groups returning the visits. The attendants of both sanctuaries pretended that the Sun's wife [the Moon] sent him messages, however this might have been done by the Moon in the Indian's estimation. The Sun answered these messages with caresses of tender fondness and mutual love, and this took up a great deal of time. For this purpose a great many rafts were used that went back and forth from one island to the other. And in order to show a live representation of this, the chief attendant at the site of the shrine took the part of representing the person of the Sun, and at the site of the other one, an Indian woman took the part of the person of the Moon. They would drink to each other's health, and the lady who represented the Moon caressed the man who had the part of the Sun. She would beg him with her caresses to shine brightly every day, never hiding his rays, so that they would make the fields fruitful until the time when the rains were necessary. In addition to this she would ask him to keep the Inca alive, in good health, and rested. She also asked the same for the others who with so much faith and devotion took care of the services and rites of the Sun. And the person who pretended to be the Sun would respond with enough flowery words to fit the occasion. In this delirium these wretched people wasted their lives in such mindless and idle pursuits. And everything ended up in a drinking bout, which was their greatest satisfaction in life. The priests of the temple of Titicaca also had the most important *mamacona* of the island take the part of the wife of the Sun. They would get her dressed up as lavishly as possible and bring her out in public, and putting her in the middle of the multitude, they would offer her gifts befitting the wife of their god.

The sacrifices made at this shrine were frequent and lavish. It is astonishing to consider the amount of blood shed by innocent victims and the treasures that were offered in these sacrifices. The following example will show how conscientious they were in doing this and in making sure the persons to be sacrificed were not ugly and had no blemishes on any part of their bodies. Once a fourteen-year-old girl was brought to this island to be sacrificed, but the chief attendant exempted her. In carefully examining her body, he had found a small mole under one of her breasts. For this reason she was not considered to be a worthy victim for their god. This woman was still living when the Spaniards came to this land, and as time passed she made friends with one of the Spaniards. She told him about the perilous situation in which she had found herself, what had helped her out, and about the great treasure that used to be offered at this temple. She did not tell this secretly, and the Indians who lived there soon found out. They say that while the Indians were having a big festival, they heard sad voices, and a while later a stag burst in among them running at full speed. From this the sorcerers determined that the Spaniards knew about their sanctuary and about the treasures that were there. In addition, they realized that very soon the Spaniards would come there, as in fact they did. And the Indians were so clever in hiding the treasure that it has never been found. It is believed that they transferred it to other islands. However, others say that the attendants who were here at that time either buried it or threw it into the lake so that the Spaniards would not be able to have it. While I was in this province in the year 1616, I heard the report that there is a great deal of wealth on Coata Island, and at that time certain Spaniards went there on a boat, but they were unable to find anything.

Chapter 19: Of the temple and buildings of Tiaguanaco

Although the temple of Tiaguanaco was a universal *guaca* and shrine, nevertheless, it was not venerated as much as the three shrines mentioned above. The people held it in high esteem principally because of the size and antiquity of its buildings, which were the most magnificent and attractive of the whole kingdom. This shrine is located on a high plain within the second level of the Sierra.[46] The plain extends for many leagues; however, it is only about one and a half leagues wide because it is surrounded by two small ranges of mountains. The town of Tiaguanaco is located in this savanna or plain next to a small river that empties into Lake Chucuito [Titicaca] four leagues from the town. The Royal Highway that goes from Cuzco to Chuquiabo [La Paz] passes through Tiaguanaco at a point just nine leagues from Chuquiabo. The natives are of the Pacage nation because it falls within the province of this name. The ancient ruins of these superb buildings are two hundred paces south of the town. And it appears that the town was previously considered part of the same complex as the buildings mentioned above and had the same name. The name of this town before it came under Inca rule was Taypicala, from the Aymara which is the native language of the region. The name of this town means "the stone in the middle" because the Indians of the Collao were of the opinion that this town was in the middle of the world, and that the people who repopulated the world after the flood came out of this place. Now I will explain why it was called Tiaguanaco. Its inhabitants say that once while the Inca was here, a messenger arrived from Cuzco in a surprisingly short time. (The Inca was informed as to the speed with which the message had been brought.) When the messenger came forth, the Inca said to him, "Tiay, guanacu," which means in their language: "Sit down and rest, guanaco." And the Inca gave the messenger the name *guanaco*, which is a very swift animal of this land, because of the speed with which he had arrived. And this name was applied to the town from that time on, except that we change some of the letters when we pronounce this name.

Now I will explain what I have been able to determine on the basis of the traces and ruins that still remained of these edifices on the occasions when I saw them and pondered over them. The size, form, and shape of these edifices is as follows. The main part of the

stonework is called Pumapuncu which means "gate of the lions." It
is a mound or flat-topped hillock two *estados* high made by hand;
it was erected on large, well-worked stones, which are in the form
of the ones we put over graves. This mound is made square, with
four sections of equal size, and each one is one hundred paces from
corner to corner. At the top are two platforms of large stone slabs,
very uniform and flat. Between the first and the second platform,
there is a space six feet wide like a large step, and the second one
has a smaller such space than the first one. The face or front of this
building is a section that faces east toward other extensive ruins
that I will tell about presently. From this front section the structure emerges with the same height and walls of stone, twenty-four
feet wide and sixty feet long; two angles are formed at the sides.
And this place that juts out from the square [mound] seems to have
been some sort of large room or hall placed in the middle of the
front of the structure. Somewhat more inside the part that juts out,
the entire ground is paved with large, magnificent stones. Therefore, this must have been the temple or the main part of it. This
paved area is one hundred fifty-four feet long and forty-six feet
wide. The stone slabs are all surprisingly large. I measured them,
and the biggest one is thirty-two feet long, sixteen feet wide, and
six feet thick. The others are somewhat smaller; some thirty feet
[long]; others smaller, but all of them are unusually large. They are
smooth and flat like a well-polished board, and they have many
decorations and moldings on the sides. At the present time there
are no walls still standing on this paved area, but judging from the
many carefully worked stones that have fallen around it, among
which pieces of doors and windows can be seen, the place must
have been enclosed by well-made walls. The only thing that is still
standing on the main stone slab is one part facing east that is dug
out of a large, well-worked stone which is nine feet high and is the
same width. And the door space is six feet high and its width is in
proportion. Near this doorway there is also an intact window which
faces south, made entirely of a single well-worked stone.

Along the front of this building the foundations of a dressed
stone wall are found. It comes out from the corners of this front
section and occupies another square space like the one for the
mound and foundations of the whole edifice. Within this wall,
about thirty feet from the edge of this building, toward the south
corner, the foundations of two small, square rooms are seen. The
foundations stand about three feet from the ground level, and they
are made of well-polished ashlar stones. These rooms look like

pools or baths or the foundations of some sort of tower or burial
place. An aqueduct of marvelous, worked stone channels goes
across the middle of the mound structure at the ground level outside. It is a canal a little more than two spans wide and about the
same height, made of square, dressed stones which do not need
mortar. The top stone fits into the walls of the above-mentioned
canal. The grooves in the top stone overlap one finger width, and it
fits into the space across the canal walls. About four hundred paces
to the east of this edifice, the ruins of another one just as big and
magnificent are seen. It is impossible to determine whether this
second edifice was separate from the first, or if they formed a single
complex. The construction may have continued some place, but
there are no traces left today. In any case, the Indians use a different name for the second edifice; it is called Acapana.

This is a mound about four or five *estados* in height which
appears to be a hill; it was erected upon a large stone foundation. In
form, it is square, and at intervals it has what resembles the cir-
cular towers of a fortress. Fifty paces to the east of the mound, a
large gateway remains intact. It consists of only three well-worked
stones, one on each side and another on top of them both. No other
parts of this structure remain here on the ground except the mound
and some worked stones that jut out from the foundations. On the
basis of this, the form of the construction can be seen. Close to
this mound is another one which is also square. A street fifty feet
wide separates the two mounds. Thus both of them seem to be part
of a single structure. The walls of the last building were admirable.
Although this building has fallen down to the ground now, its
workmanship and form can be determined on the basis of one part
of the wall that is still intact. This is because of the diligence and
care of a priest who served in Tiaguanaco. His name was Pedro del
Castillo (a conscientious man who made a careful study of the size
and antiquity of the buildings during the many years that he was a
priest in the above-mentioned town). He died in the year 1620. This
wall is made of stone blocks without mortar, and the stones are as
well fitted together as carefully finished pieces of wood. The stones
are of medium size, and other very large stones are placed at intervals like buttresses. This is similar to our buildings of adobe walls
in which brick buttresses which extend from top to bottom are
usually inserted. Thus, this wall has at intervals, in place of buttresses, some stones like square columns that are so extraordinar-
ily large that each one extends from the foundations up to the very
top of the wall, which is three or four *estados* high. And it is not

known how far these stones penetrate into the earth where they are placed. Judging by the visible traces of this wall that remain, evidently it was a large enclosure that extended to the east from this last building and covered a very large area. Here the remains of another stone canal like the first one are found, and this one seems to come from the mountain range that is in front of the building at a distance of one league.

I find two things about these constructions that should not be passed over lightly without giving some thought to them. The first is the amazing size of the stones and of the whole complex. And the second is the extraordinary antiquity of the site. Who would not be astonished to see the unusually large stones that I have described? Who would not wonder how human strength would suffice to carve such huge stones out from the quarries and carry them to where we see them now? This is all the more amazing since it is a known fact that no stones or quarries are found within several leagues of this site; moreover, none of the people of this New World have ever made use of the invention of machines, wheels, or winches for the purpose of pulling such stones, nor did they have any animals that could pull them. I must confess that I cannot fathom nor understand with what strength it would have been possible to bring these stones nor what instruments or tools would have been adequate for such a job in a place where iron was unknown. And we have to confess that in order for the stones to have been worked into the form and size in which we see them now, they must have been much bigger before they were shaped to perfection. All of these stones are of two or three different kinds; some are red sandstones [literally grindstones] and are soft to work; others are brown or ash-colored and very hard. The workmanship used is varied and very different from ours. The skillfullness of the work is most clearly shown by the fact that the stones are as smooth and flat as they could possibly be.

Since the Indians did not have any form of writing, there are many things about them that cannot be determined. Thus, in the majority of the cases we proceed with uncertainty and by conjectures, and this is what happens when we try to investigate the beginnings of this ancient place, to determine what men made these buildings, and how long the buildings have been here. Nevertheless, the fact of the matter is that the Indians do not remember any of these things; they all confess that it is such an ancient construction that their information does not go back that far. However, they do agree on one thing. The buildings were already constructed many years before the Incas started to govern. In fact, it is widely reported among the Indians themselves that the Incas made their great edifices in Cuzco as well as in other parts of their kingdom on the model of this place.[47] Some fables introduced among the Indians originated because of the great antiquity of this site. Some state that they heard from their ancestors that this construction had appeared unexpectedly in one night. Others state that the large stones that we see here were brought through the air at the sound of a trumpet played by a man. And there are other similar illusions and nonsense. In addition, I have heard several opinions given by men of good judgment, and some of them feel that this construction antedates the Flood and that it must have been a great city built by giants.[48] I would not dare to give a firm opinion on such a doubtful matter, but if conjectures are of any value, on the basis of the ones that I find here (and they are not too frivolous to carry considerable weight), I conclude that it is a construction of considerable antiquity. My first conjecture is based on the stones of the edifice themselves. These stones show that a long period of time certainly must have transpired. The rains have sufficed to wear them away to a great extent. Where the line of the wall I spoke of runs, one sees many of those large standing stones set in the earth that served as buttresses. And although all of them were of the size that I have stated and cut with four corners, some of them are so worn down that they are no more than one *estado* high, and some are even smaller. The part of them which has remained above the ground hardly shows any signs of having been worked. They look rough and pointed. Moreover, it is evident that the rains have disfigured them and diminished them because they are much more worn on the top, but toward the base, the original form and workmanship that they had can be observed. And this cannot have happened in a short time. Certainly these stones have endured for many centuries because the rains could not have damaged them so much in any other way.

The second argument that I find in support of the antiquity of this site is more convincing to me than the first one. And it is the vast number of cut stones that there are beneath the surface of the earth. In fact, besides the stones seen on the surface, including those that have fallen from the buildings, and other larger ones located some distance away, it is amazing both to see the ones taken from beneath the earth's surface, and the method of finding them. In spite of the fact that the surface of the entire countryside is flat, even, and covered with grass, without any sign of ravines or cliffs, any place where the earth is dug up within more than one-half league from the above-mentioned ruins, in going down one or two *estados* the earth is found to be full of these cut stones, including some large, beautiful slabs. Thus it appears that a great city was buried here. After I visited these buildings for the first time in the year 1610, a huge cut stone was unearthed. On another occasion when I returned here, this stone was shown to me, and I measured it myself; it was twenty feet long by fifteen feet wide, and it was as polished and as smooth as it could be. I discussed this matter at length with the priest of Tiaguanaco, whom I mentioned above, and he assured me that while the patio of his house was being dug up in order to put in a pond as an adornment in honor of the arrival of the first Bishop who was coming from Chuquiabo, some of these cut stones were found. In addition, he told me that when the church of that town was being built, he was in charge of the construction, and he ordered the craftsman to make two stone statues of Saint Peter and Saint Paul which stand today above the main doorway to the church. And since the craftsman wanted to avoid doing the job on the pretext that there were no stones with which to make the statues, this priest told him that was no excuse since there were so many cut stones of all sizes wherever he might dig, and in order to prove this, the priest ordered that they dig in the very place where they happened to be when they were discussing this matter. The priest's orders were carried out, and before they had dug down very far, stones were found of sufficient size to use in making the statues mentioned above. Another unusual thing is that inside these constructions they found large stone statues that certainly are the size of giants.[49]

The main reason why the Indians held this shrine in such high esteem must have been its great antiquity. The natives adored it from time immemorial before they were conquered by the kings of Cuzco, and these kings did the same thing after they became lords of this province. They considered the above-mentioned temple of Pumapuncu to be remarkable, and they enhanced it by increasing the amount of decoration as well as the number of attendants and sacrifices. Next to it they constructed royal palaces where they say Guayna Capac's son Manco Capac was born. The ruins of this place are seen today, and it was a very big building with many rooms and apartments.

Because of reports spread throughout this kingdom that there are extensive buried treasures within these buildings, many Spaniards have taken the initiative to dig at this site in search of treasure, and at different times they have found many pieces of gold and silver. However, there seems to have been more than has been found. As a matter of fact, what has contributed most to the tearing down and destroying of this construction has been this greed to take the treasures that, according to well-known reports, are hidden here. Nevertheless, it is also true that this place has been torn down in order to make use of the stones; the church of Tiaguanaco was built with them, and the citizens of Chuquiabo [La Paz] have carried away many of them in order to build their houses, and even the Indians of the town of Tiaguanaco make their graves with excellent slabs that they take from these ruins. And I am convinced that if these ruins were close to any of the major cities of this kingdom, these stones would have been extremely useful and not a single one would have been left lying on the ground. However, since the ruins are located on a bleak plateau far from the towns populated by Spaniards, there are still so many stones left that they will not be gone for many years.

Before continuing further, I wish to relate a notable incident that occurred within these edifices, and it is as follows. The first encomendero [grantee][50] of the town of Tiaguanaco was a resident of Chuquiabo [La Paz] named Captain Juan de Vargas. He had been sent to Spain during the civil wars of this land on a mission pertaining to these wars. During his stay at the Court, he found himself very much distressed because it did not look as if he would resolve his business as soon as he wished. One day while he was out on the patio of the palace, a stranger approached him and asked him why he was so sad, for he was the lord of the richest town in the world, which was Tiaguanaco. And the stranger gave him an account showing the location of these buildings and the place within them where the treasure to which he referred was located as well as the way to find it. After concluding the business for which he had gone to Spain, the captain returned to this kingdom [of Peru], and in accordance with the account that was given to him by that man or demon in human form (which is what it seems to have been), he ordered that the site of the above-mentioned building be dug up, and judging from the evidence that he found, the account that he had was entirely accurate and valid. At first he took out numerous large earthen jars full of clothing made of very fine *cumbi* cloth, *tianas* or seats and jugs made of silver, as well as a large amount of *chaquira* beads and vermilion. He uncovered a skeleton or the remains of a human body the size of a giant, and as he continued making more discoveries, he was very pleased to see that he was locating all the clues that were set down in the account. One day he found a large human head made of gold; its face was similar to the stone idols mentioned above. This whetted his greed to find more treasure, and he was as pleased as he could be, but his pleasure was short-lived because the following night his course of action was cut off by the hand of death, which came suddenly, though he had gone to bed healthy, with no ailment. Such an eventuality was so frightening that it stripped the greed from those who wanted to continue digging in search of the treasures that presumably are buried in the aforementioned buildings.

Chapter 20: Of the temple of Apurima

On the banks of the Apurima [Apurimac] River there was a very colorful temple which was a famous shrine. A post the thickness of a man was set inside of it, and this post was covered with blood from the sacrifices that were made to it. A gold band the thickness of one hand was wrapped around it; this band had a pair of solid gold breasts on it, like a woman's breasts. This post or idol was dressed in a woman's costume which included clothing made of very fine gold and many *topos* or large pins of the type that were used by the Indian women. On each side of this idol there were other small ones that occupied the width of the room. These [idols] were also covered with blood and dressed in women's costumes. The major idol was called Apurimac, and the devil customarily spoke to the Indians through it. The guardian of this idol and temple was a lady of Inca lineage named Sarpay who hurled herself from a high cliff overlooking the river. As she threw herself from these heights, she covered her head and called out to her god Apurima. She did this because of her sorrow over the fact that her shrine had fallen under the power of the Spaniards. It was very common for the devil to speak with the Indians through this idol. During Manco Capac's rebellion, he made the idol speak to him in the presence of a Spaniard named Francisco Martin who was being held prisoner. Later Martin stated that he heard the voice of the devil answer the questions that Manco Inca asked. And according to Martin the Inca himself said to him, "Notice how my god speaks to me." There were many other famous temples throughout this kingdom, but those that I have described were held to be the most important sanctuaries.

Chapter 21: Of the sacrifices that they made to their gods

Some aspects of the subject matter of this chapter have already been covered within what has been said in the enumeration of the *guacas* of Cuzco and of the offerings made to them.[51] For this reason and since I am going to make an extensive description further ahead of the regular and special sacrifices that these Indians made during the course of the year in celebrating their festivals, here I am only going to tell about the things that were offered in the sacrifices and the manner in which these things were consumed in honor of their false gods. Not all the sacrifices were voluntary offerings. Since some of them were general and solemn and others were private, there was a different way of making the sacrifice for each one. Some of the general and solemn sacrifices were made with the property of the Religion and with that of the Inca, and others were made with what the community contributed in the apportionments made to cover the necessities that came up. Such apportionments were made when this type of [general] sacrifice was held. The towns were compelled to contribute for both kinds of sacrifices, and no one was exempted from this tribute. This is because for the first kind [of sacrifices] regular taxes and tribute were paid, and for the other kind [of sacrifices] another special type of tribute was paid, similar to our custom of paying the *sisa*[52] or any other special contribution for some public work. And thus, what was spent on these general sacrifices could be called a voluntary offering in a certain sense, if it is considered after being collected from the community and from the point of view of the king and the others who handled it. Nevertheless, from the point of view of those who made the contribution for the sacrifices, the offering was made more under force than willingly.

The first solemn sacrifices were made to each god from the personal property of that god, and the sacrifices made to Viracocha were made from the property of all the gods. Sacrifices were made for each one of the gods of particular things and second causes.[53] These sacrifices came from the property which was assigned to them for this purpose from the major income [property]. It was collected in the name of the Religion and it benefited the Religion. In addition, the gods of particular things made offerings themselves from this very property to Viracocha, as a universal lord over everything. These sacrifices were made by the priests of each god in the name of their god. Also considered general and solemn in the same way were the sacrifices that the Inca made from his own personal possessions to Viracocha as well as to the Sun and the other gods. These sacrifices were so common and costly that most of the Inca's income was consumed by them.

Among the second kind of solemn sacrifices, there was a very great variety with respect to the material [offerings were made of] and the amount [of offerings made]. Since the needs and the occasions were different, the sacrifices were also different. The choice of the type of sacrifice depended on the will of the conjurers and sorcerers. Before any of these sacrifices that they made on behalf of the needs and troubles that usually came up, the above-mentioned sorcerers cast lots, and on the basis of the results, they chose the type of sacrifice that seemed appropriate to them, and then all of the people made a contribution, and what was gathered was turned over to the priests who were in charge of the offering. The special and private sacrifices that each person made because of his own vow and devotion were really voluntary offerings. Part of these offerings was consumed in honor of their gods and part was offered to support the priests and attendants, and this was what was given in the way of remuneration to the priests for their work, especially to the medical practitioners and diviners for the work of curing or answering the questions that were asked of them. Actually these occupations of medical practitioner, diviner, and sorcerer usually went together.

The form to be followed in the sacrifices was so well established, with the rites and ceremonies designated for each one, that no one was permitted to exercise his own free will in changing, adding, or eliminating anything from what was ordained, particularly with respect to the general and public ceremonies. The offerings were not made in the same way to all the gods and shrines, nor were the same things offered. Moreover, the offerings were not made for the same purpose. However, everything was done in a very orderly and careful manner. The priests of one *guaca* did not interfere with the priests of another *guaca*, nor were the occupations and affairs [of one priest] confused with those of another. At every town and *guaca* attendants were assigned for each sacrifice, and it was stipulated when each sacrifice was to be made, the form and manner in which it was to be carried out, as well as the different types of things for it, according to the importance of the *guaca* and shrine and the purpose for which the sacrifice was made. They also made a distinction in the words that were used at the time of making the offering. Even though the sacrifice was directed to any one of the special gods, they spoke first to Viracocha, whom they considered to be the Creator. For example, when sacrifices were made to springs, besides speaking to him first, they would say: "Lord, who created all things and among them you saw fit to create me, and you created the water of this spring for my sustenance, I beseech you to keep it from drying up and keep water flowing as you have done in past years so that we can harvest the crops we have sown." After this they directed their words to the fountain itself, and they spoke to it in this way: "O source of water who have irrigated my field for so many years, and by means of this benefaction that you confer upon me I obtain my food, do the same this year, and even increase the amount of water so that the harvest will be more abundant." After saying this, the sacrifice that they were carrying was made. The same form and order was followed when they made sacrifices to the Sun so that he would make the plants grow, to the Thunder so that he would make it rain and not hail or freeze, and to the rest of the special gods and second causes. First they would speak with Viracocha and afterward they would speak with the special gods. And in their sacrifices to all the universal *guacas* they would plead for the health of the Inca.

In their sacrifices they used all the things they had and whatever else they could lay their hands on. Actually, they prided themselves so much on being religious and they were so conscientious about it, that their main purpose in keeping whatever they had, whatever they raised and harvested, and in whatever they hoped to achieve, was to dedicate it to their gods and *guacas* and offer it to them as a sacrifice. Thus they gave everything from the children that they begat to the fruits of their harvests. First of all, the most authoritative and important sacrifice was that of human blood, but it was not as common as the others because the sacrifice of human blood was only offered to the major gods and *guacas* for important purposes and on special occasions. When they conquered and subjugated some nation of Indians, they would select a large number of the most attractive individuals that there were among them, and these individuals were brought to Cuzco, where they were sacrificed to the Sun for the victory that they said the Sun had achieved for them. However, this sacrifice was not very common because the occasion on which it was offered did not come up often. In the human sacrifices that were most frequently made, they offered the children that the Inca collected by way of tribute throughout the kingdom. In addition, because of some grave necessity that came up, some children would be voluntarily offered by their parents. Among those of the first group selected for this cruel and inhuman sacrifice there were some males and some females, but more females were killed than males. The males were children of about ten years of age or younger, and some females included in the sacrifices were the same age as the boys, others were maidens fifteen or sixteen years of age. These maidens were kept in the enclosures or convents of the *mamaconas*. They could not have any blemish or even a mole on their entire body. They were given plenty to eat and drink before their lives were taken. And the small children who were too young to eat were allowed to breast feed with their mothers. It was said that they did this so that the little ones would not be hungry or unhappy when they reached the place where the Maker was. Usually they would make the older ones drunk first. All of them were taken around the idol two or three times, and they were sacrificed by being strangled with a cord or by having their throats slit. Some had their hearts cut out, and while they were still beating, their hearts were offered to the gods to whom the sacrifice was directed.

The faces of the idols and the embalmed bodies of the lords and kings were smeared with the blood of those whose hearts were cut out and that of those whose throats were cut. This was done when the offering was made, and a line was made on the face of the idol or embalmed body from ear to ear across the middle of the nose. On other occasions the same blood would be spread over the entire bodies of the idols. In addition, they would usually pour some blood on the ground for ceremonial purposes. Finally, the bodies were buried with gold and silver and other things and with special superstitions. The hole could not be made with copper nor with any other metal; it was made with sharp sticks while certain grimaces and ceremonies were made. There were also some regular and other special sacrifices of this kind. The special sacrifices were only made for things of great importance such as times of pestilence, famine, war, or other great disasters. Nevertheless, the most common ones were usually made because of things that were of importance to the Inca, such as when the Inca took the crown and sceptre of the kingdom. On this solemn occasion, two hundred children were usually killed. Other such sacrifices were made when the Inca went to war in person, when he got sick, so that he would get well, and on other similar occasions. When some Indian was sick and his life was in danger, whether he was a noble or a plebeian, if the diviner or sorcerer said that he would surely die of

that sickness, the man would sacrifice his own son to Viracocha or
to the Sun, asking the god to receive his son's life in exchange for
his own, and being pleased with the death of his son, not to take
the life of the father.

The sacrifice of domesticated animals was valued and esteemed second only to that of humans. And sacrifices were made
only of the domestic animals, not of wild animals. The reason they
gave for this is that sacrifices should be made only of those animals
that were raised [by the Indians] and not of the others that were
born and raised on their own. The Indians assumed that whatever
was given for the health and affairs of men, must have been acquired and kept with some effort on their part. (Actually, this is a
faulty explanation because it also takes work to hunt animals; in
fact, usually hunting is more work. Besides, this explanation could
also be shown to be invalid if we wished to take into account their
own nonsense in order to convince them, for they also sacrificed
wild birds and a thousand other things that grew up in the wild
without any human assistance.) Since they had only two kinds of
tame animals, namely, llamas, which we call sheep of the land, and
guancos or *cuis* [guinea pigs] which are the same thing, all of the
sacrifices of animals were taken from these two kinds. The most
acceptable and principal sacrifice was that of sheep, and a larger
amount of them were used.

This sacrifice [of llamas] was done in an orderly fashion in accordance with their customs, both with regard to the number of
animals offered, as well as to the color and other markings, according to the god to whom the offering was made, according to the
festival, and according to the result for which the sacrifice was
made. Each one of the gods was assigned certain of these animals
according to the color and markings. Brown sheep of the color of
guanacos were sacrificed to Viracocha; white ones to the Sun, and
of these, the smooth-furred [llamas] were sacrificed for certain
purposes and with different ceremonies, and the woolly-furred
[alpacas] with others so that the Sun would shine and make things
grow. In the city of Cuzco, a smooth-furred sheep was sacrificed to
the Sun every day. This animal was dressed in a red vest before it
was burned. This was called the Sun's offering. When the animal
was burned, some baskets of coca were thrown into the fire with it.
There were people assigned to do nothing else but oversee this
ceremony. There were also animals used exclusively for it. And a
world of nonsense was involved in this sacrifice. Likewise, every
morning they made the Sun a fire of carved wood, and as the Sun

appeared in the sky, the fire was lighted, and food prepared in the
same way as for the Inca was brought there for the Sun, and as they
threw part of the food into the fire, they would say, "Eat this, Lord
Sun, in recognition of the fact that we are your children." The rest
of the food, which was a large amount, was eaten by the priests and
the other persons who served with them, which amounted to a
large number of people. Apart from these daily sacrifices, other
general sacrifices, including prayers and fasting, were made to the
Sun at specified times. In particular, each month when the Sun
reached the markers or posts that designated the months[54] sacrifices were made to him. They said that two benefits resulted from
this. The first one was to thank him for the trouble he took in
giving light to the earth and in helping the earth produce food for
mankind. The other one was to give the Sun enough strength to
always continue doing these things. This they begged of Viracocha.
And they said to the Sun himself, when they offered a sacrifice to
him, that they wished for him to always remain young and for him
to come up every day making light and shining brightly. Parti-
colored sheep were sacrificed to the Thunder so that rains would
not be lacking, and to other gods other different sacrifices were
made. The method they used in killing any animals whether large
or small, and especially the sheep, was that after having led the
animals around the idol several times, the priest took them over
his right arm, and turning the animal's eyes toward the god to whom
the sacrifice was directed, the offering was made with certain words
appropriate for the occasion, and the victim's throat was cut.

Chapter 22: Of the rest of the things that were offered in the sacrifices

The sacrifice of *cuis* [guinea pigs] was also considered quite acceptable. And it was very common to use these little animals to see the outcome of future events by slicing them open and looking at them for certain signs. They were also used for many other purposes, but it would take too long to tell about them. The sheep were used for the same purposes in matters of more importance.

The sacrifice of birds was uncommon. I can only find one kind of sacrifice in which birds were used; it was when they hunted down many wild birds, and made a huge fire with a certain thorn wood. Then the birds were tossed into the fire all together. The attendants of the sacrifice walked around [the fire] holding certain round and angular stones on which toads, snakes, tigers [jaguars], and lions [pumas] were painted, saying in their language: "Let us be victorious, and may the *guacas* of our enemies lose their strength." Then they brought out some black sheep that had been kept in prison with nothing to eat for several days, and they killed them, saying that in the same way that the hearts of those animals were weakened, so may their enemies lose heart. If by chance, on looking inside these sheep, they found that a certain lump of flesh located behind the heart had not been consumed while the animals were fasting in that prison, it was taken as a bad omen. And they brought out certain black dogs which were killed and thrown on a place of flat ground. Then they made a certain kind of people eat the dog meat, and special ceremonies and superstitious acts were performed. This same sacrifice was also performed so that the Inca would not be attacked with poison. When they were going to perform this sacrifice, they did not eat from morning until a star or Venus came out at night, and then they would eat their fill. They considered this sacrifice to be the most important and effective way to counter the powers of their enemies' gods.

Moreover, they offered their food and drink to their gods, and it was their understanding that the gods ate these things wherever they happened to be. The food was carried to the hilltops, and there it was burned and the *chicha* was poured out onto the ground. Those who were in charge of the dead bodies of the lords did not let a single day pass without giving them the same kind of food that they used to eat when they were alive. This food was burned, and the drink was poured out onto the ground. They believed that from the place where the soul was located, it would receive the thing offered and eat it. Generally food was sacrificed by burning it, and *chicha* was offered by pouring it on the ground. However, the *chicha* that the Inca offered to the Sun in the solemn festivals was poured into a large gold cup that was located in front of the statue of the Sun, and the priest took the cup and poured the *chicha* into that stone sheathed inside with gold, that was kept in the square for this purpose. When the food for the Sun was burned, one Indian stood up, and he announced this to the people in a loud voice. All the Indians, both inside and outside the square, sat down and re-mained quiet without speaking or coughing until the sacrifice was consumed, which did not take long because the fire was big and the wood was very dry.

In addition to this sacrifice, they sacrificed some kinds of flour made from certain vegetables. For instance, white maize flour and red ocher, along with some other things, were thrown as an offer-ing to the sea. They made a certain preparation or dough with the flour mentioned above and other mixtures; this was sacrificed. Among other things, they made dough of maize flour, fat, and wool which was offered by burning it, and fat by itself was commonly burned as a sacrifice. Among the sacrifices of plants, vegetables, and fruits of the land, none was as highly esteemed as coca. It was offered in many ways. Sometimes the whole coca [leaf] was offered, and other times the leaf was offered after it had been chewed and the juice sucked out. Sacrifices were made to the Earth by scatter-ing coca on it, by pouring *chicha* out on it, and by offering other things. Ordinary sacrifices were made to the Earth at the time of plowing, sowing, and harvesting the crops; this was accompanied by much dancing and drinking. On passing by the *apachitas*[55] [passes] and some other *guacas*, chewed coca and feathers of vari-ous colors were tossed to it as an offering, and when they had noth-ing else with them, they would throw old sandals, a rag, or a stone, and along the roads today we see many piles of stones offered in this way. They made this offering when they were walking along a road so that the above-mentioned *guacas* would let them go by and give them strength, and thus they said that they were strengthened by this, and if they had nothing else, they gave another offering as ridiculous as the ones already described. This consisted in pulling out their eyelashes or eyebrows and making an offering of them. Moreover, it was very common for them to make offerings of silver and gold, sometimes in small lumps of different sizes, and at other times they offered these metals in the form of human or animal images, some small and others large. And the sacrifice was made by burying the things at the *guacas* and places consecrated to the gods in whose honor the sacrifices were made, or they would place them [sacrificial objects] along the walls of their temples, as we make votive offerings in our sanctuaries and places of devotion.

Fine clothing was just as common as that of the most frequent offerings. It was a part of nearly every major sacrifice. Clothing was made for this purpose with certain ceremonies and in different ways. Part of it was men's garments and part of it was women's; some of the garments were large, some small. They dressed the idols and dead bodies of the lords in this clothing, and put alongside them folded garments. Thus, not counting the garment that each idol already had, they put another folded garment next to it. However, the amount of clothing that was burned was so much greater that there was no comparison. In this there was also diversity. Sometimes they burned clothing alone, and other times they set fire to statues of men and women made of carved wood, dressed in this clothing, and in this way they burned them. These Indians were also accustomed to sacrifice seashells, especially when they made offerings to the springs. They said that this was a very appropriate sacrifice because the springs are the daughters of the sea, which is the mother of the waters. According to the color, the shells were offered for different purposes, sometimes whole, other times ground into powder, other times broken into pieces, and in addition, some figurines were made from the powder. This sacrifice was offered to the above-mentioned springs after the planting was done so that the springs would not dry up that year and so that these springs would flow with abundance and irrigate their sown fields as had happened in past years. They also made offerings in their sacrifices of carved and scented wood, *chaquira* [seashell beads], and in short, of all the things that the land produces. And it should not be understood that the sacrifices of each one of these things were made alone with only one kind of thing, because it was not done in this way. Actually, almost all of these things were used in practically all of their sacrifices. Therefore, the human sacrifices were accompanied by sacrifices of sheep, clothing, gold, silver, and the other things. And the other sacrifices were similar. The fire for the sacrifices that were made in Cuzco was taken from a stone brazier which was located next to the Temple of the Sun, and the flame could not be taken from any other place. This fire was not started and fed with just any wood; it was done with a certain kind of wood which was scented, carefully carved, and very colorful.

Chapter 23: Of the exterior acts with which they worshiped and showed reverence to their gods, and some of the prayers that they said while they made the sacrifices to their gods

Since these people were so careful and diligent in worshiping their gods, they used every possible way to show their devotion and affection. Thus, apart from the recognition which they gave them in continuously making sacrifices to them, they were very reverent and submissive in showing their respect for their gods. Their exterior acts of worship and their usual way of showing reverence to their gods were as follows. Facing their gods or their temples and *guacas*, they lowered their heads and their bodies in a profound show of humility, and they would stretch their arms out in front of themselves, keeping them parallel to each other from the beginning to the end, with the hands open and the palms out, a little above the level of their heads. Then they would make a kissing sound with their lips. Next they would bring their hands to their mouths and kiss the inside of their fingertips. This display of reverence was made to all of their gods and *guacas*, except that when they prayed to Viracocha, the Sun, and the Thunder, they put something like metal gloves or a gauntlet on their hands, and in this posture they offered their gifts and sacrifices to their gods, and they requested what was needed. Using this same form of reverence, they showed respect and deference to their kings and lords, and they never had the custom of kneeling down on their knees as a sign of veneration as we do.

It is also true that they had some ways of venerating and giving their regards to special *guacas*, but these practices were not the same for all the *guacas*, nor for all occasions. For instance, when they were on the road, upon passing by a river they would take a drink of water from it as a way of showing their respect for the river. The same thing was done in the case of springs. In making this gesture, the Indians would ask the rivers to let them pass safely and not carry them away in the swift current, and they would ask the springs not to do them any harm. Another way of showing respect was described in the preceding chapter in the part about what was offered to the *apachitas*. When they passed by *apachitas*, graves, and other shrines, they threw a quid of chewed coca, maize, and other things [to the holy place], asking that they be allowed to go by in peace, be relieved from the tiredness of the journey, and be given strength to finish the journey. When they drank, they would wet their fingers with the *chicha* in the tumbler from which they were drinking. Then they would spatter the *chicha* toward the Sun, or toward the Earth, or toward the Fire; in doing this they would pray for peace, life, and contentment. The way they had of making solemn declarations was also a religious act. They would touch the earth with their hand and look at the Sun. This was their way of swearing to the truth of their statements by these two gods, the Sun and the Earth, which were among the major gods that they worshiped.

In their necessities and tribulations they had recourse to penance and prayer. They performed long vigils at the site of their *guacas*, staying up at night without sleep. They prayed both silently and aloud. They did not have specific prayers for all [deities together] that were recited aloud. Therefore, the wording of their prayers was different for each one. The most common practice was to entrust their affairs to the deities and request that the deities see to it that the outcome be favorable. For instance, they did this when they had to make a long journey or when they got sick, and no more nor less than in all of their work. With regard to any work that they undertook, they would not only entrust themselves to their deities, they would also ask their priests to pray for them, and they would ask the same of their wives, relatives, and friends.

For the time of offering sacrifices, the priests had many prayers picked out which they recited. These prayers differed according to the god to whom the sacrifice was directed, the offering which was made to the god, and the purpose for which the sacrifice was being made. These prayers were composed by the Inca Pachacutic, and although these people lacked writing, the prayers were preserved by the tradition of passing them along from father to son. And I have decided to include some of them here in order to show the style and devotion expressed in them. When they made a sacrifice to Viracocha for the health and common good of the people, they said the following prayer:

> O Creator without equal, you are at the ends of the world, you gave life and valor to mankind, saying "Let there be man" and

for the women, "Let there be woman"; you made them, formed them and gave them life so that they will live safe and sound in peace and without danger! Where are you? By chance do you live high up in the sky or down below on earth or in the clouds and storms? Hear me, respond to me and consent to my plea, giving us perpetual life and taking us with your hand, and receive this offering wherever you are, O Creator!

To the same god and for the same purpose, they said this prayer:

O most happy, fortunate Creator, you have compassion on men and take pity on them! Behold your people here, your children, poor, unfortunate, whom you have made and given life; take pity on them and let them live safe and sound with their children and descendants; guide them in the ways of good health and let them not perceive or think about bad and harmful things; let them live for a long time and not die in their youth; let them eat and drink in peace.

When they made a sacrifice to the Sun for the preservation and increase of the king, they would say the following:

O Sun, my father, who said "Let there be Cuzco!" and by your will it was founded and it is preserved with such grandeur! Let these sons of yours, the Incas, be conquerors and despoilers of all mankind. We adore you and offer this sacrifice to you so that you will grant us what we beg of you. Let them be prosperous and make them happy, and do not allow them to be conquered by anyone, but let them always be conquerors, since you made them for that purpose.

In making offerings to the *guacas*, idols, and dead bodies of their ancestors, they made the following prayer:

O fathers, *guacas*, and *vilcas*, our grandfathers and ancestors! Protect these little children of yours so that they will be happy and very fortunate as you are yourself; intercede with Viracocha on their behalf; bring them closer to him so he will give them the protection that he gives to you."

Moreover, they also said this to Viracocha himself:

Remain perpetually young and never grow old; let all things remain in peace and let the people multiply; let there be an abundance of food, and let all things always be on the increase.

In this style, they had many other prayers for the rest of their gods and *guacas*. These prayers were said only by the priests at the

time they offered the sacrifice. To end this chapter, it should be
pointed out that both in the public and general sacrifices and in the
private and special sacrifices, and when they made public prayers
or when they each prayed for themselves, invariably their sacrifices
and prayers were accompanied by banquets and drinking bouts,
where they enjoyed themselves with dances, games, and songs
which they had especially for each *guaca* and festival that they
put on.

Chapter 24: Of the opinion that the Indians had about sin; how they confessed their sins, and the penance that they did, as well as their fasts

It is a most astonishing thing to see that the devil had introduced the use of vocal confessions among these Indians. This custom was so universally accepted that it came to be one of their most common ceremonies, and it was practiced with much devotion. They confessed everything that they understood to be a sin. However, they were quite mistaken in the opinion they held about sin. In the first place, they never paid any attention to what went on in a person's mind, such as perverted desires or inclinations. Such things were neither mentioned in confession nor were they considered to be sins. With respect to overt acts, they believed that there were many ways to sin. Among the ones that concerned them the most were the following. Murder, except as an act of war, either by use of violence or by witchcraft and poisoning; stealing; carelessness in worshiping the *guacas* and shrines; missing festivals and failing to participate in them with sufficient reverence; and cursing the Inca or not obeying him. Although taking another man's wife and seducing a maiden were both considered sins, it was not because they felt that fornication itself was a sin. These acts were considered sinful because they were contrary to the Inca's commandments. The Inca had forbidden these acts. It must also be pointed out that all the labors and adversities which befall a man were due to sins, and therefore those who were the biggest sinners suffered the gravest tribulations and calamities. Thus when a person's children died, it was felt that his sins were very serious. They based this belief on the fact that according to the natural order of things, parents will die before their children. And they not only thought that the people's problems were caused by their own sins, they also believed that when the king became ill or suffered some other adversity, it was caused by the sins of his subjects, rather than by the king's sins. Therefore, when they found out that the king was sick, all of the provinces made confessions, especially those of the Collao region, and they made large sacrifices for his health. The persons assigned to practice the occupation of confessor were usually sorcerers in charge of *guacas;* both men and women were involved because females also practiced this occupation. The above-mentioned confessors were also ranked as high or low, and some sins were reserved for the highest-ranking confessors.

Although the use of vocal confessions was general throughout all of the provinces of the Inca Empire, it was even more common in the provinces of the Collao, and it seems that the people from the Collao must have been the inventors of this custom because they were universally held to be the best teachers of this occupation. All kinds of people were obliged to make confessions, with the exception of the Incas. They were not obliged to confess their sins to anybody. This was based on the idea that since they were among the offspring of the king and of his same lineage, and since their god Viracocha maintained such close relations with the king, if the Incas sinned, it was unjust for them to be forgiven so easily. If their offense was obvious, they should die for it, and if it was not, they should confess it to the Sun, and the Sun would act as their intercessor with Viracocha so that they would be forgiven. However, they usually ended up saying that it was not proper for the Incas to tell other people of their sins, nor for anyone to find out about their shortcomings. Finally, be that as it may, the Incas did not confess vocally; rather they confessed in the manner already mentioned. Afterward, they took baths, and it was their belief that with these baths they would thoroughly cleanse themselves of their sins. For this purpose, they would immerse themselves in the current of a river, and they would say these words: "I have confessed my sins to the Sun, and since I was raised by Viracocha, he has forgiven me; river, you receive my sins; take them to the sea where they will never reappear."

The most usual time for confessions was just before a sacrifice. After confessing and giving penance, they made their offering. This matter of confession and offering a sacrifice was commonly done not only because of someone's own illness; it was also done for the illness of one's wife, husband, child, or for some important person such as a *cacique* or someone of this status. The confessors were bound to secrecy, although with certain limitations, and the penitent was bound to tell the truth. To cover up a sin in confession was considered a grave sin, and the confessors were the judges of this matter. The confessors would determine whether the confession was complete and true by casting lots with certain small stones and looking at the entrails of an animal. If the augury was unfavorable on the basis of the inquiry made by the sorcerer and it seemed to him that the penitent had either told a lie or had been too vague, the penitent was punished on the spot. The confessor struck the penitent a certain number of times on the back with a stone and made him confess again until the said confessor was convinced that the confession was satisfactory. Once this was done, the penance was determined according to the gravity of the sins, and sometimes these penances were very severe, especially if the man who had committed the sin was poor and unable to give anything to the confessor.

After the confession, everyone was ordered to go wash in some river in the same way as has been described for those of Inca lineage. These baths were taken by all, both those who confessed their sins to the Sun and those who did it in the ordinary way, and in addition to baths, other forms of penance were imposed. However, almost all of them involved some days of fasting in accordance with their custom. When the confessor judged the penitent to be a great sinner, as would be done in the case of someone whose children were dying off, the penance was increased in the following way. They looked for a person who had been born deformed and marked by nature, and this person would go with the penitent to the river where it was necessary to take the usual bath. When the penitent had finished washing in the ceremonial way mentioned above, the deformed person would whip him with nettles. And for this purpose there were ordinarily in Cuzco certain small Indians, bent over at the waist, with large hunchbacks, who were born this way. Finally, there were included in this rite and these ceremonies many other arrangements and rules, all of which were quite ridiculous.

Thus in order to comply with the penance imposed in the confession, the most rigorous penance that they had was fasting, which was very different from our fasting. There was nothing more, even when they wanted to punish themselves and give themselves over to acts of severe self-castigation. Their fasts did not consist in abstaining from all foods for a specified period of time, nor did they involve eating fewer times than was customary or smaller amounts. For the whole time of fasting, the Indians only abstained from using salt or *aji*, which were their spices and tastiest seasoning. As long as they abstained from these things, even though they overindulged in everything else, they did not feel that

they were breaking the fast. It is true that sometimes and for certain grave occasions, in addition they abstained from eating meat,
drinking *chicha,* and having recourse to their wives. This they considered to be an extreme penalty. But the common and ordinary
fast was the one mentioned above, which did not require any more
rigorous abstenance than giving up salt and *aji.*

Chapter 25: Of the festival called Capac Raymi, which the Incas held in the first month of the year

The Incas had two kinds of festivals and solemn occasions; some were regular festivals and others special. It was established that the first kind be held at certain times of the year. Each festival had its own month, and they were held in order, for various purposes and with certain rites and sacrifices. But there was no predetermined time for the others because they were only held for unusual situations such as times of drought, the beginning of an important war, the coronation of the king, and on other occasions similar to these.

The most solemn regular festival was called Capac Raymi, which means "sumptuous" or "principal festival," and to them it was as Easter is for us. The festival is celebrated in the first month of the year which is called Raymi,[56] and on this occasion the Inca boys were initiated and knighted. These boys were relatives and direct descendents of the Inca kings. This even included the prince who was to succeed to the throne and his brothers, if he had any. This sign of nobility was not given to anyone else. This festival and ceremony was held mainly in Cuzco, and there the festival included more spectators and greater ostentation because the number of boys who were knighted was large. The festival was also held at the same time by all of the governors of royal blood who held office in the provinces. Each one did this where he was located, knighting his sons along with the rest of the young nobles of their generation. This status or order of knighthood was conferred on boys between twelve and fifteen years of age, and the major ceremonies involved piercing the boy's ears [for earplugs] and putting on their *guaras* or loincloths which they used for breeches or trousers. Far in advance preparations were started. Clothing was made, adornments were made, and everything else necessary for this solemn festival. Before anything else, they gathered a goodly number of noble maidens from twelve to thirteen or fourteen years of age, who, richly dressed, would serve on the occasion. Some days before, these girls would be at the hill called Chacaguanacauri spinning the thread for the fringe of the *guaras* which the boys would have to put on as they were made *orejones* or knights. The boys would also go to the same hill to get a certain kind of straw which they had to carry on their staffs, and the straw that was left over from what they had brought was divided up among their relatives. Moreover, all during the time that the maidens spent on their task at that hill, the *guaca* or idol of Guanacauri was left on the said hill. The rest of what was needed for this solemn occasion was provided by the parents and relatives of the boys. This included the sacrifice that they had to offer, the gifts that had to be given, the *chicha* for the dances and festivities, and the clothing and emblems that the boys needed to wear as they came forth. The latter were as follows: for shoes, some *ojotas* made of a certain very fine straw called *coya* which was gold colored; the [sleeveless] tunics were short, made of fine light brown wool, with black fringe about one and a half spans long, also of wool, which seemed like silk; white cloaks that were two spans wide and reached down to their shins; these cloaks were tied around their necks with a knot, and attached here was a thick string made of wool with a red tassel on the end; black *llautos* [bands] around their heads, and slings made of *cabuya*[57] and sheep [llama] sinew carried in their hands. It is said that they carried these slings because when their ancestors left the cave of Pacari-tampu, they carried slings in that way. Their parents and relatives also showed up in special clothing and outfits with light brown cloaks and black feathers.

When the first of the month came, the principal Incas got together in the Temple of the Sun, and there they organized the festival and everything that needed to be done for it. They ordered all of the provincials to leave the city, and none of them returned until the end of the festival. Both those who were leaving and those coming to the court [Cuzco] were instructed to stay at a certain place designated for this purpose at the beginning of each road, and at each of these places the people gathered who were from the *suyu* [quarter] to which that road went. There they would gather up the tribute and goods of the Religion, which were brought at that time from all of the provinces of the kingdom. Those who brought the tribute would wait until the attendants of the king and the *guacas* came to receive them. On this same day, each one of the nobles would bring the boys that he had who were to become *orejones*, and the noble would present the boys in the Temple of the Sun. In the plaza of the temple, the statues of Viracocha, the Sun, the Moon, and the Thunder would be placed on some low benches that were adorned with feathers. Some claim that these feathers were made of gold. Those charged with this duty would bring out into the said square the embalmed bodies of the dead lords, and this [custom] of bringing out in public the said idols and embalmed bodies was done on this day as well as on all of the solemn days of other months. The reason they brought out these dead bodies was so that their descendants could drink with them as if they were alive, and particularly on this occasion so that those who were knighted could ask the deceased to make them as brave and fortunate as they had been.

Once this was done, the Inca came out of his house with a large accompaniment, and when he reached the place where the statues were located, he sat down next to the statue of the Sun, and then the great lords and knights who were present at court were seated in a tight circle around the Inca. Next, one hundred large sheep were brought out with great solemnity. These animals were selected from among all those that had been gathered that year. The ones selected would have to be healthy and without any blemishes, and they would also have long wool and stiff straight tails. The major priest of the Sun would stand up at this time, and making a reverent gesture first to Viracocha and then to the rest of the statues, he had the sheep led four times around the statues, and after this the animals were offered on behalf of the Sun to Viracocha, and after offering them, they were turned over to thirty Indians who were assigned to take them, and each day they sacrificed three of them. Therefore, at the end of the month, all of them would be gone because on some days four of them would be sacrificed, and the sacrifice was performed in the following way. A big fire was built with *quinoa*[58] wood which was very clean and carved; the sheep were cut into four quarters. Then without losing any blood or anything else, all of this was placed on the fire, and they waited for it to burn thoroughly. The bones that remained unburned were completely ground, and each one took some of that powder and blew it away, while saying certain words. What was left over was taken to a *buhio* [hut] that was in the Pomachupa district. In that place they had the storehouse for this [powder] which had been kept for many years with great veneration, and at the time that the said sheep was burned, white maize, ground *aji*, and coca were thrown on the fire.

On the second day of the month, six very old sheep were brought. These animals were called *aporucos*, and six Indians led these animals by their halters. These Indians each had a load of maize and coca which they say was food for them [the *aporucos*]. And they led them for four days with a special solemnity, and on the fifth day all of those who were to be knighted came out into the square. They were accompanied by their parents and relatives, and after doing reverence to the idols and to the Inca, who were located in their places as has been explained above, they asked the Inca for permission to make the sacrifices and perform the ceremonies that were customary during this festival. Once permission was granted, they left for the hill named Guanacauri with the same accompaniment of relatives that they had brought. The royal insignias were kept ahead of all the people. These insignias were a sheep and a standard or pennant called *sunturpaucar.* The sheep was pure white, dressed in a red garment and gold ear ornaments, and the animal was accompanied by two *mamaconas* who were designated for this, with two jugs of *chicha* on their shoulders. This is because they had this sheep trained to drink *chicha* and eat coca, and they said that it symbolized the first of its species that had appeared after the Flood, and they imagined it to be white like this one. They always had a group of these sheep in reserve for this purpose, and these animals were never killed; rather, at the time of death, these animals were burned with solemnity. And the *aporucos* went along with this sheep. Each of the young men carried in his left hand one of the slings that had been made previously, and in his right hand he carried a tuft of *cabyua,* which was their hemp. That day they slept at the foot of the hill, and on the next day, as the sun came up, they went up on top where the temple and *guaca* were located. They handed over their slings to the attendants of this place, and these attendants returned the slings the next day, saying that the *guaca* gave the slings to them so that they could use them in fighting. Then those *aporucos* were bled from a certain vein which is above the right front foot, and without touching hands, the boys stopped face to face and smeared that blood on each other's faces. When they had all done it, the wounds of the sheep were closed, and the animals were dressed with vests and ear decorations. The clothing and the rest of the things that had been brought for the sacrifice were burned, along with six lambs that were brought from the livestock of the Sun and some others that the boys brought for this purpose. These lambs were not killed right away; rather they were bled from a certain vein, and they were allowed to bleed while they were led around the hill. In the place where the lambs fell dead, they were burned. Before killing them, the priests pulled a little bit of wool from each one; it was handed out among the boys who were being knighted and to the most important people who accompanied the boys. They blew the wool into the air while the sacrifice was offered, praying to the idol of Guanacauri for the health and prosperity of the Inca and that the idol protect them and be generous with them.

Moreover, the Inca gave six small figurines of sheep made of silver and gold to be used in this sacrifice. These figurines were buried at the above-mentioned *guaca.* Once this was done, they returned with the *aporucos* and the royal insignias of the sheep and the *sunturpaucar.* In a ravine located along the road, their fathers and relatives took the slings that the boys were carrying in their hands, beating them with the slings on the arms and legs. At the same time they said to the boys: "Be good brave men like we are, and receive the virtue and grace that we have, so that you can imitate us." Then the slings were returned to the boys, and they performed a dance called *guari* which included singing. When the dance was over, they came to Cuzco with the same accompaniment and solemnity as when they had left. When they arrived at the main square, which is called Aucaypata, they made a reverent gesture to the *guacas,* and the boys' fathers and relatives beat them once again with the slings as they had done before. After this all of the people who were present performed the said *taqui* or dance called *guari,* playing a certain large seashell. After this, the boys gave their fathers and relatives something to drink. When the dancing and drinking was concluded, the *aporuco* sheep were killed by the priests with certain ceremonies, and the meat was handed out among the young men. Each one received a small portion which he ate raw, saying that with this he would receive strength forever. Once this was over, everyone returned home and the priests put the idols of the Sun and the rest of the gods back in their places.

During the next six days, the only thing that they did was enjoy themselves at home and the boys rested from their hard labors and prepared for the ones yet to come. At the middle of the month, they returned to the square with their fathers and relatives as they had the first time, and as they stood in the presence of the Inca, the priest of the Sun gave them certain clothing: a vest with red and white stripes and a white mantle with a blue cord and a red tassel. The relatives gave them the said *ojotas* made of the straw called *coya.* The priest of the Sun also gave a red and white dress to each one of the maidens picked out to serve in this festival. All this clothing which was given to each of these groups was from the goods that were made as tribute for the Religion, and for that reason, the clothes were handed out by the priest in the name of the Sun. Once the boys were dressed in this fashion, they took in their hands some palm wood staffs called *yauri,* which had copper blades on the ends, though some were gold. These staffs were similar to hatchets; hanging from them there was a little bit of wool, the *guaracas* or slings, and the straw that we mentioned above. Holding these staffs straight like pikes, they expressed their adoration to the *guacas* and their customary deference to the Inca. Then they left with their family unit and relatives for the hill of Anaguarque, which is near Guanacauri.

The maidens that had received the dresses went along with this accompaniment. They carried some very small jugs of *chicha* in order to provide those in the group with a drink. Also with the group were the above-mentioned royal insignias, the *sunturpaucar*, and the sheep with clothing, along with six *aporucos* like those mentioned above, and the same thing was done to them, and six more small lambs that were sacrificed at Guanacauri. The reason they went to this hill and shrine was to prove themselves by running, and they performed this ceremony there because it was said that this *guaca* became so swift after the time of the Flood that it would run as fast as a falcon flies. When they reached the said *guaca*, the boys made an offering of a little wool, and the priests performed the same ceremonies and sacrifices that had been performed on the first hill. Once again, the boys' older male relatives beat them with slings, telling the boys not to be lazy in serving the Inca, warning them that they would be punished for it, and reminding them of the reason that solemnity was performed and of the victories that had been achieved by the Incas through the efforts of their fathers. After this was over, everyone sat down, and they performed the *taqui* called *guari*. While this was performed, the new knights were standing with their staffs in their hands, which were the arms given to them.

After this *taqui*, all of the maidens stood up and ran down to the bottom of the hill, and there they waited with their jars of *chicha* for the young men in order to give them something to drink. Then the girls would start to call the young men, shouting: "Come quickly, brave young men, for we are waiting for you." And then the boys formed many lines, one after another, and behind each line of the said boys there was another line of older men who acted as sponsors for the boys. Each one of the men was responsible for one of the young knights, and if the boy were to tire, the man was to help him. One handsomely dressed Indian stationed himself ahead of all the lines, and as he shouted, all of the boys started running at top speed, and some of the runners were often injured seriously. After the men and boys reached the bottom, the maidens would give them something to drink, first to the sponsors and then to their protégés.

They would also go to the hill of Sabaraura; there they would burn six more lambs, and they would bury six more. In addition to this each one made an offering of what he was carrying. Once again the boys were beaten as before, and from there they would return to Cuzco. As they entered the square, they would make their gestures of humiliation to the *guacas* and to the Inca, and as the sectional units of Hanancuzco and Hurincuzco sat down, each group separately, the young knights remained standing for a short time. Once again they performed the said dance and song called *guari*, and once again the boys were beaten in the way already stated. Since it was time to retire, the Inca would go to his palace accompanied by the people of the court, and the young knights, along with the same accompaniment as before, left for the hill of Yauira, which is straight ahead of Carmenga, where they offered the same sacrifice as at the other hills and received the *guaras*, their breeches or loincloths, which they were not allowed to wear until that time and with those ceremonies. They also put a certain type of helmet on the boys' heads, and on behalf of the Inca the boys were given certain ear ornaments, which were attached to their ears, as well as diadems of feathers and patens of silver and gold, which were hung around their necks. When this was finished, they performed the said dance again and the boys were whipped. With this they returned to Cuzco again, and they made the usual reverent gestures to the *guacas.*

After all of the ceremonies mentioned, these knights would go to a spring called Calispuquiu, which is behind the fortress, almost a mile from the city. After they returned to the square, their relatives offered them gifts. They started with each boy's most important uncle, who gave his nephew a shield, a sling, and a mace with which to fight in wars. After this the other relatives would present gifts to each boy. Therefore, the boy who was knighted would always end up rewarded and rich. Each one of those who presented the boy with a gift would give him one lash, making a brief speech to the boy; he was advised to be brave, loyal to the Inca, and very conscientious in complying with the rituals and veneration of the *guacas.* When the prince who was to be the successor to the crown was knighted, all of the most important *caciques* from all the land who were present would give him great and valuable gifts. The solemnities of this day concluded with a certain sacrifice that they made to the *guacas.* At the end of the month, the newly knighted boys would be brought out to the *chacaras* [fields], and their ears were pierced. This was the last ceremony that they performed in knighting the young men.

As the finishing touch to this month and festival, all of the people assembled in the square to enjoy themselves and perform a dance called *cayo*. For this occasion, they made a great number of small cakes of maize flour mixed with the blood of the sheep that were sacrificed that day in a certain way and with special solemnity. All of the people from every province in Peru who had been detained were ordered to come into the city. Once the attendants of these sacrifices, who were from the *ayllu* and lineage of Tarpuntay, were in their places, they gave one of those cakes to every person present, telling them that they should eat that food, for it was given to them by the Sun so that they would be content and not say that the Sun had neglected them by paying attention only to those who had participated in that festival. They brought out these cakes on some large silver and gold plates from the service of the Sun. These plates were consecrated for this purpose. On receiving these cakes, they expressed their gratitude to the Sun with words and gestures. After the people had eaten the cakes, the priests would say to them: "What you have been given is the food of the Sun, and it will be present in your bodies as a witness; if you ever were to speak evil of the Sun or of the Inca, this would be revealed and you would be punished for it." The people promised that never in their lives would they do such a thing, and they received that food on this condition. Some days were spent performing these dances, and all the while they would drink without resting. They made the rhythm with four big drums that belonged to the Sun, and each drum was played by four important Indians who were dressed in a special fashion. They wore red tunics down to their feet with red and white fringe; on top of this they wore lion [puma] skins. The entire animal's body was skinned, and their heads were empty. Patens were placed on these heads, rings in their ears, and in place of their natural teeth, others of the same size and shape were used, with *aljorcas* [probably like sequins] on their paws. All of these things were made of gold. These skins were worn in such a way that the head and neck of the lion came down over the head of the person wearing it and the animal's skin came down over the person's back. In order to start the dance, two lambs were sacrificed. The lambs were given to four old men who were designated for this. These men made the offering with a thousand ceremonies.

Once this was concluded, thirty sheep were brought from the

livestock of the Inca, and these animals were distributed among those who were in charge of the sacrifices. The Inca ordered them to sacrifice these animals in his name to all of the *guacas* of Cuzco. The animals were distributed among them along with thirty articles of clothing. In addition to this, they took thirty statues of carved wood, dressed like men and women, and the statues were burned as an offering to the Sun. This offering was made for the strength of those whose ears had been pierced and so that they would see many more days like those.

On the last day of the month, they would go to the square on the hill of Puquin. They took two big sheep, one made of silver and the other of gold, six lambs, and the same number of *aporucos* which were dressed, along with six lambs of gold and silver, seashells, thirty white sheep, and the same number of articles of clothing. They burned everything, except the articles of silver and gold, on the said hill. And with this they ended the festival of Capac Raymi, which was the most serious and solemn festival of the whole year. Ear piercing was held in such high esteem and honor among these people that anyone who by chance had an ear torn when the ears were pierced, or afterward, would be considered most unfortunate. And they took great care to make the ear holes very large. Some cotton threads were put into the ear holes so that the holes would stretch open and become very large, and every day thicker threads were inserted. Thus the holes became so big that they were able to wear as earrings inserted into their ears cylinders [earplugs] each bigger than a piece of eight [Spanish dollar].

Chapter 26: Of the festivals and sacrifices that were performed during the second month, which was called Camay

On the first day of this month, the Inca came out to the square. The *guacas* had been placed in the square in the way already described, and the Inca sat down next to the *guaca* of the Sun. One hundred more sheep were brought. However, these were light brown in color and white from the knees down, with white heads, if such were available. These animals were brought from the livestock of the Sun by each of the four *suyus* [quarters], each one bringing its own part, and they were also offered on behalf of the Sun, as they were during the previous month. The same ceremonies were performed when they were sacrificed. Those who were designated to perform this [sacrifice] stationed themselves next to the statue of the Sun, and the animals were offered on behalf of the Sun to Viracocha with these words: "The Sun offers you these sheep for his preservation and strength and so that he will always give more and more light." At the same time that these sheep circled around, the statues were surrounded by all the *caciques* and leaders, and each one of them took out a bit of wool; when it was gathered together, the wool was burned by itself.

One day when the new moon could be seen this month, those who had been knighted came to the square with new clothing, black tunics, tawny mantles, and bunches of white feathers, and with their slings in their hands, they divided into bands, one composed of those from Hanancuzco and the other of those from Hurincuzco. They threw a certain fruit at each other. This is a fruit like the *tunas* that we call *pitahayas*. Sometimes they would come to blows to test their strength. This would last until the Inca stood up and made them stop. This was done so that it would be known who among them were the bravest and strongest. Afterward they sat down together with their sectional units, and all together they made an offering of a lamb to the new moon. The same as the others, this offering was made by the *ayllu* of Tarpuntay. They made this sacrifice only as a sign of gratitude that the moon had come up quickly. It must be pointed out that from the first day that they started the festival of Capac Raymi until this new moon came out,

they fasted without eating salt or *aji,* and there were people designated to find out if anyone broke this fast. Then many old sheep
were brought to the square, and with great solemnity their ears
were pierced, and these animals were distributed among the people
of all four *suyus* so that each one could look after their part and
bring it with them at the time of the Raymi festival. This was because these were the *aporucos,* and it was necessary to consecrate
them with great solemnity. After this, they started a dance called
yaguayra which lasted for two days.

At the first full moon, they assembled again at the same place.
At this time a sacrifice of ten sheep of all colors was made to the
Sun for the health of the Inca, and the night of the following day,
they all stayed awake until morning dancing and singing the said
dance called *yaguayra* through all the streets of the city. In the
square they burned ten articles of very fine red and white clothing
that were contributed by all the kinship units: two made the offering to the Sun, two to the Moon, two others to the Thunder, to
Viracocha two others, and to the Earth two others. In the morning,
when the sun came up across the horizon, they made it an offering
of two white lambs for the universal health of the people. All the
people of the dance mentioned above went to a house that was next
to the Temple of the Sun, and they got out a very long rope that
was kept there. The rope was made of four colors: black, white,
bright red, and tawny, and it looked like a snake, and for the head it
had a ball of red wool. They danced as they carried the rope. All of
the dancers held on to the rope with their hands, the men on one
side and the women on the other. As they entered through the
square, the dancers in front made reverent gestures to the *guacas*
and to the Inca, and the others did the same as they came by. They
would go around the square, and when the dancers in front started
catching up with those at the end, they would wind themselves
together as they continued with their dance, in such a way that
they ended up in the form of a spiral; then dropping the rope all at
the same time, they left it rolled up on the ground like a snake.
They performed this festival with certain clothing consecrated for
it. This included black tunics that had the hem trimmed in a white
border and with white fringe at the bottom. On their heads they
wore white feathers from birds called *tocto.*[59] After the dance was
over, they gave a lamb to be sacrificed for the rope, and they spent
the rest of this day drinking and enjoying themselves.

Six days after the full moon, having made some dams at intervals on the stream that passed by the square, they took out the ashes and charcoals that they had kept from what was left over of the bones from the sacrifices of the whole year. They ground them up with two *cestos* [bundles] of coca, many flowers of diverse colors, *aji*, salt, and burned *mani* [peanuts], and all together made into powder, they took out a certain amount and put it into the storehouse. They would take the rest [of the powder] to a place below the district of Pumachupa where the said stream joins another stream.[60] Accompanying this sacrifice were the statues of the Sun and the rest of the gods that they usually placed out in the square for the important festivals and the Inca himself with the whole court. All went to the place mentioned above, including two hundred men with staffs in their hands. On arriving at the said place where the streams meet, the Indians carrying staffs put them aside and each one took two tumblers of *chicha*. They gave one of these as an offering to the water of the stream and they drank the other tumbler of *chicha* themselves. After dancing around the statues for a while with great rejoicing, a little before nightfall, they threw all of that ash into the stream, cleaning thoroughly the vessels in which it was brought so that none of it would remain. Then they took up their staffs and stationed themselves on either side of the river. The Inca ordered them to go with that sacrifice down the river to the town of Tambo. Following the turns and roundabout way of the river, the town is ten leagues from the city, although by a direct route the distance is no more than seven leagues. At this point they opened up the first dam, and the water rushed down with so much force that it would break the others.

The said two hundred Indians went down river after the sacrifice until they reached Tambo. With their staffs, they would push away anything [of the sacrificial ash] that got stuck along the edges. Many of the Indians of the towns located along the river were stationed at stopping places. These Indians made light with beacons of straw so that none of the sacrifice would be left unnoticed along the banks of the river that night. When they arrived at Tambo, they let it go saying: "Water, it is in your power to carry these ashes as far as the sea, to Viracocha, to whom our republic sends them, and thus we beg the wind to help you because we cannot go any further than here." They begged the water to give part of that offering to the Inca Yupanqui, as the inventor of that ceremony and because he left them instructions when he died that they should send the sacrifices to him and that the sacrifices to be made should be performed in the way just described. Pachacuti [Inca Yupanqui] had left orders for the water to bring the sacrifices to him wherever he might be. Those who had accompanied the said ashes remained in Tambo for two days resting and drinking, after which they returned to Cuzco. And with this the sacrifices of the second month were concluded.

Chapter 27: Of the festivals and sacrifices of the following four months

The third month was called Hatun Puquy. This was the height of the rainy season. On the first day, the same sacrifice of one hundred sheep was made, and it was performed in the same order as in the first month, except that these animals were chestnut colored. They all gathered together in the countryside at the time when they were ready to break the ground of the *chacaras*, and they made an offering to the Sun of twenty big *cuis* [guinea pigs] with twenty loads of firewood, and after the sacrifice was burned, they begged the Sun to help them work their fields so that the crops would be good. The *mamaconas* of the Sun were present, and a certain food was given to them. Once this was done, and it was done with solemnity, they occupied themselves with the work in their fields.

[Nothing was mentioned for the fourth month.]

The fifth month was named Ariguaquiz. On the first day of the month the same sacrifice was made of one hundred spotted sheep of diverse colors, which the Indians call *moromoros*. This month they brought out that old sheep that had been led during the festival of Raymi [see Chapter 25], and it was put in the square. Two *yanaconas*[61] were in charge of it and stayed there the whole month. They gave the animal *chicha* every day, and the sheep itself spilled the *chicha* by kicking [jars of it] over, and this way, an offering of *chicha* was made in the animal's name. In addition, fifteen sheep were burned there. This was done so that the maize seeds would develop. This sacrifice was called *napa*. Along with the said sheep, they had in the square a highly venerated object that was called *sundorpauca* [sic; for *sunturpaucar*]. And at the end they burned a large number of *cuis*, *agi*, and other things. With this the festival was over.

The sixth month, which corresponds to May, was named Hatun Cuzqui. Another hundred sheep of all colors were burned for order itself and solemnity. During this month, the maize was harvested and stored with a certain festival called Aymoray. They celebrated it by bringing the maize from the *chacaras* and fields to their houses, all the while dancing with certain songs in which they asked that the maize last a long time and not run out before the next harvest. They came together doing this dance up to the houses that belonged to Diego de los Rios. Two girls were ahead holding some feathered things in their hands and they were accompanied by one of those white sheep from the festival of Raymi, which was called *napa*. They made a sacrifice to the Sun of a large number of sheep, of which some were burned and others were distributed among all the people of the city, and they ate their flesh raw with toasted maize. There was no one, neither young nor old, who did not eat some of that meat. One day this month, thirty sheep were distributed for all the *guacas*, and a little of the meat was burned at each *guaca*. The amount varied according to the importance of the *guaca*. A lot was assigned to the great ones and a small amount to the lesser ones. The amounts were already established and well known.

On the fifteenth day of this month, they brought out five *aporucos* in a procession with great solemnity, and the animals were killed and distributed; each person ate a little of the raw meat. After this the statues of the Sun made a sacrifice themselves of six lambs, each lamb with different ceremonies. In the name of the Sun, the most important priest made the offering as a sign of respect for the maize of the coming year. Those who had been knighted appeared at a certain *chacara* named Sausero, which is located along the road to San Sebastian, to bring the maize that had been harvested. They carried it in small sacks, singing a song called *aravi*.[62] On the first day, the said new knights, handsomely dressed, brought it alone. On the rest of the days, all of the people of Cuzco came to do the same. A little later, all of the lords and important people of Cuzco, accompanied by a large number of other people, went to the same *chacara* with their plows, and they plowed the field. After this was finished, they returned with great rejoicing to the main square, wearing the tunics that they had won in war. When they reached the square, four small sheep were released, and all of the young men rushed after them. The young man who caught one of them was highly esteemed, and he shared it among the others as a great honor. They cut the animal up with their knives, and it was considered a privilege to get part of it because this was the sacrifice that they made for their victories.

This month certain ceremonies were made to *mamazara*,[63] which was a universal *guaca*. Everyone had one in his home, and these *guacas* were made in the following way. Each person would take a certain part of the most unusual [ears of] maize, which would be a small amount, and with certain ceremonies, he would put the maize in a storage bin called a *pirua*. The maize would be wrapped in the richest mantles that the person had, and there he would watch over it for three nights. After they had covered the said bin, they worshiped it and held it in high esteem, saying that it was the mother of the maize of their *chacara* and by virtue of it [the bin], each year maize was produced and preserved. At this time each year, they made a special sacrifice to the bin. In this sacrifice the sorcerers would ask the said *pirua* if it had strength enough to last for the coming year. If the sorcerers felt like saying "no" and that this was the bin's answer, they took that maize to their *chacaras* and burned it with certain rites. Then they made another *pirua* with special ceremonies, saying that they were renewing it so that the seed of the maize would not perish. And if it answered that it had enough strength to last longer, they would leave it for another year. This *guaca* was universal only in a certain sense. Although it was present in all the homes, each person worshiped only his own *guaca*, and paid no attention to the one his neighbor had. This *guaca* was called *mamazara*, which means mother of maize.

Chapter 28: Of the festivals and sacrifices that were performed during the seventh, eighth, and ninth months

The seventh month corresponded to June, and it was called Aucay Cuzqui. During this month the most important festival of the Sun was performed; it was called Inti Raymi. On the first day, an offering was made of one hundred brown sheep of the Sun. It was made in the way that has been described above. They performed this festival and sacrifice on the hill of Manturcalla, where the Inca would go and remain until the festival was over, drinking and enjoying himself. This festival was performed only by the Incas of royal blood, and not even their wives participated in it; instead the wives stayed away in a patio. The *mamaconas*, wives of the Sun, would give drink to the Incas, and all of the vessels from which they ate or drank were made of gold. An offering was made to the said statues on behalf of the Incas. It included thirty sheep: ten to Viracocha, ten to the Sun, and ten more to the Thunder, and thirty articles of clothing made of very colorful *cumbi*. Moreover, on that same hill they made a large number of statues from carved *quishuar* wood.[64] These statues were dressed in rich clothing and were there from the beginning of the festival. At the end of it, they set fire to the statues and burned them. They also took to the said hill six *aporucos* that were burned with everything else. After all the many sacrifices were concluded, in order to start the dance called *cayo*, which was performed four times a day, all of the Indians divided up. Half of them remained there dancing and drinking. Of the other half, part of them went to Chuquichanca, and part of them went to Paucarcancha. On these hills six more *aporucos* were distributed, and these animals were sacrificed with great solemnity.

During this festival the Sun would send, on behalf of his statues and with those who cared for them, two little lambs, one silver and the other gold, to Paucarcancha, and two others made of seashells to Pilcocancha, and two others to the hill of Manturcalla. All of them were buried in these hills after an offering had been made of the lambs. As they finished performing the said dance called *cayo*, the statues of the Sun would send large sheep made of certain materials and two lambs to the hill of Manturcalla. These animals were carried on a litter with a large retinue. The litter was held on the shoulders of important lords who were richly dressed. Leading the way were the royal insignia of the *sunturpaucar* and the white sheep in a red tunic with gold ear ornaments. On reaching the said hill, an offering was made of the animals to Viracocha, and they were burned with many ceremonies.

After the foregoing was completed, this festival, which was held in honor of the Sun each year at this time, was finished. All of the charcoal and burned bones of the offerings were collected, and all this was thrown out on a flat place just next to the hill mentioned above. No one could enter this place except those carrying these offerings. All of the people returned to the city square accompanied by the Inca, and all along the way they scattered coca, flowers, and feathers. On returning, they were all painted with a certain pitch that was made from ground seashells. The lords and knights wore small gold patens on their chins. They all sang until their arrival at the square. There they stayed and drank for the rest of the day. At nightfall, the Inca returned home, and everyone did the same. With this the festival of Inti Raymi was over.

The eighth month was named Chahua Huarquis. During this month, one hundred brown sheep were burned, just like the ones of the previous month. In addition, they took two more on the first day of the month to burn at the *guaca* of Tocori. One was taken to where they started to irrigate the valley and the other to where they ended their irrigation. This was done to preserve the water. This sacrifice was established by Inca Roca, and the Indians tell this fable about him. Very little water used to come out of that spring, but after making certain sacrifices, Inca Roca thrust his arm into the spring, and this made the water gush out as abundantly as it does now. This they considered to be such an established fact that the members of his family unit and lineage used it as justification for laying claim to that water for their own use exclusively, and during the time of the Incas, they succeeded in getting it. After the Spaniards took control of this land, they tried getting it with the same justification, but their illusions were dispelled, and the water was distributed equally. During this month, the people busied themselves with repairing the irrigation ditches.

During the ninth month, called Yapaquis, one hundred chestnut sheep without any blemishes were burned with the ceremonies described above, and they had a festival called *guayara* in which they asked for a good and abundant year. Fifteen sheep were distributed for all of the *guacas* of the area surrounding Cuzco. These sheep were from the livestock of the Sun, and with this sacrifice the *chacara* called Saucero was sown. This job of seeding was done with great solemnity because this *chacara* belonged to the Sun. What was harvested from it was for the ordinary sacrifices made in addition to the ones described above. All during the time that the seeding was done, in the middle of the field there was a white sheep with its ears of gold, and with this sheep there were numerous Indians and *mamaconas* of the Sun pouring out much *chicha* in the name of this sheep. Since they were finishing the sowing, a thousand *cuis* were brought by shares from all the provinces. Each province brought a designated amount, according to the distribution that was established. With great solemnity they slit the throats of the animals and burned them at this *chacara*, except a certain number of them that were distributed among the *guacas* and shrines of the city in the name of the Sun. This sacrifice was made to the Frost, the Wind, and the Sun, and to all things that seemed to them capable of making their sown fields grow or capable of harming them. The Tarpuntay priests fasted by not eating anything other than cooked maize and herbs without salt, and the only thing they drank was dark *chicha* which they called *concho*. They continued this fast until the maize grew up one finger above the ground. Moreover, during this month all of the people did the *taqui* or dance called *guayara*. They performed this dance in red tunics that reached to their feet, informally with no mantle or cape. When this festival and its sacrifices were over they went out to do their farming.

Chapter 29: Of the festivals and sacrifices that were made during the tenth month, called Coya

Raymi During this month one hundred white woolly sheep were burned in the same way as has been described for the other months, and they had a very solemn festival that was called Citua. The reason they had this festival this month was because the rains would start at this time, and as the rain first started to fall, some people would usually get sick. Thus in this festival they asked Viracocha if he would see fit to prevent sickness that year in Cuzco and throughout all of the Inca Empire. And this festival was celebrated in the following way. First, all people from the provinces and all people with their ears torn or any other lesion or physical defect, such as the hunchbacked, crippled, and deformed, were made to leave the city. These people were told that they were not to be present at that festival because they suffered those evils due to their own sins. They were unfortunate men, and their misfortune might very well dampen the good fortune of everyone else. Dogs were also made to leave town so that they would not howl. One day after the conjunction of the moon, the Inca and lords, along with the majority of the townspeople, went to the Coricancha [Temple of the Sun]. There they remained awake waiting for the new moon to come out, and as soon as they saw it, they started shouting with torches in their hands, saying, "Sickness, disasters, and misfortune, get out of this land!" They all repeated in loud voices, "Go away, evil!" At the same time they struck at each other in fun with the lighted torches.

Later this shouting extended throughout the whole town, and they all, old and young alike, came out to the doorway of their houses shouting the same thing: "Go away, evil! How anxiously we have waited for this festival! O Creator, let us reach the end of another year so that we will see another festival like this one!" While they were shouting in this way, they would shake their mantles and clothing as though they were casting the evil out of their houses with this act. In addition, from before the time that the new moon appeared, a goodly number of Indians armed for war according to their customs, with spears in their hands, were at the Square of Coricancha, and likewise in the Main Square there were people ready for war, four hundred of them, divided in four troops around a certain font which was there. This was the font into which they poured the beverages offered as a sacrifice.[65] These troops were from different lineages of the natives of Cuzco, and the members of each troop stood facing the direction in which they would have to run. This corresponded to the four quarters of the world, east, west, north, and south, the directions of the four quarters of the Peruvian Kingdom. At the moment when the moon came out, the shouting started. First those who were inside the Temple of the Sun started. The priests came out shouting in the temple square. The people bearing arms in this square took up the cry from the priests and immediately started to run, shouting the same thing, "Go away, evil!" This they continued until they reached the Main Square. As soon as the four hundred people bearing arms there heard the shouts, they ran off, each troop in the direction they were facing, repeating the same cry and running without stopping for a considerable distance. At the stopping places along the roads, there were many groups of runners, some awaiting the first ones and others awaiting the second ones, receiving from one to another the same cries in succession and carrying them ahead until they reached the place to stop. The one hundred who ran from the square toward the provinces of Collasuyu kept on running until they reached Angostura, and there they passed the cry on to others who were ready to go. These second runners, having covered the distance assigned to them, were followed by the third group of runners. They ran and repeated the same cries in this order until the last runners reached the Quiquijana River, which lies nine leagues from the city [of Cuzco]. This point was the stopping place for the runners who went in this direction. When they reached this river, they bathed in it and washed their weapons. This same thing was done in the same fashion by the runners who went along the other three roads, and the last ones would bathe in the rivers designated as the stopping point of their course. The runners who went in the direction of Chinchaysuyu bathed in the Apurimac River. Those going toward Antisuyu, in the Yucay River, and those going toward Cuntisuyu, in the Cusipampa River. They bathed in these rivers because they were large and extended all the way to the sea. This bathing was done so that their diseases would be carried away to the sea. They believed that with these ceremonies their diseases would be banished from the land. At the same time, it was the general practice for the people in the city to cleanse themselves by going to the rivers and fountains found on their own *ceques*, saying that in this way sickness would leave their bodies.

Once this was finished, they took a long drink, and afterward they went to their homes, where they had a *mazamorra* porridge of partly ground maize which was called *sanco*. While it was still hot, they would smear it on their faces, on the lintels of their doorways, and on the places where they kept their food and clothing. While doing this, they would tell sickness not to enter into their houses. They would also take plenty of this *sanco* to their fountains, and throwing it into the water, they would tell the fountains not to get sick. After this they would eat the tastiest foods and drink the finest *chichas* that they could make. This was done with much rejoicing and merriment. The reason for this was that for this day, everyone, no matter how poor, set aside the very best food and drink available because they thought that the people who did not enjoy themselves by eating and drinking splendidly this day would be plagued by bad luck and hardships throughout the year. They did not quarrel with each other during this time, nor did they speak angrily to each other, nor ask their debtors to pay, because they believed that whoever got upset or had a quarrel on that day would suffer the same way the whole year. Moreover, they offered their idols the finest and best-prepared foods available. These foods were received by their priests, and the foods were burned as a sacrifice.

After this they brought the statues of their gods and the richly dressed embalmed bodies out to the Main Square. The Inca as well as the priests, knights, and ordinary people came with their finest clothing, and, seated by order of rank, the only thing they did was eat, drink, and enjoy themselves. They did a special dance for this festival, and those who participated in it came wearing certain red tunics that reached down to their feet and feather diadems on their heads. All the while they played [instruments made of] long and short tubes [probably the *antara*] that were placed like organ pipes. On this day they gave thanks to their idols for having allowed them to attend that festival, and they begged their idols to allow them to reach the end of another year. The Inca would toast the idols, pouring out much *chicha* in their honor, and the priests drank toasts to each other. With this the day would end, and they put the statues and bodies back in their places.

Another day they came out as the day before to the same square. They ordered those who had been put out of the city to come back. From the four *suyus* of the kingdom, they brought much livestock that was healthy, clean, without blemishes or deformities of any kind, and woolly, that had never been sheared before, and all of this livestock was from the lands of the Religion. Then the priests of the Sun picked out thirty sheep. The animals were richly dressed and were burned along with thirty bundles of *quishuar* wood. After this sacrifice was concluded, the *mamaconas* of the Sun brought out some large gold plates with many lumps of maize flour mixed with the blood from a certain sacrifice of white sheep. A mouthful of this maize was given to each one of the people from the provinces so that they too could enjoy the sacrifices and take part in them as they did in the Raymi festival. For the same purpose, as a sign of confederation with the Inca, they were admonished not to say anything bad about the Inca or the Sun. Since they had eaten that morsel, their sin could not be kept a secret. Lumps of this maize were also sent to the provincial *guacas* of the entire kingdom, and for the purpose of taking the maize lumps there were Indians in Cuzco from every quarter of the kingdom who received them. These Indians were told that those maize lumps were sent out by the Sun as a sign that the Sun wanted them all to venerate and honor him. Moreover, the *caciques* of the provinces were sent their share of the maize lumps as a special favor.

As the final part of this festival, four sheep were sacrificed. The priests pulled out their lungs and inflated them by blowing into them. Once the lungs were inflated, the priests examined them to see, on the basis of certain signs in them (according to their imagination) whether the year would be prosperous or not. Afterward, the lungs were burned, and the meat of the said sheep was distributed among those present as something sacred. Each person was given only a tiny portion, and they ate it raw. All the rest of the livestock was distributed to all the people of Cuzco for them to eat. As this livestock was entering the square, a little bit of wool was pulled from each animal, and it was sacrificed to the Sun. Once this was done, they would drink and dance. All of the nations that obeyed the Inca, each dressed in the style of their region, participated in this dance. The priests assigned to them would bring out the *guacas* on litters, and upon reaching the place where the idols and the Inca were located, they made a reverent gesture to them and went on to take their places. During the rest of this day, each nation performed the dances and songs that were done before they had become the subjects of the Inca. At the end of this month, the charcoal was gathered from all of the sacrifices made in it, and this was ground together. Then with great solemnity the dust and ashes were taken away and spread across the pastures and punas to fertilize the grass.

Chapter 30: Of the last two months and the festivals performed then

The eleventh month was called Homa Raymi Puchayquiz. During this month the ordinary sacrifice of one hundred sheep was made. If there was a shortage of water this month, they selected a sheep that was solid black from those of the Sun. The animal was tied, placed on a flat plain, and a large amount of *chicha* was poured out around it while certain ceremonies were performed. The animal was not given anything to eat until it rained. They said that seeing this animal suffer would cause the Sun to feel so sorry that he would make it rain. And if the rains did not come, all of the Indians who were involved in making sacrifices would assemble there. Each one would have two tumblers of *chicha* in his hands, and while drinking one, they would pour out the other one as a sacrifice. Women whose sons were to have their ears pierced and be knighted in the Raymi festival, which was coming soon, busied themselves in spinning and sewing the clothing that their sons were to wear during the festival mentioned above. Some women from their lineage would get together with them in their houses to help them and drink during those days. And each of the men spent his time on whatever the Inca had assigned to him. Thus this month came to a close.

The last month was called Ayamarca. The first day the hundred sheep were sacrificed, the same as in the other months and with the same solemnity. The second day the boys who were to be knighted the following month went to Huanacauri hill. They offered a certain sacrifice to that *guaca*, and since it was their major idol and it was said to be the brother of Manco Capac, from whom they had descended, they asked the idol to grant them permission to be knighted. The boys slept there that night, imitating the pilgrimage that their ancestors had made there,[66] and the priests of this *guaca* who were assigned to do this, would give each boy a sling. Then they drew blood from the sheep that each one of the boys brought. With this blood they made a line on each boy's face, and later the animals were sacrificed. On the next day in the afternoon, the boys returned to the city, each one carrying his bundle of straw on which their parents and relatives would sit during the Raymi festival, and on this day the boys would fast. Their relatives would bring very nicely woven tunics and give one to each of the boys.

Later all of these young men would get together and chew the maize to make the *chicha* for the festival, and their parents and aunts would go to Calispuquiu and get the water to make the *chicha*. While this leaven was being made for the *chicha*, a woolly white sheep was burned with great solemnity so that the *chicha* would be good. The relatives of these young men would bring the jars and the firewood to make the *chicha*. They spent the whole month performing great ceremonies while preparing what was necessary for this Capac Raymi festival. The young men paraded for inspection, and the elders instructed them, going around the square with the boys every day. After this was concluded, they drank and made some sacrifices so that the boys would turn out to be good knights. These parades could not be seen by anyone from the provinces. They were reserved only for the residents of Cuzco. And in order to perform them, everyone who was not a resident of Cuzco was ordered to leave. This festival was called Itu Raymi. It was also customary to perform it when it rained too much or very little or when there was a plague, and whenever this festival was done in this city, as has been said, all the people from the provinces left the city, and guards were stationed so that the provincials could not come in. The people of Hanan Cuzco would kill four sheep, and those of Hurin Cuzco would do the same, after having first gone around with the sheep in a certain way. After this was done, the people who were detained [outside the city] were permitted to return, and with this the obligatory festivals and sacrifices of the year were concluded. These were regular ceremonies, and there were set days for them and people designated to perform them. In addition to these, there were numerous personal festivals that each one performed. If they were nobles, this was done with their family unit on behalf of their dead, and there were numerous other personal festivals that the Indians performed with the members of their family and household. Therefore, if an account of all of them were made, there would be no end to it.

Chapter 31: Of the Itu festival, and the ceremonies with which it was celebrated

In addition to the festivals already mentioned, which were the regular ones, others were special. These ceremonies were established, as was the solemnity with which they were performed. Nevertheless, there was no fixed time to hold them nor was everyone permitted to celebrate them. The most important of these was the Itu festival, which was very famous, magnificent and performed with joy and devotion. It was done only at unspecified times according to the need that might arise, and then not everyone was permitted to celebrate it in the same way. During all of the preceding days, the men fasted and stayed away from their women, ate nothing with salt or *aji*, nor did they drink *chicha*, which was the important part of their fast. Later all of the people came together with the Inca and the statues of their gods in the main square, and all of the women who had dogs and other animals were sent out of the city and ordered to stay with their animals at a considerable distance from where the festival was being held. They looked to see if there were any people from the provinces, and the provincials were also ordered to leave town. Guards were placed on the roads so that no one would enter town while they were celebrating this festival. Moreover, they were especially careful not to let any animal enter into that place where the people [doing the ceremony] were congregated. They said that it would be an insult to communicate among animals with the Sun and Viracocha about such important things.

Once these steps were taken, two sheep of a certain color, depending on what they wanted to achieve with the festival, were sacrificed with great ceremony and solemnity. If there was a great need, some children were killed, but this was when the Inca ordered that the festival be general. After the sacrifice, those who were required to celebrate this solemn occasion put on the costumes and ornaments reserved for it. They wore red tunics made of *cumbi* with long fringes of the same color. Wrapped around the waist, they had long braids that hung down to their feet. On their heads they wore large, very well made diadems of feathers in a variety of colors. Around their necks they wore necklaces made from strings of shells. In their hands they carried a small pouch called *sundorpauca* [*sic*; for *sunturpaucar*, a misnomer here]. Some also carried a dried green bird with its feathers, and each one had a small white drum that was very well made. These articles of clothing and instruments were kept in a house in Cuzco that the Inca had designated exclusively for this purpose, and there were a great many of these things kept in storage. Those who wore the costumes described here were young men up to twenty years of age. The rest of the people kept their heads covered with mantles or capes. And thus the young men as well as the others remained quite silent, for this was such a serious obligation that they refrained from speaking to each other during the whole day.

The boys mentioned above started to move around the square very slowly in a procession, all playing their drums at the same time and making certain grimaces. They continued in this way rhythmically until they completed the circle around the square. Once around, they sat down all together without saying anything. A noble stood up and circled around in the same way as the procession had done, spreading coca on the ground. After a short while the attendants [i.e., the boys mentioned above] got up again and went around again the same as was done at first. After they sat down, more coca was spread about as before. They planned and arranged this whole day in such a way that during this time they would circle around the square eight times. All of the following night they remained in the square praying with great care and using the Sun as an intercessor for the needs they had. When morning came, they took off that clothing and stored it as a sacred thing in the place mentioned above. Next they started to drink with great rejoicing, singing and dancing for two days and nights, as a sign that their prayer had been accepted.

This was a specifically Inca festival, and they were the only ones to perform it for a long time, but later, as a means of showing favor, permission was granted for the festival to be held in their lands by other lords who were ruled by the Incas. Such permission was granted mainly when the Inca married one of his daughters or nieces to some provincial lord. Many times such marriages were arranged for a variety of purposes. The Inca spoke highly of the favor done by the lord in taking his relative, and he emphasized the obligation which the lord had as a consequence [of the marriage]. The Inca also made the lord realize that he had become a relative by marriage of the Sun, from whom the Incas descended. As a sign of this, and as a very special favor, the Inca granted the lord permission to celebrate this Itu festival in his land, and by means of this festival the lord would receive help with the needs for which the

festival had been instituted. Along with the authorization to perform the festival, the Inca gave these lords the clothing and instruments with which it was performed. These things came from the
storehouse that they had for them in Cuzco. Giving them these
things was the last and most esteemed favor that the Inca could
grant. Later, in the land where permission was given to celebrate
this festival, a house was designated in which the clothing and apparatus for the festival were stored.

This festival was performed in the city of Cuzco as well as
other places in times of great need, such as when a severe earthquake occurred, when there was a severe pestilence, when the rains
were late in coming and there was much need of them, and, especially, when the Inca decided to go to war in person. In this latter
case, it was a general festival and everyone who had authorization
to do so got the order to perform it. At the court the festival was
performed with more ostentation and solemnity than for anything
else. On this occasion, the young men who participated on other
occasions did not perform. Instead it was done by the most important nobles and knights of Cuzco. They dressed in the costumes
already described, and they would play the drums while their wives
followed carrying the men's weapons in their hands. In addition,
the sacrifices were more solemn, and there were more of them.
They offered everything that was normally sacrificed in every one
of the other festivals, and the sacrifices were distributed to all of
the *guacas* of the city. The amount going to each one depended on
how much the *guaca* was venerated.

Furthermore, it must be pointed out that although everyone
was not authorized to perform this festival with the ceremonies
that we have mentioned, nevertheless, on the same occasions for
which it was generally performed in Cuzco and in the same locali-
ties authorized to perform it, in its place another festival called
Ayma was performed in all of the provinces. This other festival was
done in almost the same way [as Itu] except that the clothing was
different and so were some of the ceremonies. Moreover, there were
storehouses everywhere for the clothing and adornments with
which it was done.

Chapter 32: Of the solemnity with which the coronation of the king was celebrated

A special and very solemn festival was also celebrated after the death of the Inca when his successor took the fringe which was the insignia of the king. The purpose of this festival was to pray to the gods for the health, preservation, and prosperity of the Inca who was to be crowned. Although they were mistaken in these superstitions, there certainly is no denying that the great care taken in all the sacrifices for the health of the king was most praiseworthy. This festival was performed in the following way. After it was determined who was to be the successor and the lamentations and ceremonies were performed with the body of the dead king, the one to be crowned fulfilled the customary obligations to his many ancestors. All of the great lords who were able to be present for this act, depending on the distance they would have to travel, gathered together at the court, and there was a deputy representing each one of the *guacas* and shrines of the empire. Normally this was the guardian or attendant in charge of the *guaca*. All of them went to the square called Hurinaucaypata, which was located at the edge of town on the road to Collao. The statues of the Sun and of the rest of the major gods were placed in this square, and from all of the provinces of the kingdom, the things that were to be offered in the sacrifice were brought, namely, two hundred children from four to ten years of age, a large amount of gold and silver made into tumblers and figurines of sheep and other animals, much very well made clothing of *cumbi*, both large and small, a large amount of seashells of all kinds, colored feathers, and up to a thousand sheep of all colors, which were gathered together outside the square. Once all of this was brought together and the festival was arranged and those who were to be present in it were assembled, the high priest or attendant in charge of the sacrifice, dressed in certain clothing appropriate for the festival, would stand up. With many ceremonies he took a child in his arms from among those youngsters, and while the other children were together with the rest of the sacrifices, he turned toward Viracocha and said, "Lord, this we offer to you so that you will be at peace with us and help us in our wars and preserve the Inca's greatness and his state and let it always be expanding, and give the Inca much knowledge so that he will govern wisely." The priest did the same thing with each kind of sacrifice, going around the statues in a certain way with the insignia of each thing that was to be sacrificed.

Later all of the attendants of the provincial *guacas* and those of the native Cuzco *guacas* gathered together, and the Inca ordered the distribution among them of the sacrifices that had to be offered at the *guacas* of the city and at the provincial *guacas* from throughout his kingdom. The portion set aside for the provincial *guacas* was separated into four parts, one for each of the four *suyus* into which the empire was divided. This was because the Inca had *vilca camayos* for each one of the *suyus*. They were like accountants whose only responsibility was to keep track of the *guacas* from their districts and the sacrifices that needed to be offered to each one. These *vilca camayos* would summon before them all of the attendants of the *guacas* of the kingdom. From the sacrifices which had been brought to Cuzco for this festival, they would distribute among the attendants that portion which was to go to the *guacas* of the provinces. This was done in such an orderly and careful fashion that there was never an error in the reckoning, nor did they ever confuse one place with another. The things that were to be sacrificed were very well distributed when they left Cuzco, even though the amount of things for this sacrifice was excessive and the places where the sacrifices were to be made were practically countless. These things were distributed in such a way that no *guaca* or shrine, no matter how small it might be, would be left without a sacrifice. This was accomplished because the things to be offered to each *guaca* were already designated and agreed upon.

The reason why all of the *guacas* were included in this sacrifice was because it was held to be an omen that if any *guaca* did not receive an offering, it would become angry with the Inca and take its vengeance on him, punishing him for this oversight. They were very careful and conscientious in this, for if they could not reach certain hills that were shrines to make the offerings, due to the rough terrain or because they were covered with snow, the attendants went up as far as possible, and from there, with slings, they would throw the sacrifice to the top of the hills.

Once what was to be allotted to each *guaca* was determined, and once the sacrifices were distributed in the order already stated, they started to make the offerings, first to the statues that were present in Cuzco. The first sacrifice was Viracocha's. His priests received it and made the offering, praying that Viracocha see fit to give the Inca health and long life, and that he not take the Inca

away in his youth, that he allow the Inca to be victorious over his
enemies and that the Inca have sons to succeed him and to preserve the royal lineage, and that while the Inca governed all the
nations of his empire be at peace, multiply, and have an abundance
of food. After this prayer was over, the children were strangled and
buried with gold and silver on the hill of Chuquichanca, which is
half a league from the city above San Sebastian, and the sheep,
clothing, and other things were burned. After this, on the Inca's
same order, the priests of the Sun, the Thunder, and the other great
gods received what was assigned to their *guacas* and made the
offerings with the same ceremonies as the first ones, asking in
their prayers that the same things be granted for the Inca and the
welfare of the kingdom, and after the sacrifice was made to the
gods just mentioned, the priests of the rest of the *guacas* of Cuzco
received what they were to offer and left with it. Starting with
Guanacauri, as the major shrine, they set out making offerings of
what had been allotted to the rest of the *guacas*.

Once the sacrifices for all the *guacas* of Cuzco were concluded,
the Inca ordered the provincial priests to take what had been allotted to the *guacas* of their lands in the distribution that had been
made and offer it to them. The priests left at once to carry out the
order, walking according to the following arrangement. The livestock went alone along the royal road, and the throng of people
carrying the other sacrifices, off the road in parties somewhat separated and lined up in single file with the sacrifices ahead. They
went straight toward the place where they were going without
turning anywhere, going over hills and through ravines until each
one reached his land. The children who could walk went on foot,
but they carried the very tiny ones on their backs, along with the
gold and other things. From time to time they raised their voices in
a loud shout, starting with one person who was designated for this
purpose, and all of the others joined in in the same way as the first
one. In shouting like this they would pray to Viracocha for the
health and prosperity of the Inca. This sacrifice taken from Cuzco
was so highly venerated that if it happened that as the sacrifice was
being taken through the wilderness and other places, some people
came upon it, those who came upon the sacrifice would not dare to
raise their eyes and look at it. They would prostrate themselves on
the ground until the sacrifice had gone. When the sacrifice was carried into towns, the inhabitants would remain inside their houses,
being very reverent and humble inside there, until those carrying
the sacrifice would be handed over to those who cared for the ma-

jor *guaca* of each capital. Those attendants also kept an orderly account of the shrines that fell within their district and the sacrifices that were to remain in each province for all the shrines. However, since they sometimes increased or decreased these sacrifices, according to the will of the Inca, they took an explanation every time from Cuzco of what was to be done in each place. The order followed in the provinces for offering this sacrifice was as follows. First a festival was celebrated as it was offered at the major *guacas* of each district by those of that place, imitating the festival held at Cuzco, and then to all of the *guacas* and shrines of that province, they offered what corresponded to each one according to the allotment made in Cuzco.

These Indians customarily held many general festivals in which they made notable sacrifices. Many of the festivals were established for their wars and for the occasion when they entered the court with the prisoners who had been captured in the wars, and for other purposes. This is without taking into consideration the different festivals customary in each province. However, no account will be made of them because they did not differ greatly from those that have been described here and because it is possible to determine what the others would be like on the basis of those already mentioned.

Chapter 33: Of the priests and the functions that they had

Included under the name of priests were all of the men who dedicated themselves to the cult of their false gods and were in charge of offering them sacrifices and performing all of their usual superstitious acts. And since there were numerous superstitions, it follows that there were numerous kinds of priests. In the first place, some acted as caretakers and attendants of the *guacas* and offered them the sacrifices. These sacrifices were sustained from the income of the Religion. Nevertheless, not being content with this stipend, they were very skillful in getting as much as possible from the community, and in order to accomplish this they invented all sorts of nonsense, saying that the *guacas* complained to them at night in their dreams of how they were neglected, and for this reason the *guacas* brought about all of the hardships that the people had to suffer. As a result, the ignorant people would be moved to multiply the sacrifices and offerings, which was just what the priests wanted. Among themselves the priests had their ranks and grades of higher and lower officials. They had special clothing which they put on for the sacrifices. Some were instituted by election or appointment of the Inca or his governors; others by succession within certain *ayllus* and lineages for the service and care of different gods, and others by offer of their parents, *caciques*, or elders, and this did not happen by chance; rather, it resulted from a number of events or situations.

The priests of the Sun were of the *ayllu* and family of Tarpuntay, and for this reason they were called Tarpuntaes, and the priests of the Sun could not be from any other lineage. Their high priest, or their bishop as we would say, was the one who presided in the Temple of the Sun, located in the city of Cuzco. He was the highest-ranking dignitary among them and the superior and prelate over the rest of the priests, both those dedicated to the Sun and those dedicated to the rest of the gods. The high priest was called *villac umu* which means "diviner or sorcerer who speaks." Using their corrupted form of the word, the Spaniards call him *vilaoma*. He always resided in Cuzco at the temple called Coricancha [Temple of the Sun]. Those who were designated for this occupation [priesthood] were selected in the following manner. If some male child was born in the country while there was a storm and thunder, the people kept track of him, and when he was an old man, he was ordered to dedicate himself to this [the priesthood]. From the time he was born, he was called "son of the Thunder," and it was believed that the sacrifice made in person by this man was more acceptable to their *guacas* than the sacrifice made by anyone else. Moreover, it was said that priests were not selected by chance nor without some mystery that marked them. This happened to those born of women who stated that they had conceived and given birth from the Thunder and to those born as twins or triplets from the same womb, and finally to those given by nature something out of the ordinary. All of these individuals were consecrated as priests when they were old because all priests, or at least the majority who had this occupation, were old, and they were not admitted to the priesthood until they reached the age at which they could not do other types of work. There was an excessively large number of priests because there was not a shrine, large or small, whether it be a stream, a spring, a hill, or any other place of veneration, for which attendants and caretakers were not designated. In addition to taking care of the sacrifices that corresponded to each *guaca,* they took care to perpetuate the memory of the *guacas;* that is, the function and special purpose that corresponded to each *guaca,* the reason why sacrifices were made to it, and the things with which the sacrifice was to be made. They undertook this endeavor in a very studious and careful manner, and the attendants themselves educated those who were to take their places, instructing them diligently in these things.

There were also many others who specialized in casting lots. These we call *sortilegos,* and there were numerous types of sorcerers, diviners, and augurs. Associated with all of them were the occupations of confessor and of curing superstitiously. Many times these occupations [confessor and curer] were confused with the first type of priests because the same person practiced them all together. Other times these occupations were separated because each person attended to his own task. Nevertheless, the first situation was the most common. More often than not the same priests were confessors, doctors, and sorcerers. Therefore, although we are going to separate these functions and discuss each one in its own chapter, it must not be understood that the individuals in charge of these duties were always different.

Chapter 34: Of the sortilegos

We use the name sorcerers to mean all types of people who use superstitions and illicit arts in order to do strange things and go beyond human faculties. These things are achieved by the invocation of and help from the devil. All of their power and science stems from an explicit or implicit pact with the devil. Theologians usually divide this diabolic superstition into four types. The first is called the art of magic, and this occurs when by it one tries to produce an incredible effect or knowledge of something. The second is divination, and this occurs when one tries to obtain knowledge of things yet to happen or things at the present time or in the past about which an understanding cannot be achieved in a natural way. The third is the way in which those who are called sorcerers in the strict sense or evildoers endeavor to be instructed and helped, not for anything beneficial but in order to harm others, and this is called a curse or sorcery. The fourth and last is that which is called vain observance. Without harming or damaging anyone, those who profess this art use it to help themselves in things that are personally useful or enjoyable to them. Among the Indians there were individuals who were very skilled and experienced in all four types of superstitions. Nevertheless, many used some of these vanities without having any communication or pact with the devil. This was the case of the majority of the *sortilegos* and doctors, who had the people fooled, though their methods were useless and ridiculous and did not produce the results that they proclaimed to be the effects of their art. Nevertheless, some of them had an understanding of the devil. In this chapter I will only cover the *sortilegos* who made predictions by casting lots, without having any pact or communication with the devil. In the following two chapters I will discuss the doctors and sorcerers who made use of diabolic arts.

These Indians considered the occupation of *sortilego* not only to be permissible but also useful and necessary for the republic. It was practiced by men and women alike, although more commonly by men, and every town had many of them. In the city of Cuzco, the Incas always had officials designated for this occupation. Normally they were from the province of Condesuyo, ever since the time that one came from there named Galina, who was considered very eminent in this occupation. All of those involved in it were useless, poor, and unfortunate like the rest of the sorcerers. The *cacique* of each town would select all of them after they had become too weak to work. The selection was preceded by diverse ceremonies and rites which these *caciques* ordered them to perform. In fact, these Indians often tried to make use of lots and sorcery, and this practice was so common and frequent that they would never embark on any important endeavour without first referring the matter to the sorcerers and "sortilegos" for inquiry. In spite of all this, they always considered it to be a low and undignified occupation. Thus it was delegated to persons of such condition and needs. Regarding this situation, they gave some explanations that are not very convincing. It seems to me that only one of their explanations is based on their customs and type of government, and it is that the general aim of the Incas was to keep all of their vassals busy. Thus all were to be responsible for something in the republic, and since this occupation of sorcerer was necessary, those individuals who were unable to handle any other occupation because of their age and poverty were ordered to practice it.

First it must be understood that before starting any acts of sorcery, casting lots, or any of the other things done by those who practiced this occupation, some kind of sacrifice had to be made. This sacrifice could be of much or little importance, according to the intention and reason for making it, and once what they considered to be a satisfactory part of these sacrifices was consumed, those in charge of the sacrifice ate the rest and sustained themselves on it. They say that since they were not strong enough to work, it was only fair that they should have an occupation by which they could sustain themselves without any effort. This was another of the explanations that they gave on the basis of the principle that has been established here. They even added another explanation which seems to be more or less probable. They say that once, while Viracocha was feeling sorry about the poverty and hunger of the elderly and needy, he saw fit to allow their predictions to be correct. He did this so that everyone would come to them, and they could compensate for their poverty with this occupation. The principal basis for all of these explanations was, in my opinion, the fact that these people had little or no sense of charity for each other. They were negligent in fulfilling the needs of their own poor, elderly, or disabled. Since this occupation was open to both men and women, so suitable for human sustenance, and since it was the only recourse for the poor after they had lost the strength to work, it is no wonder that so many people practiced it. In fact, there were so many of them that in his account the Licentiate Polo

de Ondegardo[67] tells that on the basis of the inquiry made by the
Indian mayors in the city of Cuzco on his orders, just from among
the inhabitants of that city there were four hundred seventy-five
men and women who had no other occupation. Each of them was
brought before him with the instruments that they used. Although
everyone was permitted to cast lots for his own purposes, only
those named by the *caciques* as public officials who made their
living by this occupation were permitted to cast lots on behalf of
other people. In this, the same thing happened as in everything
else; some turned out to be more skillful than others in their
speech and their make-believe, adding and creating more than what
was usual. Thus they earned more than others because more people
came to them.

They practiced this occupation with different types of instruments and contrivances. The most common was with maize,
beans, and black pebbles and other pebbles of different colors. The
sorcerers and their successors were very careful to keep these things
when the one who used them died, and when they got old, they
used the same things.

What they told about how they got these pebbles is a long
story. Some stated that the Thunder gave the pebbles to them or to
their ancestors. Others said that they got them from some *guaca*.
Others said that a deceased person came at night in their dreams
and brought the pebbles to them. Some women let it be known
that while they were in the fields during a storm, the Thunder
made them pregnant, and after nine months the pebbles were born
to them with a great deal of pain. In their dreams they were told
that the predictions made with these pebbles would be true. In this
way they told a thousand other foolish stories. Thus with the poverty of one group, the simplicity of the other, and the diligence of
the devil, things were established that are not only harmful but
also difficult to eradicate, as experience has shown.

The second way of making these predictions was by using
some big spiders that they kept in tightly covered jars, and in there
the spiders were given a certain kind of food on which they kept
alive. When someone came to find out from them the outcome of
what that person wanted to do, the following was done. After some
sacrifice had been made, the jar was uncovered. If the spider had
any of its legs pulled in, it was a sign that the outcome would be
bad, and if it had all of its legs spread out and in view, the outcome
would be good. This type of sorcery was more commonly used by
those of Chinchaysuyu, where spiders were much venerated. In

some other places snakes were used for this purpose, and in other places, other types of animals were used.

The third manner of lots and inquiry into the future was as follows. They would chew coca and spit its juice with saliva into the palm of their hand while extending their two longest fingers. If it ran down both fingers equally, they said it was a sign of good luck, but if it ran down only one finger, it was a sign of bad luck. Before this test, they made a sacrifice and expressed their adoration to the Sun.

The fourth manner was the following. They would kill birds, sheep, or lambs. Then by blowing into a certain vein in the [animal's] lungs, they said that they would find signs in the lungs by which to foretell what was going to happen. Other times for this same purpose, they would burn sheep's fat and coca. By a certain fluid that appeared and by other signs that were seen at the time of burning, they said that they knew what was going to happen to the one who hired them.

They cast lots for all the things that they wanted to undertake, such as planting, harvesting, storing bread, going on a trip, building a house, getting married or leaving the wife one had, piercing ears with the solemnity that was customary, going to war, and for all other important matters. Therefore, they never started anything without two precautionary measures. The first one was to cast lots, and the second was to make some sacrifice, or the reverse. For he who cast lots also showed deference to the *guacas* and to one in particular from his town or settlement or *suyu*, and he offered some sacrifice to it. They not only used these lots in order to find out if the outcome would be good or bad for the things they wanted to do, no matter what type of things they were, but they also used them to find out which sacrifices would be the most agreeable to Viracocha or the Sun, or to any of their other gods of whom they wanted to make a request. The sacrifice also depended on the importance of what they hoped to achieve. In sum, they did not start anything without casting lots, nor did they cast them without a sacrifice. And it was laughable to see the simplicity that these Indians exhibited in the credence they gave to such childish notions. If one asks them if they ever refrained from planting their fields because the lot cast so indicated, they answer that the lots always told them to plant, and nevertheless, they always cast lots because they were so pleased that these lots told them the truth.

Chapter 35: Of the sorcerer-doctors and the superstitions that they used in curing

There were many Indians, both men and women, who cured sicknesses. Some of them had a little knowledge and knew about medicinal plants with which they were sometimes able to heal. Nevertheless, they all generally cured with superstitious words and actions, and they did not bring about any cures without making previous sacrifices and casting lots. These doctors were called *camasca* or *soncoyoc*. When they were asked to tell who gave them or taught them the occupation that they practiced, the majority of them would give as the main cause that it came to them in a dream. They said that while they were asleep, someone appeared to them grieving about their plight. This person told them that they were being authorized to cure the sicknesses that they cured. And whenever they started giving a cure, they would sacrifice something to that person who, as they claimed, had appeared to them in their dreams and taught them how to cure and what instruments to use in doing it. There were others who cured fractures and dislocations. As long as the treatment lasted they took great pains to make sacrifices in the place where the injured person suffered the fracture or dislocation. The way in which many of them took up this occupation is as follows. Whoever had broken an arm or leg or any other bone in their body and got well in less than the normal time was taken among them to be an expert in curing such maladies, and they made up great things to explain how they had gotten well, including dreams in which they were given power to cure. Many of them claimed to have had certain sicknesses and to have gotten well very quickly. This was taken as a miracle by the people, and more sick people came to them.

There were also midwives. Some of them said that they had received that occupation in their dreams, and being poor, others took it up when they gave birth to twins. At this time many ceremonies, fasts, and sacrifices were performed. They concerned themselves with curing pregnant women by massaging their abdomens in order to straighten out the unborn child, and they even had great contrivances for killing the child in the mother's body, provided they were paid for it.

Many of these doctors or sorcerers were very skilled in making preparations of poison herbs and things with which they would kill anyone they wanted. They had herbs for different purposes. Some would kill quickly, others slowly, according to the way the herbs were mixed and prepared. And there is no doubt about it. A great many Indians died from these magic charms. Individuals who were known for their skill in making it [poison] were greatly feared by the unfortunate Indians. As a last resort, even though they were *caciques* and nobles, they would make contributions to the sorcerers with gifts and do whatever they could do to please them. With the herbs and poisoned food customarily given by these sorcerers, the one who fell prey to the magic charms would slowly lose weight until overcome by death. The instruments and materials normally used for their magic charms were molars, teeth, hair, fingernails, shells of different types and colors, animal figurines made of different things, live and dead toads, the heads of various animals, small dried animals, large hairy spiders that were kept alive in jars with clay lids, a great many different kinds of roots, pots and other vessels full of preparations made of herbs and other ointments. When they described in detail the effects that each one of these things produced, the nonsense that they told was infinite. Although all of these Indians believed it as they were told, the truth is that not all of these things produced the effects that the sorcerers said they did. In fact, they pretended to have extraordinary things in order to frighten those who saw the things, and thus frighten everyone into making contributions to them by giving the sorcerers part of what they had.

When these Indians felt sick, they got carried to the sorcerers or called them to their houses. Before doing anything else, the sorcerers would offer sacrifices and cast lots. They believed so strongly that their sacrifices and superstitions were useful for restoring health and were accurate in everything that if by their tricks and lots they concluded that someone was certain to die and if the man saw that he was afflicted by the malady, he would not hesitate to kill his own son, even though he had no other. Moreover, it was their opinion that in this way they would regain their health. Thus the offering was made with words to this effect. It was stated that since his death was inevitable and could not be avoided, that his son was being offered in his place as a sacrifice. When they got sick from any kind of illness, the majority of these Indians generally believed that they had been given some magic charm or poisoned

food, and thus they went to experts in this art so that the harm
they suspected them of doing could be undone. As a result of what
these sorcerers gave them so they would get well, they often suffered the very fate that they feared because frequently many of
them would die of it [the remedy]. The superstitious acts they carried out and the grimaces that they made in order to cause this
harm were numerous. The sorcerers made the common people believe that for them alone that occupation was reserved and that no
other person could perform it properly. They would tell the ways
that the devil had to teach it to them and the hardships they had to
suffer in order to learn it. This kind of magic charm was considered
necessary for curing in this way. However, to kill with magic
charms was a very serious crime.

The other doctors who did not use poisonous preparations had
various methods of curing. First they made a certain flour of black
and white maize and other colors and seashells of as many colors
as they could obtain. This was put on the sick man's hand, and he
was ordered to blow it as a sacrifice to the *guacas* while saying
certain words. They also made him blow a little coca to the Sun as
an offering and at the same time ask the Sun for good health. The
same was also done for the other gods. And taking a small amount
of gold and silver of little value, the sick man himself offered it to
Viracocha by scattering it about. After this the sorcerer asked the
sick man to feed his ancestors. The food was to be placed over their
graves, if the graves were in a place where this could be done, and
chicha was to be poured out to them. But if this were not possible,
it could be done in any part of his house that he considered appropriate. The sick man was made to believe that since his ancestors
were suffering from hunger, they had put a curse on him, and for
this reason he had gotten sick.

If the sick man could do it, he was made to go on foot to where
two rivers met. His body was washed with water and white flour,
and they said that he left the sickness there. If he was in no condition to walk, the sick man was given the bath at home. It was also
customary for them to cure by rubbing and sucking the sick man's
abdomen and other parts of his body while smearing the same parts
with grease or with the meat and fat of the *cui* [guinea pig] or of a
toad, and such ointments were applied with other filth or with
herbs. The sick were made to believe the following. By sucking the
part of the body where pain was felt, the [sorcerer] would draw out
blood or worms or small stones, and he would show them to the
patient stating that the sickness left through that place. The fact is

that the [sorcerers] brought these things with them and put these
things in their mouth at the time they were to suck. Later they
would show them to the patient and to his relatives, saying that
the malady had gone out and that the person would soon be well.
Along with this, they did a thousand other tricks.

For very grave illnesses that could not be cured with ordinary
medications and remedies, the sorcerers had the patient put in a
secret room. First the place was prepared in the following way. It
was cleaned very well, and in order to purify it, they filled their
hands with black maize which they brought [to the room]. They
scrubbed the walls and floor with it, blowing everywhere while
they did this, and they would burn the maize in the same room.
Later they would take white maize and do the same thing. Afterward they would sprinkle the whole room with a mixture of water
and maize flour, and in this way they purified the room. Once the
room was cleaned and purified this way, the patient was placed on
his back in the middle of it. If the patient was the wife or son of
the Inca, he would be present himself. Next, by illusions and tricks
of the devil, the patient was caused to fall into a deep sleep and
trance. The sorcerers pretended to cut his body up the middle with
crystal knives, and out of his abdomen they took snakes, toads, and
other filthy things, burning them all in the fire that they had there.
All the while they carried out many superstitious acts. These doctors were paid with food, clothing, silver, and other things.

Chapter 36: Of the diviners and how they summoned the devil

The Indians had extensive knowledge of the devil. They called him *zupay,* and they knew very well that he was an evil spirit and a deceiver of men. But the devil had achieved such authority and power over them that they obeyed and served him with great respect. Nevertheless, it is true that they venerated him more because they feared that he would do evil to them than because they believed that there was some deity in him. In spite of the fact that they knew that there was a creator of all things, they were blinded and deceived by this cruel tyrant, and they also knew that he had a hand in all things. At times some of them were on bad terms with him, and they hated him because they were aware of his intrigues and wickedness and that he never used or spoke the truth. However, because of their sins (God permitting it) the devil had the Indians so subjected to his will that they could not escape being blindly imprisoned by his trickery. Everywhere the devil had numerous subjects and attendants. In order to be such followers, they offered and consecrated themselves to him in diverse ways. Sometimes they let their hair grow down to their waist; other times they cut it in a certain style. They also conducted other ceremonies and superstitious acts, and as a sign of their submission to him, they customarily carried with them his likeness made of a hollow bone with his statue on top of it in black wax. The name of these disciples of the devil was *umu.* The people considered them to be diviners, and they came to ask them about stolen or lost things, events yet to happen, and what was happening in distant or far-off places. And they consulted the devil about this. They spoke to him and had conversations with him in dark places. He answered them in a harsh and frightening voice which other people often heard without understanding it or seeing who was speaking. And it is true that with regard to stolen or lost things these diviners made admirable inquiries. In many instances the diviners accurately stated where the things were located. Other times they told what had happened in far-off places before the news arrived or could possibly arrive in any normal way.

It is true enough that they normally lied in the answers that they gave about future events, but their reputations were not damaged as a result of this, because they claimed that the devil had changed his mind. They commonly summoned the devil in a number of different ways. Sometimes they did it by drawing certain lines and circles on the ground and saying appropriate words. Other times they went into a room; closing it from inside, they used certain ointments and got so drunk they lost consciousness. One day later they answered the questions asked of them. For these consultations and conversations with the devil, they performed countless ceremonies and sacrifices. The most important one was to get drunk on *chicha* which had the juice of a certain plant called *vilca*[68] added to it. In several parts of the kingdom there were famous idols which were held to be major oracles. The devil spoke through them and answered questions. Included among the oracles were the *guaca* of Guanacauri in the Cuzco area, the oracle of Pachacama, four leagues from the city of Los Reyes [Lima], and many others. In conjunction with these oracles, the Indians invented many superstitions and magic charms. In other instances, the devil answered his attendants from a stone or from some other thing that was venerated by them. On many occasions he appeared visibly to them in several frightening forms, such as that of a snake or other wild animal, and he spoke with them.

The method of summoning the devil that these "ariolos"[69] employed with the most authority was by fire, which they venerated and worshiped as a major *guaca*. The devil was summoned in the following way. They took two braziers made of silver, copper, or clay, which were about the size of a large still without a beak that had many openings all around it and another larger opening in the top from where the flame came out. The braziers were placed facing each other, full of slivers of wood soaked in fat. The braziers were lit up, and the attendants blew into them with tubes about the size and shape of an harquebus. These tubes were made of copper from the middle upward, and the other half was silver. Around these braziers many vessels made of gold, silver, wood, and clay were set with various kinds of food and drink. Later the principal attendant, with the others, chewing coca, first chanting then weeping, started with words that they knew for this purpose to summon the spirits of those persons about whom they wanted to know something. The spirits were invited to come to the banquet that had been prepared for them in the presence of the sacred Fire, the Sun, and the mother Earth, Pachamama. Once the fire was burning well in the braziers, its flames started coming out through the vents, and then the devil would come. Without being seen, he spoke to them, saying that he was the spirit of the person about whom they were asking. That person might be dead or alive, in a nearby place or far away. The first thing that the devil did was to make it known that he had accepted the invitation to the banquet, and later he proceeded to answer as many questions as they might ask him.

Finally, in order to confirm everything that he had said, with incantations and magic charms they forced him into one of the braziers. They made him go through the opening around the brazier which was designated by them. Then they ordered him to repeat and verify everything he had said by means of the flame coming out through the opening. In this way, with the flame he answered everything that they asked him. If the diviners felt that it was necessary to challenge and compare the answers, they made other spirits or devils go into the other brazier, and by the openings in it that they indicated to them [the other spirits], they answered the first [devil]. Finally, in order to confirm that the truth had been spoken, they made the fire approve of what had been said by a response from the principal flame that came out of the opening in the top. They employed this method of divination only for very serious and important matters, such as when it was suspected that some province wanted to rebel or was plotting against the Inca and it was impossible to find out what was happening through witnesses, torture, or any other method, and in similar cases. This summoning of evil spirits was not performed without great sacrifices of children, gold, silver, spotless white lambs, and other valuable things that they customarily sacrificed to their *guacas*. The children were buried alive, and the rest was burned. Sometimes the Inca was present at these sacrifices, appearances, and illusions of the devil. The Inca would prepare himself by having previously fasted for two or three days without tasting *agi*, salt, or meat. Diviners of this kind were called *yacarca*, and they were usually natives of the town of Guaro, diocese of Cuzco. They were greatly feared by the Inca as well as by the rest of the people, and wherever he went, the Inca took them with him.

There was another type of sorcerer permitted by the Inca in a certain way. Although they were not among those considered necessary for the republic, no effort was made to punish them. Their status was that of wizards who changed into whatever form they pleased (according to them), traveled through the air covering great distances in a brief time, and saw everything that was happening. Upon returning to the place from which they had left, they told about what they had seen.

Men also came to these sorcerers for help in attracting some woman or capturing her affection, and in keeping their mistress from leaving them. And women customarily came to them for the same reasons. For this purpose the sorcerers were given some part of their clothing and some of their hair, or that of their accomplice; sometimes some of their blood itself was given. With these things the sorcerers made their magic charms. Moreover, these tricksters would carry with them a certain kind of magic charm or diabolical spell that they called *huacanqui*. Such charms would be given to other men so that they could carry them in order to attract women and capture their affection, or for women to attract men, or the charms were placed in the clothing or bed of the one they wanted to entice, or in some place that seemed appropriate to produce the desired effect. Other similar magic charms were made from herbs and other things. These *huacanquis* were certain figurines made of feathers or of other different things. And there was no end to these kinds of tricks, magic charms, and superstitions employed by these people who were deceived by the devil.

Chapter 37: Of the cloisters or convents of maidens dedicated to their vain gods

As we have seen, a great many men were dedicated to the service and ministry of their false religion. However, the number of women dedicated to it was just as great. From childhood, they were consecrated to the idols and lived in a cloistered and chaste manner, as nuns do among us. In each major town and provincial capital in which there was a temple dedicated to the Sun, next to it they also constructed a convent or cloister called *acllaguaci*, which means "house of the chosen women." In it there lived a number of virgins called *mamaconas*, which means "esteemed mothers." The number of them at any given place was greater or lesser according to the size and authority of the temple which they served, and in some of them there were as many as two hundred. They were enclosed in these convents from the time they were girls of ten to twelve years of age. This did not happen due to any personal devotion on their part, nor on the part of their parents. It happened by the will of the Inca and the observance of their religion. These girls were from the ones gathered as tribute throughout the entire kingdom, and care was taken to select from these girls the most noble and beautiful for this profession. Along with the *mamaconas* the rest of the girls from the tribute lived within these cloisters until they were old enough to be available for the Inca. These secular girls were called *acllas*, which means the same as "chosen women." This is because they were chosen from among the girls throughout the Inca's kingdom, as has been stated above.[70] Here these girls learned the things pertaining to their religion, its rites and ceremonies, as well as the occupations that correspond to women and that are necessary to human life. The *mamaconas* taught them both of these things.

The governor or commissioner, called *apupanaca*, who collected the tribute of girls, was in charge of each convent. He looked after the safekeeping, administration, and sustenance of the convent. The number of *mamaconas* who died was replaced from among the girls raised at these cloisters. These virgins were responsible for the service of their gods, but not for all of them, only the major ones such as Viracocha, the Sun, the Thunder, and a few others. It was a necessary prerequisite to be admitted to this status and profession that the girls be virgins and remain virgins for the rest of their lives. If it was found that one of these girls had lost her feminine virtue, she would be given the death penalty, and it would be carried out by burying the girl alive or by some equally cruel death. The same punishment would be applied to her accomplice, no matter what his social status might be, except in the case of the Inca. It is said that sometimes the Inca would indulge himself and that he had access to the favors of some of these women. In spite of this, they retained their cloistered status, serving the idols to whom they were dedicated, and they were watched over the same as before, without being taken out of their cloister. But the guards and doorkeepers had a way of proving how very careful they were in their vigilance. Once they found out that the Inca had entered some night, the next day when the Inca was present in the Square of the Sun attending the ordinary daily sacrifice, one of these guards, who were always very old men, approached the Inca from the rear, and sitting down beside him, he would grasp the Inca's mantle and say in a very low voice. "Inca, last night you went into the House of the Sun, and you were with one of his women." The Inca responded, also in a very low voice, "I sinned." And with this the guard would return assured that his job of safekeeping and vigilance had been properly performed.

These maidens were consecrated to their gods in the following way. The maidens were married to the gods with special ceremonies and solemnity, and from that time forward, the maidens were considered to be their wives. Although it is true that this name [wife] was applied to all of them, nevertheless some of them were more important than others, and specifically in each house or convent there was one woman who with more legitimate title was considered to be the wife of the Sun or of the idol to whom she had been consecrated. And she was always the one with the noblest lineage. As a result, at the main temple of Cuzco, the Sun's wife was normally a sister of the king himself. This lady was in charge of governing the convent, and the others respected and obeyed her. She alone dealt with the stewards and people who served outside the convent, handled matters pertaining to income and business transactions, and could allow her relatives and devout friends to visit her. None of the others were permitted to have visitors, be it their relatives or anyone else.

Generally the people greatly respected these women. They looked up to them as saints who had intimate dealings and communication with their gods. Thus the people would not even dare touch the clothing of these women. Their profession was the same as that of the vestal virgins of Rome, and they observed almost the same rules as the vestals. Their ordinary activities included taking great care in the service and worship of the temple. They spun and wove clothing of wool, cotton, and vicuña which was very fine and delicate, of excellent quality, and in a variety of very bright colors. This clothing was used to dress the idols, and it was offered in the sacrifices; it was also used for the garments of the Inca. These women made large amounts of high-quality *chicha* which was for offerings to the gods and for the priests to drink. Every day they cooked the food that was offered in the sacrifices and was eaten by the priests and attendants of the idols. The women who resided in the temple of Cuzco were in charge of lighting and stirring the fire that burned in the temple for the sacrifices. This fire was not fed with ordinary wood but with a very special kind of carefully carved and painted wood. The women got up early every day to cook the food for the Sun and his attendants. As the Sun appeared on the horizon and struck with its rays at the Punchao, which was a golden image of the Sun placed so that as the Sun came up its light would bathe the image, the women offered the Sun this food that they had prepared, burning it with special solemnity and songs. They would say, "Sun, eat this food that your wives have cooked for you." After this a sacrifice was made, some of the same food was given to the priests of the Sun and to the rest of the attendants of the temple as well as to the people who were guarding the convent, and the women also ate.

These women were not totally confined. They did go out at times, not only to the temple but also to other places. However, this was only so that they could be present for the sacrifices made to the Sun wherever he might go. And they were not allowed to leave their cloister for any other occasion. Moreover, the only reason they were permitted to go out for these sacrifices was that they had an important part in them. They were the wives of the Sun for whom the sacrifices were made. Thus they were required to perform certain tasks. This included bringing the idol of the Moon out in public, a job that could be performed only by them, carrying out the *chicha*, which they had prepared previously, to be used in the sacrifices, giving this drink to the priests of the Sun, and other similar things. Therefore, some of these *mamaconas* were always present to assist during any festival dedicated to the Sun himself.

Chapter 38: Of the omens and superstitions that these Indians

had The superstitions and omens of these Indians were so numerous that it is not easy to make a record of them all. In this chapter I will be content to tell about the most ordinary and general ones. Commonly, when they saw snakes, either alone or joined together, serpents, vipers, lizards, spiders, toads, large worms, moths, foxes, and other similar things, they thought it was an evil omen and that some misfortune would befall the one who saw such things, especially if the things were seen at home. On finding a snake, an Indian would kill it, urinate on it, and step on it with his left foot so that in this way he could ward off the evil omen. They also performed other ceremonies for the same purpose. When they heard the hooting of an owl or some other strange bird or the howling of a dog, they took it as an evil omen which foretold their own death or that of their children or neighbors. The omen was especially directed to the owner of the house or place where the hooting or howling was heard. And they made offerings of coca or other things to the birds or dogs, asking these animals to harm their enemies, not them. Moreover, when they heard the song of a nightingale or finch, they took it to mean that they would quarrel with someone.

Lunar and solar eclipses were interpreted as evil omens, foretelling misfortune and calamities. Seeing a rainbow was also considered to be an evil omen which meant death or some serious injury. But sometimes it was taken as a good omen. The rainbow was much venerated, and they did not dare look at it. However, if they happened to look at one, they would not dare point their finger at it because they thought they would die. They believed that the end of the rainbow was a frightful place where there was a *guaca* or some other thing that should be feared and venerated. When a comet appeared, or hail or snow fell, or it became very stormy, they would shout, hoping that this would be of help, and they would make some sacrifices and do other superstitious things. Furthermore, when there was a falling star, the shouting would be tremendous, and they became as sad as they did when there was an eclipse or a comet. When the earth shook, they poured water on it, saying that the earth was thirsty and wanted to drink, and they also performed other ceremonies. Twitching of the eyelid, lip or other part of the body, buzzing in the ears, or stumbling were said to mean that something good or bad was going to happen or be heard, good if it was the right eye, ear or foot and bad if it was the left.

When they were sick, the Indians of the [coastal] plains would place their clothing on the roads so that their illness would be carried away by someone walking that way or so their clothing would be purified by the winds. This was also the custom in some parts of the sierra. And in order to cure illnesses, a standard practice was to smear maize or other things on themselves or on other people. With *llimpi*, which is the metal of mercury [mercuric ore or vermilion], they customarily did a number of superstitious things. They would smear it or other earth colors on themselves at the time of their festivals or for other evil purposes, adding ceremonies and superstitious acts. They bathed in order to cleanse themselves of their sins, and they would spit in the grass called *hicho* when they confessed their sins to the sorcerers. They also burned the clothing they were wearing when they sinned. They believed that the fire would consume their sins and leave them cleansed of all guilt and free of any punishment.

When the fire jumped and gave off sparks, they poured maize, *chicha*, or something else on it in order to calm it by this veneration. In order to bring illness or death to an enemy, they would make a statue in the name of the enemy, dress it in his clothes, and curse it by hanging it up and spitting on it. Moreover, they made small statues of wax or clay or dough, and they put them into the fire so that the wax would melt there, or so the clay and dough would harden, or so as to produce other effects that they sought. They believed that in this way they would be avenged and do evil to their enemies. The women often broke their *topos* or pins used to fasten their clothing, thinking that this would render a man powerless to lie with them or soon take away whatever powers he had. It was also considered an evil omen for a pregnant or menstruating woman to pass through the sown fields. Finally, they paid close attention to dreams, and they would ask the sorcerers and diviners to interpret them. The Indians gave complete credence to what the sorcerers told them. This covers the major idolatries, gods, ceremonies, rites, and superstitions that these Peruvian Indians had. However, since these people were beastly, filthy, and disciples of the devil, they had vile and obscene habits which were included along with these rites. Such things will not be treated here, but in this respect the Indians were no better than the pagans of the Old World. In fact, the guide and master of their blindness and ignorance was one and the same. But I did not want to put anything in this account of their false religion that would offend the chaste sensibilities of the Christian reader. Therefore, I have purposely omitted the vile aspects of their religion which accompanied many of their idolatries and superstitions.

BOOK II
CUSTOMS

Chapter 1: Of the Quichua language, which is the general language of Peru

I will begin this book on the customs of the Peruvian Indians with their language, since it is something so very closely associated with man. Thus my point of departure is the customs that are most intrinsic and close to these people. From there I will proceed to those that are most extrinsic and removed. Many languages were spoken in the Inca Empire. In fact, every province and nation had its own language, and some were more widely spoken than others. The language of the Indians of Trujillo extended for many leagues along the seacoast, and likewise some others were common to several provinces. However, only two languages were considered to be general. These were Quichua and Aymará. The second was spoken by the nations of the Collao, and it extended across the land for more than one hundred fifty leagues. Quichua was spoken by all the vassals of the Inca, including the Aymará Indians themselves. Therefore, we consider Quichua to be absolutely general. Quichua was the language of the people of Cuzco, and they considered it to be their mother tongue. The Inca kings required all the people that they conquered and placed under their dominion to learn Quichua, but they did not take away from them their own native languages that they spoke before. Thus, in discussing the language of this kingdom, I speak only of Quichua, since it was the general language, common to all of its inhabitants. We call this language Quichua, taking the name from the Indian nation called the Quichuas who had it originally, and it was derived from them by the rest. In the same way we refer to the Castilian language with this term because it is the mother tongue that we Castilians speak.

It is very easy to learn to speak this Quichua language, and its pronunciation is soft and sweet. Moreover, the emotions of the spirit are expressed in it with great feeling. The Indians pronounce some words gutturally, and those who make the effort to learn this language do not master them easily. However, those who learn the language from infancy articulate and pronounce these guttural words with the same facility and ease as the Indians themselves. In their pronunciation these Quichuas lacked the following letters: b, d, f, g, x, z; the pronunciation of the "r" was not harsh, but rather soft, as in this noun, *"caridad."* When they borrow our words, the

Indians who are not Spanish speakers nor raised among the Spaniards use "p" in place of "b," and what we say with "d" they pronounce with "t". In this way they accommodate our words to their manner of speaking, substituting for the letters that they lack the letters of their own language that most resemble them. In accordance with this, they say Tios instead of Dios [God] and instead of saying Blas, they say Plas.

This language has the eight parts of speech that Latin has, namely, noun, pronoun, verb, along with the rest.[1] Nevertheless, except for that similarity, in other respects it does not resemble the European languages. On the contrary, it seems to be quite different. Although there are some words in Quichua that are similar to the words of those languages, the resemblance is only in the sound of the word, but in meaning there is rarely or never any similarity. Nouns, both substantive and adjective, have only one declension, and nouns are recognized and distinguished only by their meaning. Adjectives do not have the different endings that they have in the Latin language, rather one ending serves for different genders. Since there is only one ending for adjectives and substantives, the declension is not produced by inflections for case, as in Latin or Greek; cases are expressed by adding certain particles to the nominative. These particles are always placed after the noun in the phrase and sentence. There were no particles for the nominative and vocative cases. The plural is formed from the singular by adding a certain particle, which is also placed after the noun, and this same declension is used for all nouns, pronouns, participles, and indeed for all words that can be declined as nouns.

The verbs of this language are of the same types as Latin verbs, except that verbs are recognized by their meaning rather than by their endings. All verbs end in the same way. The first person singular is formed with "ni," as in "cani," "I am," or "cuyani," "I love." There are two types of conjugations: one simple and the other compound. The simple one is formed by conjugating the verb according to its moods and tenses without inserting any element at all. The compound one is formed by the addition of certain particles and insertions which indicate the transition of the verb from one person to another, as for example, "cuyayqui," "I love you." The first person plural of verbs, the plural of the pronoun "ñoca," which means "I," and possessive pronouns, have two endings, one inclusive and the other exclusive. The inclusive ending includes in its meaning those with whom one is speaking. So for example, speaking with Christians, we would say, "We Christians know the true God." The word used to say this includes both those who are speaking and those spoken to. The exclusive means only those who are speaking, and it excludes those to whom one is speaking. For example, if in speaking with pagans we said the same sentence, we would form it with different words than those used the first time because then it was inclusive and here exclusive. This feature is a peculiarity of this language. All the words in this language are normally stressed on the next-to-last syllable.

Examining the etymology and origin of their words, we find that some words were assigned, because they were perceived to resemble the thing signified; these were simple words which were applied from the beginning to the things they designate. Other words designate some property of the thing they signify; these are ordinarily compounds, the parts of which have meanings by themselves. The majority of the names of animals are of the first kind; these words resemble the sound of the animal's voice, its songs, cries, or howls in the following way. Small birds are called *pisco* because of their thin and delicate song. In imitation of its voice, the partridge is called *yutu,* and for the same reason, the ibis is called *caquingora.* The *guanaco* was named for a neighing sound that it makes, because in making this sound it seems to say its name. This same explanation applies to the *cui* [guinea pig] and to many other animals. But this is most clearly proven in the case of the viscacha; this little animal makes a squeal that is so similar to its name that it seems as if the animal itself is pronouncing its own name. Of the second kind are most names of places, towns, fields, rivers, mountains, and other inanimate things. These names were given in accordance with the attributes, features, and qualities that the places or things have. For example, "Province of Stones," "Town of the Terrace," "Land of Salt," "Place of the Fortress," "Place of Gold, of Silver, of Water," "River of Salt," "River of *Aji*" [capsicum pepper], "Boggy Land," "New Place," "Site of the Ravine," "Plain of Gold, Storage Bins," "Battle Field," "Smoky Place," and so on for the rest.

Quichua is generally a limited language, and the same word is used for diverse meanings. This may be done without altering the word; or it may be done by some change that is made in the stress and pronunciation. Nevertheless, it has more than enough terms for some things such as the names for relatives. A brother uses a different word for his brother than the word his sister uses, and the word used by a mother for her son is different from the one used by the father. This same procedure is followed for all relatives. The

same abundance is found in the many verbs whose actions we signify with one single word. They have different verbs to signify
carrying inanimate things or carrying animate things. With certain
particles which they insert in the simple forms of verbs, the meaning is changed to express the action with some modification. For
example, when the particle "chca" is inserted in a verb, it means
the action is being performed. The verb "micuni" means "I eat";
and "micuhcani" means "I am eating." When the particle "mu" is
inserted, it gives the verb the meaning of physical or spiritual movement; thus, "micumuni" means "I come to eat." There are many
particles that are inserted in verbs in this way in order to modify
their meaning. In spite of this abundance of words, in an absolute
sense, this is a limited language, and it is very difficult to accommodate our expressions to it, especially expressions of courtesy and
politeness, and it is even more difficult to express the mysteries of
our Holy Faith in it. Because of the danger of some error slipping
into these translations, the Provincial Council of this Kingdom has
prohibited explanations of Christian doctrine and its mysteries in
this language, except for what has been done in the catechisms
printed with the authorization of the above-mentioned Council.
This material is used at the present time to teach the Indians about
our Holy Faith.[2]

The Indians have taken many words from us, and they have
accommodated these words to their language so much that we
understand them no less than the Indian words. When the Indians
use the verb *"azotar"* [whip or flog] they say *"azutini,"* and they
use the rest of these words in a similar way. The words that they
have most frequently introduced into their language are all the
ones that refer to the mysteries of our Holy Faith, to our sciences,
arts, and occupations, and to the instruments and equipment for
them. These words refer to all the things we have brought from
Europe and that the Indians did not know before. Thus, they have
received the thing right along with its name. They have also received other common words such as *"perdon"* [pardon] and *"per-
donar"* [to forgive] because what they had for this really meant "to
forget." Moreover, they also received the verbs "to sell," "to buy,"
and "to pay" because the word that they used for "sell" meant to
barter one thing for another. And they received innumerable other
words with which their language has been enriched and enlarged
with our words much more than our language has with what we
have taken from them.

Chapter 2: Of the dress and garments of these Indians

There is nothing special to add here to what was already stated above in the ninth book [*sic*; Book 11][3] about the color and physical features of the Indians. There we were speaking about the Indians in general, for in this respect they are all similar and look alike. The men make their hair into a kind of medium-sized bob which is very becoming to them. They cut the part of their hair which falls over the face at about the middle of the forehead, and from the temples the rest comes down even with the mouth, covering the ears, and they wear it cut at that length all around the head. Both men and women are very careful to wash and comb their hair. Previously they cut it and made it even all around with sharp pieces of obsidian. After the arrival of the Spaniards, they became accustomed to our combs and scissors. The combs that they had were very crude; they were made of the same thorns that were used to make needles, or of other similar thorns which were tied between two small pieces of reed. These combs were not used for cleaning the head because the teeth were too far apart; they were used to untangle the hair and make it lie straight. The Indians identify their honor with their hair to such an extent that the worst disgrace that one can inflict on them is to cut their hair, and for that reason, the judicial authorities are accustomed to pass this sentence on those who commit grave and infamous crimes. The headdress of the Incas and natives of Cuzco (whose dress is the only kind I am describing here) is the braid or band woven of wool, called *llauto,* which has been mentioned above.[4] The *llauto* is half a finger thick and the width of one finger straight through. By wrapping it around the head many times, they made of it a kind of garland or crown the width of a hand, with which they bound the hair above the forehead. The noblemen of high lineage had holes pierced in their ears so large that, in place of earrings, they wore plugs almost the size of the palm of the hand. These plugs were made of light material, well wrought and painted. They did not wear these plugs hanging from their ears but actually inserted and fitted into their earlobes in such a way that, although the plugs seemed to be dangling, they were bounded all around by the flesh of the ear. This was the reason we gave them the name of *"orejones"* [big ears].

The footwear that they used was called *usuta.*[5] They made it

of a sole which was shorter than the length of the foot, so that
their toes extend out beyond the end of the sole, permitting them
to grip with their toes when they are climbing uphill. Making these
shoes is very simple. The soles already mentioned are tied from the
heel to the instep of the foot with certain wool cords about the
thickness of the finger. These cords are made with great care; they
are round and soft because the fiber ends are turned outward like
velvet or like the pile of a carpet; they are of bright colors and
handsome patterns. In fact all of the adornment of their footwear is
put into these fastenings. They make certain attractive loops with
them on the instep in such a way as to cover a large part of the
foot, and from there the cords are wrapped around the ankle. The
soles of this footwear are of untanned leather which is taken from
the neck of their sheep because the hide from that part is thicker
than that of any other part of these animals. Since the leather is
untanned, when it gets wet, it becomes as soft as tripe. For this
reason they remove their shoes when it rains or when the ground is
wet. Men and women used the same kind of footwear without any
distinction whatsoever. However, the women and even most of the
men are starting to adopt our shoes.

Their dress was simple, consisting of only two parts, also
simple, without lining or pleats. In place of underpants or shorts,
the men wear a thin strip of cloth which is a little wider than the
hand; it is fastened around the waist and passes through the crotch
in order to cover the private parts. Since their dress is short and
loose, if they did not use this undergarment, which they call a *guara*,
when they work in the fields they would not keep very much covered up. They do not start using the *guara* until they are fourteen
or fifteen years old. Over it they wear a light garment without
sleeves or collar, which they call *uncu* and we call a "camiseta"
(tunic) because it is shaped like our shirts [*camisas*]. Each one is
woven separately; they are not in the habit of making long pieces
of cloth that are cut to measure as we do. The material used to
make this tunic is a long piece of coarse cloth; it is three and one-
half spans wide and two *varas* long.[6] The hole for the neck is left
while the piece is still at the loom, so that no cutting will be necessary. When it is taken off the loom, all that needs to be done is
double it over and sew up the sides with the same thread of which
it was woven, as one sews up a sack, leaving at the upper part of
each side just enough space open for the arms to fit through. Normally this garment reaches down to their knees or more or less to
within three or four fingers of the knees. The cape is less compli-

cated; it is made of two pieces sewn up the middle, two and a quarter *varas* long and one and three-quarters *varas* wide. The result is that it has four corners like a blanket or bedspread, and for that reason we call it a "manta" [blanket or mantle], while the name the Indians give it is *yacolla.* They wear it over their shoulders, and when they dance, work, or do something for which it could be a hindrance, they tie it by two corners over their left shoulder so that the right arm remains outside. Underneath this mantle and over the tunic they carry a small bag called a *chuspa* which hangs around the neck. It is more or less one span in length and about the same width. This bag hangs down by their waist under the right arm, and the strap from which it hangs passes over the left shoulder. They use this bag for the same purpose for which we use pockets. This is the common and ordinary dress of the men, which did not cover either their arms or their legs. It was made of wool in the sierra and of cotton in hot country. The clothing which was worn by the lords in ancient times was very elegant and of many very fine colors.

Over these ordinary garments they put their adornments and finery when they went to war and in their celebrations and solemn festivals. The majority of these ornaments were made of feathers which came in a variety of attractive colors. Above the forehead they put a large diadem of feathers standing up high in the form of a crown or garland; it was called *pilcocata.* They wore another string of the same feathers around the neck like a Vandyke collar, and still another across the chest like a gorget which ended at the shoulder. Hanging from the *llauto* they had several flowers and other finely made feather decorations. It was also their custom to wear over their chest or on their head disks of gold or silver called *canipos,* the size and form of our plates. They adorned their arms and wrists with bracelets of gold that they call *chipana,* and they adorned their feet with miniature masks of gold and silver, and also of wool. These masks were attached to the band or string of the *ojota* [sandals], and others were put on the shoulders and on the knees. For their most solemn festivals, they had very bright garments made of feathers, which were their richest and most esteemed apparel. And on such festive days, especially when they were going to war, in place of chains and necklaces of gold, they wore strings of human teeth that were from the enemies that they themselves or their ancestors had slain in war.

The women's garment, which served them as a dress and a cloak, consists of two blankets. They wear one of them like a sleeveless soutane or tunic the same width at the top as at the bottom; it covers them from the neck to the feet. No hole is made for their head to fit through. They put it on the following way. They wind it around the body under the arms, and pulling the edges over the shoulders, they bring them together and fasten them with their pins. From the waist down, they tie and squeeze the abdomen by wrapping around many times a sash called *chumpi* that is wide, thick, and attractive. This dress or soutane is called *anacu*. It leaves the arms uncovered, and it is open on one side. Thus even though one edge overlaps the other a little, when they walk, the edges are pulled apart from the *chumpi* or sash on down exposing part of the leg and thigh. For this reason, now that the women are Christians and profess more decency, they are in the habit of sewing up the side in order to avoid that immodesty. The other blanket is called *lliclla*. They put it over their shoulders, and bringing the corners together over the chest, they fasten it with a pin. These are their cloaks or mantles which come halfway down the leg. They remove them in order to work or when they are at home.

The pins that they use to fasten their clothes are called *tupus*. These pins are very special; in size they vary from one *tercia*[7] [11 inches] on down, and the smallest ones were one-half span and as thick as spindles. At the end, the head is a small, thin round plate of the same metal, about the size of a piece of eight, more or less, according to the size of the *tupu*; the edges of the head are so thin and sharp that many things are cut with them. Some of these *tupus* or *topos* have many little gold and silver bells hanging from the head. These pins are by far the most decorative ornament that they wear. In ancient times the pins were made of gold, silver, and copper. At the present time, most of them are made of silver with some decorations and painting on the heads, which are wrought with excellent workmanship.

They adorn their hair by wearing it long, very long, washed and combed. Some wear it loose, and others braid it. They bind their hair with a band the width of one finger, which is colored and attractive. This band, called *vincha*, is worn around the forehead. For their headdress, they wear a piece of rich *cumbi* cloth called *pampacona*, and they do not wear it spread out; they fold it up three or four times in such a way that it is about one-half *tercia* [5½ inches] wide. They let one edge drop down over the forehead, and the rest passes on over the head, leaving the other end hanging down the back and the hair uncovered on the sides. Across their chest, from one shoulder to the other, they wore strings of certain beads called *chaquira*. These beads were made of bone and sea-shells of various colors. They were not accustomed to wearing ear-rings nor to piercing their ears. In order to make these garments and clothing, and even to mend them, the only instrument they need is a needle, which they call *ciracuna*. This needle is made from a thorn which is one-half *geme*[8] [3½ inches] long, about the thickness of our mattress needles, with a hole at one end and a very sharp point at the other end. With this needle and the same thread used to make the garments, they sew and mend them. They are not accustomed to adding another piece of cloth over the torn place as we do. They darn what has worn out of the warp with a thread of the same wool.

Chapter 3: Of their towns and houses

The city of Cuzco and some of the large settlements were built like towns. However, none of the other settlements were. The houses were jumbled together with no order or coherent relation between them; each house was separate with no links or continuity among them. Therefore, the houses were not arranged to form streets or central squares. The settlements were small, like villages of about one hundred inhabitants, and very few were any larger. They had no defensive castles, walls, or other implements for defense in times of war. An effort was made to select building sites in places that did not include land that could be cultivated. For this reason, where there were valleys surrounded by hills, the towns were on the slopes, and many towns were on rocky, uneven places. Where towns were located on fertile farmland, the houses were more widely separated so that the Indians would have space to plant maize and other vegetables. The Quichua call a town *llacta*, and the Aymará call it *marca*.

The form and structure of the houses is different according to the weather and natural resources. In this respect, there is great diversity in such an extensive kingdom. There are also great differences in the method of construction because everywhere it depends on the type of climate and the materials that the land produces. The *yunca* Indians who inhabit the provinces east of the Andes make their houses large, airy, and of wood. This is due to the extremely hot climate and the abundance of trees. They do not put up walls; instead they use posts or wooden columns which are set in the ground. On the posts they construct the roof, which they cover with tree leaves carefully placed for protection from the rain and the wind, or they cover them with the tops of giant bamboo plants or palm trees. The ridges of the roofs are very well made. According to its size and spaciousness, more or less ten or twelve persons live in each one of these houses. This is a one-room house or *galpon*;[9] it is very long and open on the sides, with nothing more for walls than the posts mentioned above. Usually all of the members of one lineage and family live in each house. In keeping with their paganism, when they finished a new house they celebrated, as in honoring Vesta, keeping vigil over the house with dancing, drinking, and many sacrifices and superstitious acts.

On the plains of the seacoast, there are two types of houses. Some are of *bahareque*[10] and others are of earth and adobe. Those of *bahareque* have for walls and enclosures a very tight lattice woven like wattle. In making it they set certain thick canes or poles in the ground very close together, and at about two cubits from the ground, they run a reed in between in the way of a weft, leaving on each side half of the above-mentioned poles set in the ground, which cross over that lateral reed like interweaving; at a similar distance another lateral reed is placed, and in this way with three or four lateral reeds which are crisscrossed and interwoven between those poles that stand upright, they have a completed wall more or less two *estados*[11] in height. We call this type of wall *bahareque*, taking the word from the Island of Hispaniola or Tierra Firme, while the natives of this kingdom use the term *quencha*. Some daub this *bahareque* or wattle with mud; others do not. The roof is constructed over this wattle, and since in this land it never rains, the roof requires no more workmanship than a covering of branches for protection from the sun; it was made with lateral poles and a matting of reeds on top. This is not a sloping roof; rather it is flat and level like a terrace. These houses of *bahareque* are in the form of a square, very humble, small, and low. This is the style of the majority of the houses of small towns and settlements of the Indian fishermen who live on the coast.

The other type of house has mud block walls, and some of these have adobe walls. In ancient times the Indians did not make these mud block walls as we do, of loose earth slightly dampened. They made them from well-mixed, soft mud, the way we make adobes. They made them very straight and smooth because instead of lining the sides up along wooden molds, they used blankets and wattle. Later they plastered them with the same mud. There are many ancient walls of this type still standing. This whole Valley of Lima is full of them, and on the basis of the ones here we can ascertain their form and proportions. Some walls were made straight and vertical, and others were sloping, wide at the bottom and progressively narrower as they went up. Some were three or four *estados* high, others were as low as one *estado*. Finally, some were as thin as two or three feet, and others were as thick as strong ramparts. Today we see in the vicinity of this city of Los Reyes [Lima] parts of ancient walls that are ten or twelve feet thick. But in regard to them, there was a difference. The high, thick walls were normally made to fence the roads and enclose their fields, not for building their houses. The walls for their houses were lower and thinner, except for the walls of their *guacas*;[12] some of these were thick and tall. There were few adobe buildings whose walls were not as strong as the *bahareque* ones. The adobes were bigger and thicker than the ones we make, as we see by observing the ruins of their ancient towns, especially those of Surco el Viejo and Maranga, in this Valley of Lima. The ground plan of these houses made of earth was in the form of a square, longer in length than width; some were perfectly square. They were taller than the ones of *bahareque*, and the roofs were a matting of woven canes with a little mud on top. These roofs were also flat, with no slope.

In the sierra the houses are made of stone and mud, and the roofs are made of straw. The stones are rough, and they placed them with no special order because the stones were set in place and joined together with handfuls of mud. The walls are thin, low and very weak. Some of the houses are round, and others have gabled roofs. The round houses are abundant in the cold lands, such as the provinces of Collao, because the round houses are very warm. The ordinary houses of the plebeians have walls no more than one *estado* in height, and some are much lower. These houses are made in a perfect circle of about fourteen to twenty feet in diameter, more or less, according to their capacity and size. But there are many houses so small and low that if the roof were removed, what was left would look like the round wall of a well curb. The roofs of these round houses are either in the shape of a funnel or that of a dome. For the first type, the beams used for roofing are straight poles whose ends rest on top of one another in the form of a funnel. For the other type, the poles are bent and curved so that the roofing takes on the form of a dome. It is true that we see in certain places some of these round houses which in ancient times were dwellings of *caciques*. These houses are exceptionally large, tall, and very spacious. A thick, straight tree trunk is set like a mast in the middle of the floor. The whole network of wooden poles is set on top of the central trunk. There is a large *buhio*[13] of this design located in the town of Juli, and there are some other similar ones that I have seen in the other towns of Collao. This type of dwelling is very appropriate for the Indians' way of living, or to put it more precisely, for their way of drinking. Sitting inside one of these houses in a circle, and leaning up against the wall, they often continue drinking day and night.

Houses of the other type do not differ from the round ones a great deal, except that they have a square construction, including two gables supporting the roof, which has considerable slope on both sides. Most of them are small, but there are some big ones. No nails are used in the wood framework of roofs of this type nor in that of any of the others mentioned above. Over the beams or poles they tie and weave with cords and thin branches a network of canes or of thin sticks and branches; on top of this, in place of tile, they put a large amount of *hicho*[14] grass. In ancient times the roofs were covered with so much of this *hicho* grass that I have seen some ancient houses that have a covering of it over two cubits thick. In some places the houses had flat roofs made of thin slabs of stone.

I am not referring here to the sumptuous structures of Inca masonry. I will deal with this topic further ahead in this same book. What can be said in general about all the different types of houses described in this chapter is, in the first place, that each room was separate, not connected or continued with any others. In the second place, they were not in the habit of whitewashing them as we do. However, the main houses of the *caciques* usually had the walls painted with a variety of colors and crude drawings. In the third place, doors hung in a fixed place to be opened and closed were lacking both for the houses of the nobles and for those of the plebeians. They used a fabric of canes with which to cover the doorway when they closed it up. If they went away and there was nobody at home to watch the house, they would push some stones up to the cane doorway, and they did not use any other locks, keys, or protection. They did not bother to make large carved doorways. All their doorways were small and simple, and the majority were so low and narrow that they look like oven doors. Thus, when we go to confess their sick, the only way we can enter is by stooping over or even crawling. Finally, except for the houses of the *caciques*, all of the houses are so narrow and humble it would be more proper to call them huts or cabins than houses. The houses do not have attics; all of them are one story. Windows are not put in them so light can enter, nor do they have chimneys or even vents for smoke. These houses lack apartments, patios, and diversity of rooms and offices. Only the houses of the *caciques* had large patios where the townspeople got together to drink during their festivals and celebrations, and the *caciques'* houses had more spacious rooms. The general word for house in the Quichua language is *guaci*, and in Aymará, *uta*.

Chapter 4: Of the furnishings and valuables that they had in their

houses We can classify into three categories all of the personal possessions and supplies that are usually stored in the home. The first category would be the things that pertain to the household decorations and adornments. The second is the stock of food and what pertains to it. And the third includes the things that they acquire for their personal warmth, adornment, and comfort. In the homes of the Indians nothing from the first category is to be found. This is because they have no tapestries, portraits, or other adornments for their houses. With regard to the things in the second category, they usually keep what is necessary to live through the year from one harvest to another. Foods included in their stock are maize, *chuño*,[15] and *quinua*;[16] all three of these things are consumed by them like bread, although all of the Indians do not always eat all three. These foods are normally stored either inside their houses in large jars or in some alcove that they make for this purpose, or outside the houses in small bins that they make which are well protected from the rain. And inside their houses they have all the necessary implements to grind, prepare, and cook their bread. Actually, for this purpose they have no need of large mills, ovens, or any of the other equipment that we must use. The majority of their household equipment and fine furnishings are earthen jars or jugs. They keep no other liquor, not even water, except their wine or *chicha,* and this does not last them a very long time. For this reason, they make it often and in batches of four to six *arrobas* [sixteen to twenty-four gallons] at a time. Considering the large amounts that they drink, this much lasts a man no more than a week, more or less. To make this beverage, store it, and drink it, they have more instruments and containers than they have for their meals. They use earthen jars; the largest ones contain from four to six *arrobas,* and the others contain less. They use a large number of jars, both large and small, and three or four different kinds of cups and tumblers. In the warm lowlands, the cups and tumblers are made from dry gourds decorated in many colors which are called *mati.* The most common cups and tumblers are made of wood; they are shaped like our *cubilete* glasses, which are broader at the top than at the base and hold one *cuartillo* [approximately a pint] of wine. These tumblers were decorated on the outside with a bright varnish in a variety of colors and with various figures and paintings. These wooden tumblers are called *queros*. The wealthy people used silver tumblers called *quilla* [sic; *aquilla*] and they are made in the same shape as the wooden ones. The *caciques* and great lords had gold ones in ancient times. Once a *cacique* showed me one of the ancient tumblers made of pure gold; it was the same shape as our earthen bowls and just as thick. There is the same difference [in materials] in the earthenware and dishes from which they eat. The pieces that they use for this purpose are of only two or three different types: unglazed earthen pots which in ancient times were painted with a variety of figures the same as the jugs and other containers; plates made of dry gourds, clay, and wood, about the size of small chinaware bowls; the wooden plates are called *meca,* the earthen ones *pucu*; and medium-sized earthen casseroles are called *chuas.* The service of the most important nobles and lords in ancient times was made of silver and gold.

In order to grind their grain and bread, they have in their houses thick stone slabs; they put a small amount of grain on there, and once it is ground up, they add more. The grain is ground by rolling on top of the stone slab another stone made in the form of a half moon which is about two spans long and one span high; it is not round, rather it is oblong and three or four fingers thick. They put their hands on the corners of it, and lowering first one arm while raising the other, they rock it from side to side over the maize. With this labor they grind maize or anything else. However, now the majority of the Indians use our mills. We have given this instrument the name *batan* because it grinds like a fulling mill. The Indians call it *maray;* the bottom stone is called *callacha* and the top stone *tanay.* In order to grind small amounts of things they have a stone which is like a mortar, somewhat concave, and they grind on it with another stone which is small and elongated, like what painters use to grind their colors. In all of the houses, no matter how small they may be, there is a stove behind the door; it is shaped like a very small clay furnace, no more than one span high; it is entirely covered, except for a small hole for stoking the fire, and on top there are two or three round holes where the pots are set. This stove uses very little wood, and they never put anything in it but two small sticks placed straight in; as the sticks burn they stir them up. And just one of our ovens consumes more firewood than twenty of the Indians' houses.

Among the things that we mentioned for the third category, the most important ones are clothing and bedding. Apart from the clothing that they were actually wearing, the most that the ordinary people had was one additional change of dress for their festivals. However, the nobles had twice the garments and adornments. They kept all of this in earthen jars since they had no other chests, trunks, or wardrobe. The bed used by those of the sierra and cold lands is a thick wool blanket called *chusi* which they spread out on the floor; half of it takes the place of a mattress and the other half, which they fold up at the foot, serves as a covering or heavy blanket. Everyone from a single household, both parents and children, normally sleeps inside one *chusi*. However, now the majority are becoming more refined, and because of modesty, they sleep in separate beds. The *caciques* and people among them who enjoy greater luxury put some straw or matting under their *chusi*. On the plains and in temperate lands, the only bed they have is the bare ground, and at the most a reed mat or a cotton blanket underneath. Everywhere they sleep in the same clothing that they wear during the day, except that the men take off their *yacolla* and the women take off their *lliclla*. On getting up in the morning, all they have to do in order to get dressed is straighten their hair because when they get up it is disheveled. In the low *yunca* lands, in this kingdom as well as in other regions, hammocks are used for the bed. The hammock is made the same way everywhere, but of different materials. Most of them are made of a thick cotton blanket; it is two and one-half *varas* long and about the same width. At each end there are many threads or strings made of the same material. Each bunch of these strings comes together and ends as a thick cord. In order to set up this bed all that needs to be done is tie the cords. In a house the cords would be tied to two posts or to the two walls, and with this the bed is permanently made. It is not necessary to go to the trouble of making it every day as we do with our beds. And when someone sleeps in the country under the open sky, it is tied to two trees. Thus at home as well as in the country, it is always placed one or two cubits above the ground. Other hammocks are made of *cabuya*[17] strings or of strings made of some other plant, in a variety of colors. The strings are loosely woven in the form of nets. The advantages of this type of bed are numerous. In the first place, as has been stated, once the bed is made it stays that way for the whole year. In the second place, without carrying a heavy load or going to any special pains, it can be taken wherever one goes, and if one travels through a wooded area, in just a minute it can be set up between two trees. In the third place, since the low *yunca* lands, where it is used the most, are normally humid and full of poisonous vermin, one sleeps in a hammock with greater security from the danger of both the humidity and the vermin. Finally, the hammocks are very cool, and for this reason they are appropriate for a hot climate. The name hammock [*hamaca* in Spanish] comes from the language of Hispaniola Island, where the inhabitants have no other kind of beds. The Indians of this kingdom use the term *puñuna* for any type of bed.

In their houses, they did not have chairs, benches, or any type of seats. Everyone, both men and women, sat on the floor, except the *caciques* and great lords, who, by special favor and privilege of the Inca used a seat both inside and outside of their houses. This seat was called a *duho*, and it was a small wooden bench made of one piece of wood, about two spans wide and one span high, like an animal with short legs, lowered head, and the tail high. Usually it was made in the form of some animal. The upper surface was concave so that it would fit the part of the body where a man sits down.

Chapter 5: Of their foods and drinks, and their eating times and customs related to eating
Not very much needs to be said in this chapter about what is stated in the title because almost everything that needs to be known about this subject has already been explained above.[18] In writing about their vegetables, I have already stated that the ordinary bread that they eat is maize, *quinua*, and *chuño* or dry, fresh *papas* [potatoes].[19] Maize is toasted in clay casseroles pierced with holes, and it is their bread. It is the most usual ration of food that they take with them on journeys, especially a maize flour that they make. They toast a certain type of maize until it bursts and opens up; they call it *piscancalla*, and they consider it a delicacy. There are small cakes and rolls ordinarily made from maize flour called *tanta*. Apart from them, as a treat, from this maize flour they customarily prepare some small cakes by cooking them in a pot. These cakes are called *huminta*.

It has already been stated what wines they have and how much these people are given to drinking.[20] In ancient times they had very few viands and stews. They made a certain kind of stew called *motepatasca* from whole kernels of maize with some herbs and *aji* peppers. The maize was cooked until it split open. Another stew called *pisqui* was made from *quinua* seeds. These two stews correspond to the ones that we usually make with rice, garbanzos, and other similar things. The plebeians ate very little meat, and when they did it was at festivals and banquets. They ate more dried meat than fresh, and they prepared the dried meat without salt in the following way. They cut the meat in wide, thin slices. Then they put these slices on ice to cure. Once the slices were dried out, they pounded them between two stones to make them thinner. They call this dried meat *charqui*. From it and from fresh meat, they only knew how to make one kind of stew called *locro*. It had a lot of *aji* peppers, *chuño*, *papas*, and other vegetables. They made the same stew with dried fish, which they ate quite often. In short, their cooking was so rustic and crude that there was nothing other than poor stew and worse roast over the coals because they never even had roasting spits.

They ate two times a day, at eight or nine in the morning and in the afternoon about one or two hours before sunset. The table was the ground. They put nothing under the dishes, except that the *caciques* and important people used a blanket for a tablecloth. They did not seat their women at the table, although they all ate together. A woman would sit behind her husband facing the opposite direction. Thus the couple was situated back to back, and the woman had the pots of stew close at hand so that she could serve her husband when he asked for food or drink, although she ate at the same time. This is the way that they sat to eat in their houses and in public banquets of their town. At their major festivals the whole town ate in public on the *cacique*'s patio or some other suitable place. The *caciques* sat at the head of the table on the *duhos*, and the rest of the people sat on the ground. These banquets lasted a long time, and the people kept on drinking at them until they were drunk. They each ate and drank at their own expense because they each brought their own food to the festival. Thus the people at the table did not eat the same dishes. For this reason, the people would invite each other to try their respective dishes. They sat down to eat lined up in a row. Each section was separate: the *hanansaya* section in one place, and the *hurinsaya* section in another place, each seated facing the other, like two parallel lines.[21] Those of one section would drink a toast to those of the other section in the following way. The man proposing a toast to another would get up from his place and go toward him with two tumblers of *chicha* in his hands. He would give the other man one of the tumblers while keeping the other for himself. They would both drink together.

Whenever they sit on the ground, they do it in the following way. With their feet together, they bend their legs as much as they can; their knees come up so far as to almost touch their chins. On sitting they drop their tunic down to their feet so that their whole body fits into the tunic, except for their head, and since their legs are supported by the tunic, it is pulled tight. And they are so comfortable in this position that they commonly stay in one place like that for a whole day.

Chapter 6: Of the ceremonies observed in the education of their children from birth until they reached the age for marriage

When the women were in labor, their husbands would customarily fast. Sometimes the women would fast also by abstaining from certain foods, and the women confessed and prayed to the *guacas* so that the delivery would be a success. Normally, the women gave birth without midwives. After giving birth, without concerning themselves for a moment about the weather, they would go to the nearest stream, and there they would wash themselves and their babies. This they would do even though the climate was very cold. They considered that it was an evil omen for a woman to give birth to two babies together, and when the baby was born with some natural defect, such as six fingers on one hand or some similar defect, the parents became sad. They fasted by not eating *aji* peppers, and they performed other ceremonies.

When a child was born, it was customary among some nations to mold the child's head into different shapes. Many superstitions were employed in doing this. In addition, such rigor was used that many children died of the pain that they suffered, and it was not uncommon for their brains to be squeezed out or for them to remain sick and crippled for life. In this way, they would deform the shape of the human body. Since they were not satisfied with the heads given to them by God, they wanted to improve on the natural human body and give their heads the shape that was most pleasing to them, and the more disproportionate and deformed the heads turned out, the more attractive they judged them to be. Some nations widened their foreheads. They would squeeze their heads by securely tying on small boards to make their foreheads wide. The Collas made their heads long and pointed. They took this to such an extreme that it is amazing to see the old men that I observed with that fashion from their pagan times. And they did this because they wore wool caps called *chucos*, like a mortar or a hat with no brim. These caps were very tall and pointed. To make sure the cap would fit better, they molded the head to the shape of the headgear rather than making the headgear of the same size as the head. And in order to mold the children's heads into this shape, they bound their heads tightly with bandages which were left in place until the children were four or five years old. By this age, their heads were hardened and molded to the shape of their head-gear: long, tapering, and without a nape. They said that the children's heads were molded into this shape so that they would be healthier and work harder. And they made the children's first hat with many ceremonies and superstitious acts, both in spinning the wool and in weaving it.

On the fourth day after birth, the parents put the baby in its cradle, called *quirau*, and they called their relatives to come. Once they arrived to see the nephew, they drank that day without performing any other ceremony. This cradle is shaped like a bed the size of the baby, made of boards or poles like wattle, and has four feet. The two front feet are about a span in height, and the other two are a little shorter. A folded blanket is put over this bed so that it will be soft where the child is placed. The child is gently tied to the cradle so that it will not fall off. Above the head of the cradle they have two arches crossed which are made of thin, flexible sticks. There is another, smaller arch-stick at the foot of the cradle. And the cradle is covered with a blanket over these arches, which leaves space for the baby. As long as the baby is still nursing, the mother carries it in its cradle wherever she might go, even to church. They carry the cradle supported by a blanket on their backs. They pull the ends of the blanket over their shoulders and tie them across their chest. When they stop and sit down, lowering the cradle, they put it on the ground, where it sits on its feet. Rocking is done by moving the cradle a little from side to side without shifting it from where it is placed. In the same way that they carry the cradle, they put the child on their backs when they carry it without the cradle, and this is done when the child starts to walk. Carrying the child in a blanket this way does not hinder or impede them in moving about, even though they travel long distances. And a small boy commonly carries a baby this way for a long time without getting tired. This is the way they carry their children in their arms. However, they do not really carry them in their arms; they carry them on their backs. Since they had no linen, they could hardly be very neat and clean in changing diapers or baby clothes.

When a child was weaned, they celebrated in the following way. They invited their relatives and friends, and they all enjoyed dancing and drinking together. When the festivities were over, the child's oldest and most respected uncle cut the child's hair for the first time and trimmed its fingernails. Both the fingernails and the hair were kept with great care, and the child was given the name that it was to use until of age. Once this was done, the uncle presented some gift to the child. After the uncle, the other relatives and friends presented gifts to the child. The gifts were silver, clothing, wool, and other similar things. With this ceremony, they put their children into the service of the Sun, and they asked the Sun to allow their children to live in prosperity and to inherit from their fathers. At the same time, if it were possible to be of some help to their parents (though it was really too soon), the children were to serve their parents both in their domestic chores and in the work in the fields and care of the livestock. This applied to the boys as well as to the girls. And the children had no education in any discipline and study that would cultivate their minds other than helping their parents. Thus each child learned the profession and way of life of its parents.

When the boys were fourteen years old, more or less, a solemn reunion of their relatives was held, and the boys were given their *guaras* or breechcloth which their mothers had spun and woven with certain ceremonies and superstitions. On this solemn occasion, many rituals were performed. They danced in their fashion and drank, which was the height of their glory. At this time the boy was given his permanent name which he would use all his life. Sometimes the boys would be given the names of their fathers or grandfathers, but the lords and important people freely sought out names and nicknames that were honorable and meaningful. The ones most commonly used were names of towns, plants, birds, fish, and animals such as puma, which means lion; *cuntur* [condor], vulture; *asiro [amaro]*, snake; *guaman*, hawk; and other similar ones. Since the Indians have become Christians, these names that were their proper names previously are used as extra names by those who had them before and as family names by their descendants. This celebration which was held to give the boys their *guaras* and permanent names was called Guarachicuy, and it was very important.

Just as important was the celebration that they put on for giving names to the girls. This happened when a girl was thirteen or fourteen years old. For this celebration the girls were required to fast for three days, eating nothing the first two days, and on the third day, they were given a little raw maize; at this time they were told not to die of hunger. During these days, the girls were shut up in their houses, and on the fourth day, their mothers washed the girls and combed and braided their hair. Then the girls were dressed in elegant clothes with *ojotas* [sandals] of white wool. On this day the girls' relatives came to their house, and the girls came out to serve them food and drink. This feast lasted two days. Later the most important uncle of each girl gave her the name that she was to have permanently, admonishing her how she was to live and obey her parents. The uncle presented her with whatever he saw fit, according to his means, and each of her other relatives and friends presented something to her with certain ceremonies. This solemn act was called Quicuchicuy.

Chapter 7: Of the rites and customs that they had for marriage ceremonies

Having many wives was not a crime among the Indians. In fact, it was considered to impart authority, honor, and wealth. Moreover, it was a special favor and privilege that was given as remuneration for services rendered to the Inca or in consideration of a person's high rank or superior intelligence, ability, and competence for the government of the republic. And this was a very highly esteemed favor because it was both wealth and service. Furthermore, among these people the women were so subjugated to their husbands and obliged to serve them and comply with their wishes that even if there were many of them, it made no difference, nor did they dare to do anything other than what they were ordered to do. The women performed the household duties, and in addition, they worked outdoors, in the cultivation, sowing, and caring for their *chacaras* or fields, building their houses, and carrying loads, when their husbands traveled, both in times of peace and war. It happened with some frequency that when the women were traveling with a load they would go into labor, and in order to give birth, all they would do was go off the road a little; after giving birth, they would proceed to a place where there was water. There they would wash the baby and wash themselves. They would put the baby on top of the load that they were carrying and continue on their way the same as before giving birth. Finally, the men would do nothing without the help of their wives. Therefore, whoever had a number of wives was considered to be rich, and in fact he was.

If a man had a wife who had been given to him by the Inca or his governors, or if he had won her in a war, or gotten her by other means considered legitimate among them, there was no way for her to break away from the authority of her husband, unless he died. Moreover, the women did not dare complain about any injury they may have received, except to their husbands. Such matters would never be discussed anyplace outside the home. It must be pointed out that only the nobles had numerous wives and such authority over them. The plebeians and commoners each had only one wife. This was not because there was some precept or order concerning the number of wives a man could have. But since the lords distributed them on the basis of the criteria already stated, which was the only way a wife could be obtained, they never gave more than one wife to poor and humble men. Moreover, in addition to being limited almost invariably to one wife, many of the common and poor men had to spend long periods of time without a wife after they were old enough to have one and even after they became widowers. The loss of their first wife was considered to be extremely severe due to the dire straits that they were in until they were given another wife. It even happened that during confession the priests would give them bitter penitence, saying that their wife had died because of some grave, concealed sin, and if the wives became sick, the priests made the husbands fast and perform other acts of penitence.

From among the many wives that a man had, only one of them was his principal wife, and she was the only one who had the name of the legitimate wife. He married her with some solemnity, and both parties agreed to it. And this principal wife was obeyed by the other wives. She was their superior, and she had a different name than they did, since she was the proper and legitimate wife and the others were concubines. The solemn ceremony that was performed when a man took his legitimate wife was not repeated as long as she was alive, even though the man took another or many other wives later. In conclusion, only the principal and legitimate one was considered to be the man's wife. The rest were considered to be concubines, permitted according to their customs. The solemn ceremony that was performed among the Incas for this marriage was common in many other parts of the kingdom, but not observed in all parts of it. Within the limitations of his own possibilities, each one performed the ceremony in the following way. After the harvest was collected, the Inca called together the *aclla*[22] maidens that had been raised in the cloisters of the *mamaconas,* and he distributed them among the important men in the order that suited him, and if he gave the women to married men, it would be for concubines, and if to single men, it was for legitimate wives. In the latter case, the marriage was celebrated with the following ceremonies. All of the relatives present of each of the marriage partners got together. The groom's relatives went with him to the home of the bride's father or nearest relative who was there, and she was given to him. As evidence that he received her as his wife, the groom put an *ojota* sandal of wool on her right foot if she was a virgin, and if she was not, it was of *hicho* grass, and he took her by the hand. Then together the relatives of both the bride and the groom took her to her husband's home. When they arrived there, the bride took out from under her *chumpi* sash a fine wool tunic, a *llauto* [headband], and a flat metal ornament, and she gave these things to her husband. He put them on at once. Then the bride's older female relatives lectured her until evening on the obligation that she had to serve her husband and the way in which she was to do it. The groom's older male relatives advised him as to how he was to treat his wife. And the relatives of both the bride and the groom presented gifts to them. Each one gave from what he had, even though it was a small quantity. The duration of the celebration and drinking of the family units depended on the importance and possibilities of the bride and groom. The Incas called this solemn ceremony a wedding, and the woman to whom a man got married in this way was his legitimate wife. If a man had a wife with whom he had performed these ceremonies, even if the Inca gave him another woman who was more noble and important than the first one, no solemn ceremonies were performed with the second one, not those just mentioned nor any others. She was just sent to the man's house. But if the man to receive her was a widower whose legitimate wife had died, even though he still had many concubines, he married her with the solemn ceremony described here, and the women already in the home had to serve the new wife.

In the other provinces outside of Cuzco or where the Inca was present, on a specified day of the year the governor brought together all of the plebeian boys and girls who were of marriageable age (the boys were from fifteen to twenty years old and the girls were a little younger) and there each one was given his wife. From that day onward, the boys became part of the system of taxation or tribute, and they helped the community perform the public work projects. They were assigned their *characas* [fields]. They built their own houses, and they lived by themselves. In these marriages, the solemn ceremony of the *ojota* just described was also performed, according to each one's ability. The first woman that the Inca's governor gave a man was his legitimate wife, and as has been stated, seldom would he be given another, except in one of the cases already mentioned. But in any case, this first one was the principal wife as long as she lived.

In other provinces other ceremonies and rites were observed. In the Collao provinces, among the common people, when the governor designated a woman, it was customary for the groom to get a small coca bag and take it to his mother-in-law. When she received it, the marriage was considered to be concluded. In other places, the groom went to the home of the bride's father and told him that he had been given his daughter by the governor. In addition, the groom said he wanted to serve the bride's father. Thus the relatives of both the bride and the groom assembled, and they endeavored to gain each other's good will. The boy went to the home of his in-laws, and for a period of four or five days, he brought straw and firewood to them. In this way they made their agreement, and he took her for his wife. The governor who was giving her to him said that she was being given until death, and he accepted her under this condition. And in this fashion there were different rites in each place, but a solemn ceremony was performed everywhere with the legitimate wife. Once it was performed, it was never repeated, even though the husband was given one or more other wives. There was a great difference in many respects between the legitimate wife and the concubines. One difference, among others, was that the legitimate wife could not be repudiated nor could she be cast out of the house nor could she be given to another man, without the husband undergoing severe punishment. If the husband cast her out of the home, she was sent back to live with him again. If he cast her out a second time, he was punished publicly according to his social status. Any of the other wives could be cast out without the husband incurring any kind of punishment, but they could not be given to others, not as legitimate wives nor in any other way, without the consent of the one who had title over them.

When a man's legitimate wife died, if the husband was an important man, he did not remarry for a year, and during that whole time, he wore a black mantle. And this matter of not marrying for a year was an inviolable custom. They do not say that it was mandatory, but if a man were to remarry, he would be strongly disliked. If the man was a plebeian, often it took two years before they gave him another wife, and when they did give him another wife, he held the solemn ceremony. For this reason, the poor considered that the death of their wife was a great adversity. They had no way of obtaining another until she was given to them, and in the meantime, they suffered a severe plight.

If a man had many wives, when his legitimate wife died, there was a great deal of weeping along with the ceremonies that they had. But if one of the concubines died, only her family mourned for her, and in the home of the husband, they did not weep as they did for the legitimate wife. Once the legitimate wife was dead, the husband decided which of the concubines was to run the household and be obeyed by the others. However, one thing must be noted. Although there was no such prohibition or law among these people, nevertheless, no one remembers of anyone marrying or performing the ceremony with any of the concubines. After the period of mourning, the man would always marry another woman whom the concubines obeyed and served. Regarding this matter, it is explained that they would not marry any of the concubines because this would be an insult, but in addition it was not done because they wanted to avoid the possibility of the legitimate wife being killed by a concubine who expected to become the legitimate wife herself.

In addition to the legitimate wife, these Indians had numerous other women, and in some cases the number of them was excessive. Obtaining these additional women was achieved in a variety of ways. The first was based on a custom of theirs that was very barbarian and immoral. When the boys were very young, their parents would give them a woman to keep them clean and serve them until they were of age, and before the boys married, these mistresses would teach the boys vices and sleep with them. The parents approved of this, and the women would always stay in the home as concubines after the boys got married. The second way of obtaining women was based on another custom. On considering it for the first time and taking it at face value, this custom seemed praiseworthy. However, owing to what really happened, it was just as reprehensible as the first. Among these people, great care was taken to raise orphans, and in the case of the very poor, one of their ways of achieving this was to turn over the orphan to one of the town widows who had no children and who was not going to remarry. When the boy was of age, the woman would go to bed with him, even if she was old. This would continue until the governor gave the boy a woman and he got married. In spite of this, the woman would continue her relations as before until she was paid for the work she had done in raising the boy. This payment customarily extended for a long time, and when they could not come to an agreement themselves, the governor would determine the payment.

Another way of acquiring women was in war. The captains and important men took advantage of this type of booty, and they divided the women up among themselves. However, most women were obtained as a personal favor from the Inca. With this type of reward, the Inca paid for the notable services performed by his people. The last way of obtaining women was by inheritance. It was customary among them for a man to inherit women from his father and brothers. The inheritor of such women treated them as his own, except for the legitimate wife whom the father had mar-

ried with the solemn ceremony that was customary. Carnal relations were prohibited between the legitimate wife and her sons.
Such relations were also prohibited between a concubine and the
sons she had borne by the father. However, if they had not borne
children by the father, the concubines were inherited by the sons,
who had possession of them as their own women and were permitted to treat them as such. Brothers also inherited each other's
women, both the legitimate wives and the concubines. With regard
to the matter of who was to get preference in such successions,
there was the following custom. If the sons were grown and had
their own houses at the time of their father's death, the eldest son
took possession of the women. If any of them had recently given
birth, she would concern herself with raising her children and remain separate. If she was the legitimate wife and she had not borne
children, the deceased man's son did not take her; his brother did,
because only the son was prohibited to have carnal relations with
the legitimate wife of the father, but the brother was not prohibited to have such relations with his brother's wife.

They had their regulations governing marriage and possession
of concubines. Prohibitions were established according to degrees
of blood relationship, and different punishments were designated
for offenders and transgressors, according to the severity of the offenses which had been committed. With regard to the first matter,
marriages were prohibited with ancestors and descendants, such
as with a daughter or granddaughter, with the mother or grand-
mother. These restrictions were so strong that not only were such
marriages unprecedented, but the death penalty was designated for
anyone who committed such an offense. The same penalty was applied to anyone who had carnal relations with any woman within
these grades of blood relationships, and the penalty was applied to
both parties, regardless of their social status. The second matter
was also a general and very ancient prohibition of marriage within
the first degree of blood relationship, such as with a sister. This
prohibition lasted until the time of King Tupa Inca Yupanqui, father of Guayna Capac. Tupa Inca was the first to break it by marrying his own sister on both the paternal and maternal sides, and he
ordered that only the kings could do this and that the rest of the
important people could marry only their sisters on the paternal
side. Therefore this custom of marrying their sisters was recent.
Except for the first degree and with ancestors and descendants, as
has been stated, marriages were permitted with other family members. Moreover, not only were these other marriages sanctioned,

but if an unmarried man or his parents asked the Inca or his governors for the man's first cousin, the request was always granted. This was justified on the grounds that both parties came from the same stock and grandfather. This relates to the custom of worshiping the dead bodies of certain ancestors.[23] Each one worshiped his ancestors in a direct line, excluding the grandfather's uncle or brother. Therefore, in the case of marriage to the first cousin, they argued that both parties were obligated to worship the same grandfather, and on these grounds a man would ask to be given his first female cousin as his wife, and this was sufficient for the request to be granted if she was to become his wife but not if he wanted to take her as a concubine.

Chapter 8: Of their knowledge and practice of agriculture

The art of agriculture consists in plowing and sowing the land and raising all kinds of plants with attention to the times, places, and things required. These Peruvian Indians made a greater achievement in this art than in any of the others that are human necessities. The grains and vegetables that they had were planted and cared for in a very orderly and wise manner. They would find the land best suited to the properties of each plant, cultivate it, and irrigate it at the proper times. Thus what has happened to their other crafts has not occurred in this case. Their other crafts have been much improved with our help, for they have learned from us what they lacked in order to achieve the necessary perfection. However, with regard to the essentials of agriculture, they have taken little and changed nothing of what they did before, except adopting some of our implements, which diminished the work load that they had previously. These include using oxen to plow and doing now with iron tools what used to be done with sticks and stones and other implements of copper. In short, they were such excellent farmers, so adept in raising their vegetables and plants, and they had achieved such excellent agricultural methods, that we have learned from them their entire system of sowing and caring for their grains, as well as much for the proper care of our own grains. For example, we have learned how to *guanear* or fertilize with guano in some places, which is a very special technique and very different from what is done in Spain, and we have learned other similar techniques. No doubt what made them so skillful and outstanding in this art was the fondness with which they practiced it; this is so notable that there is no Indian who does not prefer it to any other occupation. Even the workmen skilled in our crafts, such as silversmiths, painters, and the rest, are no exception; we cannot persuade them to continue with their work instead of returning to sow their fields. When sowing time comes, they drop everything in order to return to their *chacaras*. It is amazing, and I have tried to dispel some people's illusions in this regard; in order to produce a little maize with their own efforts, they lose ten times the value of the harvest in the time they spend returning to their fields because this interrupts the work of their crafts and keeps them from earning anything from it.

In searching for the cause of this extraordinary fondness for farming that they have, I find it in the way their kings the Incas arranged and established this work so that the people came to consider it recreational and enjoyable. And this is one of the things in which the Incas proved their genius; they were able to set up an occupation requiring so much work and effort in such a way that it came to be considered an entertaining and pleasurable practice. In fact, they are still of the same opinion, especially in the Sierra. Thus friends, sections, and entire towns invite and summon one another to plow their *chacaras,* and the guests come as willingly and cheerfully as to a weding, without taking any pay or interest other than eating and drinking at the expense of the owner of the field, who prepares a large quantity of *chicha* for these gatherings. This *chicha* drink is the bait that brings them so willingly, and they continue the work as long as it lasts with the same pleasure and cheerfulness as at the beginning, rejoicing with songs according to their custom. In short, the work of the *chacaras* was one of the major forms of recreation and festivals that they had.

They always took care, to the extent that the lay of the land made it possible, that their fields be irrigated, not only where rains were lacking, but also where there were sufficient rainstorms. For this they did two things that required a great deal of work and ingenuity: the first was that they leveled the rough and uneven lands that they cultivated so that being flat, these lands could be irrigated, plowed, and cultivated more easily, and also because in this way they made use of much land that would be totally barren and useless. They also leveled the land by making terraces that they call *pata* on the hillsides. At intervals they built stone walls that held the earth, and they spread the earth out even and level from one wall to another. These terraces were wider or narrower according to how steep the slope was. On the hillsides that sloped gradually and were not very steep, we see very large terraces of fifty, one hundred, two hundred feet wide, and wider, but on the rugged hillsides the terraces are so narrow that they look like stairways; some of them are no more than three or four feet wide. Regarding these walls that they made at intervals, the highest were one or two *estados,* and the others lower, in accordance with what the lay of the land required. All of these walls were made of dry stone; in some places the stones were so well worked, with such skill and care, that, though they were not square, they were as carefully fit together as the stones of their most carefully constructed buildings. Many of the terraces that still remain in the Cuzco region are of this type. By means of this construction, the Indians planted all the hills, even the highest and steepest which would have been too rough to cultivate without terracing. As we see these hills today they look as if they are covered with flights of stairs.

They made use of the water from the rivers, irrigating with it all of the land where it would reach, and this construction of their irrigation ditches was one of the most impressive and admirable things that they had. The ditches were so well done and with such order, that it is difficult to imagine how they could build them without our tools. At the outlets where the water flowed from the rivers, they made strong barriers against floods and overflows. The ditches were built level across many leagues, and some were very large. These ditches were not built only on flat land; they were also made across slopes and high, rough hills, and what is more, across crags, boulders, and steep slabs. The ditches were made across these places with hard work and skill, digging across large sections of living stone, when there was no other way to take them. In places where even this was impossible, such as when it was necessary to take the ditches across some slab or sheer cliff, they made a dry stone wall from below many *estados* high next to the above-mentioned slabs, or away from them, when it was necessary to cross over some ravine, and the water would be taken over the top of the slabs. Where it was necessary they made these ditches with dry stone walls, and where it was not necessary, they just dug them in the earth. They took them across places that were so rough and difficult because not only did they irrigate flat land, but also rough terrain, by means of these terraces on the slopes; this way they did not lose one bit of land.

Their farming implements were few, and these were very simply made from wood or copper. The plow or spade was an implement called *taclla*, made from a stick as thick as the wrist and approximately two cubits long, in the form of a stilt. In the place where they gripped, it was curved like a staff, and at the point they tied another stick four fingers in width and one finger thick from a different and harder wood. Approximately one span from the point of it, a rest one *jeme* [about six inches] wide was secured, where they would bear down with the left foot. The manner in which they broke and plowed the land with this *taclla* was by raising the top of it up to the right shoulder and the point about two or three spans from the ground, and they would drive it down with all the force of their arms and their left foot which bore down on the above-mentioned rest; they did this so that they could make the plow strike with force and penetrate deep.

Apart from this type of plow, they had another implement made from a curved stick, which was shaped more like a carpenter's adz or a weeding hoe; it was used to break up dirt clods, weed, and loosen the earth. And these two implements were the main ones that they used to cultivate their fields. In order to weed the planted fields and make the holes where maize was buried as it was planted, they used *lampas*, which the Mexicans call *coas*. It is an implement like a hoe except that the head was made of copper and not curved, but flat like a short baker's peel. At the present time Spaniards use *lampas* made of iron much in their farming, especially for weeding the vegetable gardens and vineyards; in this land weeding is called *cuspar*.

The ropes that were used in this type of work were usually of wool in the sierra, and where there was no wool, ropes were made from *cabuya*, which is their hemp. They start to break the ground at the end of the rainy season, and where it does not rain, it was done a few months before planting. At the proper times, they weed the sown fields, cleaning out the undesirable growth. When the maize is half grown, they weed around the base of the plant, heaping earth around there. The activity that was the most work for them was plowing, but they always came willingly because they always plowed in large groups, both men and women together, in the following way. The men alone did the plowing in rows, and the women were ahead of them in another row opposite the men. When the men dug up chunks of sod with their *tacllas*, the women turned them over, breaking them completely with their wooden weeding hoes. Generally, they planted their seed in the strips of earth between the furrows; they were very well organized in making these strips, some of which were quite large. They have cheerful songs devised to accompany the plowing. They all sing together; one starts the chant, and the others follow him. They keep time so well that they never miss the beat of their chant as they strike the ground with their *tacllas*. The same as in this chant, they all work together, raising their *tacllas* and striking the earth with them in unison. And it certainly is very pleasant to see them plowing according to their custom, as I have seen them so many times. These chants are very enjoyable, and can usually be heard a half-league away.

Chapter 9: The art of warfare, how it was practiced by these Indians, their weapons, and their way of fighting

These Peruvian Indians considered the military profession to be the most serious and noble of all, and so they practiced it with more care and study than any other. The Incas paid much attention to the military and to those who practiced it, since it was the means by which they had achieved such great power and majesty, and through it they maintained this position. Among their vassals, the military profession was the only way to advance to positions of honor, and there was hardly any other way for them to move up and gain importance. Valiant, experienced captains and any others who distinguished themselves in the military were so highly esteemed that the man who had been brave and successful was not only rewarded by the kings with increased wealth and positions of honor, but the people believed that after this life, he had an important place in heaven. In the storehouses of the provinces, there were always ample supplies of food, clothing, tents, weapons, and all the implements of war; this was to provide supplies both to the garrisons that were in the fortresses and on the borders of the kingdom and to soldiers going to the wars that broke out. And in order to maintain sufficient well-trained and disciplined troops, the Incas kept a large number of captains and military officers stationed in the provinces; these men took great pains to instruct and drill the youth in the use of all the different kinds of weapons. The young men who showed the most spirit in the reviews and simulated battle maneuvers were enlisted for duty. In addition, the majority of their festivals and celebrations were like military displays and exercises similar to our jousting tournaments.

The salary and pay of those in the military was as follows. While they were absent from their homes on active duty, the Inca gave them food and clothing, weapons and munitions. Moreover, the people of the community plowed and sowed their fields. Apart from this, some men were well rewarded according to their custom; this included the captains and important people and all the soldiers who had proven their bravery when the opportunity arose.

The defensive weapons that they used were so light that none could withstand either a blow from a sword or from an iron-headed weapon. They used mantles of thin cotton wrapped many times around the body. Some wore doublets or tunics reinforced also with cotton, with helmets of the same material or wooden helmets. Other helmets used were made of plaited cane, and they were so sturdy that they could withstand any blow from a stone or club. All the men carried small round shields of woven palm slats and cotton on their backs, and they carried other, larger shields with their hands; these shields were not round but oblong for protection of the head against clubs and stones. These shields were sheathed with deerskin and covered on the outer side with a piece of fine cotton, wool, or feather-cloth, embroidered in several colors; on this cloth they would depict their devices and coats of arms. Over this defensive gear they would usually wear their most attractive and rich adornments and jewels; this included wearing fine plumes of many colors on their heads and large gold and silver plates on their chests and backs; however, the plates worn by poorer soldiers were copper. And they all generally wore the finery and jewels with which they customarily dressed for their festivities. Some painted themselves in a variety of colors and designs to frighten their enemies. To attack and make assaults on fortified positions, they used large shields similar to blankets, which were so big that one hundred men could go under each one.

With regard to the offensive weapons, some were for fighting at long range and others for close range. At long range they fought with slings made of wool or *cabuya*. They were excellent marksmen with their slings. Almost all of the Indians of this kingdom used them, especially the men of the Sierra, who were very adept with the sling. But the weapon used most extensively throughout all of the Indies, both in war and hunting, was the bow and arrow. They made the bow as long or longer than the height of a man, and some were eight to ten spans long, made of a certain black palm called *chonta*, which had very heavy, strong wood. The string was made of animal sinew, *cabuya*, or some other strong thing. The arrows were of light material, such as reed or cane or some other rod as light as these, with the tip or point of *chonta* or some other hard wood with prongs, bone or animal tooth, obsidian point, or fish spine. Many Indians used poisoned arrows, prepared by dipping the points into a strong poison made of herbs. However, the only Indian nation from this kingdom to use poison herbs on their arrows was the Chunchos.[24] Moreover, this was not made only from an herb, but a concoction made from several herbs and poisonous vermin, and it was so effective and deadly that anyone who was injured by one of these poison arrows enough to draw blood, even though no more blood was drawn than what would come from being pricked by a pin, the person would die screaming and making terrifying grimaces.

The Chunchos mentioned above made this herb concoction, and it is still made and used by Indian nations not yet conquered, such as the Indians of Urabá, on the border of the Diocese of Cartagena, and many others, in the following manner. They catch many lizards, vipers, certain black ants which are as big as beetles and very venomous, large spiders, and certain big hairy worms that live in trees. They mix bat wings, the head and tail of the fish called *pege tamborino*,[25] toads, snakes, and other poisonous vermin. Moreover, they add deadly poison herbs of many different kinds, and especially the root of the tree that bears the poisonous fruit called *manzanilla*.[26] After collecting all of this, they put it into a large container, and they seek out three women, the oldest ones they can find. These women prepare the fire and stir it by turns, one after the other. And since the poison is weak at first, the first old lady lasts longer than the others, but after a time, the fumes it gives off affect her so much that her life is taken. Once the first one is dead, the second old woman follows her in tending the fire for the brew. This one dies in a short time because the poison is getting much stronger. The second is followed by the third old woman, who dies very quickly due to the great strength of the poisonous concoction, and once this one dies so quickly, they know that the poison has reached its full strength. They take it off the fire, and once it has cooled off, they store it. They value it highly, for making it is very costly. This brew is made in an open place, far from any settlement so that no one will be harmed. In some places only one person dies when they make it, and usually the one to die is some old woman or female slave held in low esteem.

There are Indians who shoot an arrow with such force that there is hardly any weapon that it will not pierce and break. Generally all of the Indians are very able marksmen, and some are so accurate that they can hit any object thrown in the air with their arrows. There are Indians who do not aim at their target when they shoot, but they aim up in the air with such skill that when the arrow falls, it hits the target.

They also used spears or darts with fire-hardened points or equipped with fish spines, and these projectiles were cast with a spear-thrower, which the Spaniards call *tiraderas*. At a short distance, in order to catch and hold the enemy, they would throw an implement called *ayllo;*[27] it is made of two round stones slightly smaller than the fist connected with a thin cord about one *braza*[28] [approximately five and one-half feet] in length. It was thrown at the feet in order to entangle them as the cord hit the legs; with the weight of the stones at the ends, the cord swings around the legs until it comes to the end and holds them.

The close-range weapons were spears, pikes, *macanas*, clubs, hatchets, and others similar to these. They made the spears long, of hard wood with fire-hardened points of the same wood or copper points. The *macana* is a stick made of *chonta* palm wood about one *braza* long, four fingers wide, thin, and with two sharp edges; it ends in a rounded hilt and a pommel like a sword. It is held with both hands like a broadsword, and a blow with it is so effective that if a man gets hit on the head, it will crack his skull. They also had heavy round wooden clubs. They had another club called *champi* that was the favorite weapon of the Incas; it has a shaft like a halberd and a copper head on the end in the shape of a star with very sharp points or rays all around. Some of these *champis* were short like a club, and others were as long as spears, but most of them were about medium sized. The battle-axes had a copper or obsidian head or blade. Some were small, one-handed weapons, and others were large, requiring both hands. The majority of the weapons used by the captains and nobles had gold or silver heads. Each man fought with only one type of weapon; therefore, they were organized into groups based on the type of weapon each man used individually; there were the bowmen, the slingers, etc. They also had musical instruments which were used to encourage the men doing battle. There were small drums, large seashells, flutes and small trumpets both made of bone or animal shells.

The motives for the Incas to make war were normally their ambition and desire to expand the borders of their empire, to punish the provincials when they rebelled, to repress the enemies that bothered the borders, and other similar ones. But they never started war without ample advice, consulting the old captains and those who had proven their bravery in battle. And they conferred with the same men on the method and order in which the war should be conducted. Generally the king himself came out; he would be carried on a litter, and he entered in battle, directing and encouraging his men. When the king returned from a war to his court, everyone came out to meet him, dancing, singing, and doing other things to show their happiness. Other times, remaining in Cuzco, the king sent high commanders to make certain conquests, and if the mission was especially important, he put his own close relatives in charge.

The same governmental system was used in war as in peacetime. The soldiers were divided into decuries and centuries. All of the captains, field marshals, and ranking officers in the army were generally of the royal Inca lineage because they did not trust anyone else. When people were brought from the provinces, the captains who took them to Cuzco kept the posts that they had before, but the king put a commander of Inca lineage in charge of each one [of the captains]. Thus by letting them keep the posts that they had, they were converted into lieutenants under those who were newly put in charge. The entire military was governed by Incas. When the army marched in ranks for war, the men were divided into a variety of squadrons by provinces or nations. Each squadron took its place according to seniority. Thus the nations closest to the Inca were the ones that had been ruled by him for the longest time, and those that had been under his rule for the least time were placed the farthest away.

Before entering into combat with the enemy, the Inca would try to subjugate them by peaceful means. For this purpose he would send them a message, explaining to them how his father the Sun sent him to make them live by the dictates of reason and lead them out of the barbarous and bestial life that they were living. If they resisted, at first the Inca tried to press them by sieges and hunger. However, when these methods were not sufficient, he would enter into battle with them. Their method of fighting was to attack by all rushing together at their adversaries; they would shout and clamor in order to frighten them; but they would not maintain orderly squadrons formed up with the organized parts that proper military training teaches. They certainly did believe that it was permissible to take all of the goods of the conquered. They said that since it was the will of Viracocha to give them victory, it also followed that all of the belongings of the conquered belonged to them. They left the recently conquered provinces well protected by garrisons and fortresses that kept them under control. They also left personnel to instruct the new vassals about the customs, rites, and worship of their gods. Everyone who came under the dominion of the Incas was required to accept their gods and adopt their opinions on religious matters.

Chapter 10: Of their knowledge and practice of medicine

It has already been stated in the previous book that all of the treatments done by these Peruvian Indians were accompanied by superstitions and magic. I will not continue now with what was stated there about this subject of superstitions. In this chapter I will only discuss what pertains to the art of medicine, their doctors, and their methods of curing. Although they were a barbarous people with little knowledge, still, since love of life is natural to all men, it caused these Indians to look for ways to preserve and protect it from harm. Normally their doctors were old and experienced. Nevertheless, they came to understand very little about the individual names and differences among diseases. This ignorance is so general among all the Indians that not one of them, unless he is well versed in Spanish, knows how to inform the doctor about his ailment and what could have caused it. Regardless of what the illness may be, when the patient is asked what he has, he can only answer that his body hurts or that his heart is hurting and bothering him. Therefore, the doctor has to resign himself, like a veterinarian who cures an animal, to explanations made up as he sees fit. As a result, since they did not know the causes and scarcely knew the effects of ailments, they were unable to understand their opposites.[29] All they achieved was to know about some illnesses caused by cold, which is what affects them the most. Nevertheless, this nation is excessively warm, as has been stated previously.[30] And they have many herbs to cure those illnesses. They had more knowledge of wounds and sores, which are clearly visible, and of particular herbs to cure them. They never used compound medications. For all of their remedies they used simple herbs, and among them there are some great herbalists to be found; from them we have learned the healing powers of many plants that we use now in our healing. Also with simples they commonly made fomentations and fumigants which they apply to fevers and other ailments.

They were also able to find out about the benefits of evacuation by bloodletting and purges. But they did not learn about the pulse, nor to look at the urine, much less did they pay any attention to applying their medicines to physical make-up of the patients nor to the causes of their ailments. They were never aware of the four humors, except for blood, because they did not study their

nature and properties.[31] They had no knowledge of the veins, and
still they used bloodletting in their own way. It was as follows.
When they felt pain some place, they would let blood there with a
very sharp point of obsidian. The veins in the neck are the ones
that they knew best, and it was only from these veins that they
drew blood when they cut a vein; they did not use the veins in the
arms or in any other part of the body. They still use this method
of bloodletting, and useful applications have been observed of this
bloodletting, especially in that general epidemic that occurred in
this kingdom the year 1589. When they felt bloated, they used
herbs indifferently to take a purge, not knowing the humor that
was overflowing and needed to be drained; all they expected to accomplish was to alleviate the body.

Normally they were successful in curing wounds. For this purpose they knew extraordinary herbs that were very effective. In
order to make this clear, I will tell of an unusual cure that an Indian performed in the city of Chuquiabo [La Paz]; this was reported
by a gentleman named Diego Avalos, who lived in that city, in certain papers of his that came into my possession, and it is as follows. There was an Indian boy who had a bad fall; this boy was the
son of Alonso Quisumayta (from the descendants of the Incas),
cacique of the encomienda[32] and repartimiento[33] of the above-
mentioned Diego Avalos. The boy broke his leg in the middle of his
shin; the break was such that the bone broke through the skin, and
it was thrust into the ground, where a great deal of the marrow was
lost. This promised to be very difficult to cure, but since the boy
was the son of an important *cacique* of royal lineage, Diego Avalos
had the surgeons called to cure the boy with great care. When the
surgeons saw the harm that had been done to the patient's leg, they
decided to cut it off and take a chance on this approach because
otherwise they were sure that the boy would die. But since this
remedy had seldom been successful in this kingdom, those involved expressed diverse opinions, and the boy's father decided
against it. The father ordered his men to call an old Indian whose
occupation was that of healing among the Indians, and he asked
the old Indian what cure he might suggest for his son. The old Indian
stepped a little way off the road (they were outside of town), and he
picked out a certain herb which he immediately smashed between
two stones so that it could not be recognized, and it never was.
When he arrived where the sick boy was, he squeezed the herb, and
with the juice of the herb, he moistened some wool thread; this he
tied around the base of the bone that was sticking out through the

skin, promising that the patient would certainly recover his health. The next day, with Diego de Avalos and other people present, the Indian returned to cure the patient, and they all saw what happened with great surprise. The wool thread with the juice of the herb was so potent that it had cut the bone off, without causing any pain, according to what the patient said. And the old herbalist applied the same herb mixed with others to it; very soon the leg was cured, leaving only a small hole in the shin as a scar where the bone came out. But the boy was as healthy and nimble as if no such misfortune had happened to him. Diego de Avalos was left with such a strong desire to find out about that herb, and he promised that Indian such good pay, with flattery and kindness, that he promised to show it to him. Although he did make the promise, he never kept it. He kept putting the man off with a variety of excuses until winter came with its frost that made the fields wither, which the Indian considered sufficient reason to not keep his promise.

Chapter 11: Of the clothing and cloth that they used to spin and

weave These Indians of Peru had more clothing than the Indians of other regions of this New World. Cotton, which is common to all the hot lands in the New World, is also abundant in this kingdom, because of the many temperate valleys here where this plant grows very well. Moreover, the Peruvians enjoyed a plentiful supply of wool from their llamas,[34] and vicuñas, from which they made the majority of the cloth for their clothing. Both the wool and the cotton cloth are decorated with fine colors and excellent weaving. For dyeing it they have excellent colors of blue, yellow, black, and many others, and especially crimson or scarlet, which are known to be better than the dyes from many parts of the world and compete favorably with the best that can be found anywhere. The dye is applied to the wool and cotton itself before spinning it, and after a piece of cloth is removed from the loom, no dye is added at all.

The implements used to make these cloths are few and simple. The first thing that they use after dyeing the wool or cotton is the distaff for spinning; it consists of nothing more than a small stick one *tercia* [eleven inches] long and no thicker than a finger, with a little open ring on the top, the same as a bracelet, on which the bunch of cotton or wool was placed; while holding this distaff in the left hand, they have the spindle in the right hand. However, they generally spin without a distaff, winding the bunch of wool or cotton around the wrist. The Indian women spin not only at home, but when they go outside, whether they are standing in one place or walking. As long as they are not doing something [else] with their hands, walking does not interfere with their spinning, which is what most of them are doing when we meet them on the streets. When they remain seated to do their spinning, the spindle rests on one of their pottery plates. Although women are the ones who generally practice this occupation as their own, nevertheless, in some places the men consider it to be their own also. After making the thread, it is doubled and twisted; they never weave with single threads. The same women twist it in the same way as they spin it, and some of the men will generally help in this, especially the old men who are not able to do other work.

Their looms are small and so inexpensive and crude that with

two poles as thick as an arm and three or four cubits long the loom
is set up. They wrap the warp around one of the poles and on the
other pole they roll up the cloth. In order to keep it stationary and
tight, they drive four stakes, about one span long, into the ground,
two at one end and two at the other end, about one and a half
varas[35] [50 inches] apart, more or less, as they see fit, according to
the size of the cloth they are weaving. They tie one of the poles to
two stakes and the other one to the other two stakes; this keeps
the cloth stiff and at about one span above the ground. These looms
are set up just outside their doorways or in their patios, whenever
they want to weave, and when they pick up their work, they take
the two poles and on one of them they roll up the warp that was
spread out. The four stakes which hold it are always left driven in
the ground. They press down and tighten the cloth with a sharp,
smooth bone. With this and no other apparatus or implements,
they make as tight a weave as our silks. And all their textiles, the
plain ones as well as the colorfully decorated ones, the ordinary
and the fine valuable ones, were finished on both sides, a job that
requires great skill, and not surprisingly, it causes us to marvel.

They put on the clothing exactly as it comes off the loom,
without doing any additional work on it; they do not even wash it
(for they never get it wet). This is not necessary because they prepare the wool without oil or grease. It was never their custom nor
did they ever learn how to raise a nap on their cloths, and thus, all
of their textiles have the thread exposed, like our linens and taf-
fetas. But this certainly does not make their textiles ugly; on the
contrary it makes them more beautiful, especially the delicate fine
ones, because the thread is very thin, doubled, and twisted. However, because their cloth did not have any nap, their clothing was
not very warm, and it was more useful in covering their bodies
than in protecting them from the cold.

They weave clothing of thin ordinary cotton; some is white, in
its natural color, and some is of different colors; of the latter, some
pieces are made in a single color, while others come in many colors; some come with stripes, where each stripe is a different color;
others have various designs of animals, flowers, and other things.
Cotton does not hold its colors as well as wool. Newly dyed cotton
has bright colors, but with use they fade. This does not happen to
wool clothing, which always holds its original colors fully without
fading. Only the *yunca*[36] Indians and the inhabitants of the plains
and seacoast wore cotton; the Indians of the Sierra, which is the

main part of the kingdom and where the old Inca nobility and *ore-jones* lived, made their clothing of wool.

In ancient times they made five different kinds of textiles. One, called *abasca*, was coarse and ordinary; another, called *cumbi*, was fine and valuable; the third was made with colored feathers woven into and fixed over the *cumbi*; the fourth was like cloth of silver and gold embroidered in *chaquira*; and the fifth was a very thick and coarse cloth used for various rugs and blankets. The *abasca* clothing was woven of the coarsest wool from the llamas or sheep of the land, and the plebeians wore it. It was almost all made from wool of the same color. However, they did dye some of it. The *cumbi* clothing was from the finest, most select wool, and the most delicate and valuable *cumbi* was made of lamb's wool, which is very fine. They made some that were as thin and glossy as *gorboran*[37] [fine wool fabric], and they dyed it with the same colors as cotton. This clothing was worn by the kings, the great lords, and all the nobility of the kingdom, and the common people could not use it. In many places, the Inca had very special craftsmen called *cumbi camayos*[38] who did nothing but weave *cumbi*. Normally these craftsmen were men, although the *mamaconas*[39] usually made them also, and the ones made by the *mamaconas* were the finest and most delicate. The very rich cloths made for the Inca and the great lords were made entirely or partially of vicuña wool, and they mix in viscacha wool, which is very thin and soft; and bat fur was also added, which is the most delicate of all.

The looms on which this *cumbi* cloth was woven, especially the large pieces for tapestries, were different than the ordinary ones. They made them of four poles set up as a frame which was raised up and placed next to a wall. The *cumbi camayos* went there with many threads and plenty of time to do their work. Their cloths came out perfectly finished, the same on both sides. Today they normally make hangings of the same material with the coats of arms that are ordered. However, the *cumbi* that they make today is nowhere near as fine as it was in ancient times.

The feather cloths were the most esteemed and valued, and this was quite reasonable because the ones that I have seen would be highly regarded anywhere. They were made on the *cumbi* itself, but in such a way that the feathers stand out on the wool and cover it like velvet. The material that they had for this kind of cloth was extensive because incredible numbers and varieties of birds are found in this land with such excellent colors that it is beyond belief. They used only very small, fine feathers. These they fastened on the cloth with a fine, wool thread, laying them to one side, and making with them the same patterns and figures found in their handsome *cumbis*. The gloss, splendor, and sheen of this feather cloth was of such exceptional beauty that it must be seen to be appreciated. Upon entering this land, the Spaniards found the storehouses of the Inca well supplied with many things; one of the most important ones was an abundant supply of valuable feathers for these textiles. Almost all of the feathers were iridescent, with an admirable sheen which looked like very fine gold. Another kind was an iridescent golden green. And there was an immense amount of those tiny feathers which are found on the chest of the little birds that we call *tominejo* [hummingbird], in a small patch about the size of a fingernail. Some of them were strung on very thin thread, some not yet strung were put into *petacas*, which were the trunks and chests of these Indians. The clothing that was embroidered with *chaquira* [beads] was considered to be the most valuable of all. *Chaquira* refers to small, delicate beads of gold and silver. The workmanship was an astonishing thing to see because the whole cloth was so covered with these little beads that no thread was visible, like clothing made of a very tight netting.

The coarsest and thickest cloth that they made was called *chusi*; it was not for making clothing, but for blankets, rugs, and other uses. Some of this cloth was woven as thick as a finger because the thread of the weft was that thick. Comparing these different cloths with ours, we can say that the clothing of *abasca* corresponds to our woolen fabrics, that of *cumbi* to our silks, that of feathers to our silver cloth, that of *chaquira* to our brocades, and that of *chusi* to our coarse woolens; and finally, the clothing of cotton to our linen.

Chapter 12: Of the Inca buildings and how they constructed them

The Inca kings had a large number of architects and master stonemasons who became highly skilled in their occupation and made their living from it. All of the building that they did was for the king, who always kept them occupied with the many fortresses, temples, and palaces which he had built throughout all of his kingdom. And there were a great many of these magnificent buildings, as we can see today by the ruins and parts of them that have remained in many places. Actually, there was no province in all of the Inca's states that was not enhanced with these skillfully made stone structures. The design of the buildings was not very elaborate because the temples usually had only one large room. The fortresses were surrounded by a wall not very high, but thick, and continuous, without the barriers and fortifications of ours. The palaces and royal houses were encircled by a great wall like an alcazar or fortress; the wall was made square, and inside of it many rooms and lodgings were built; on the inside of them and even sometimes on the outside, there were many window spaces closed off on one side, like cupboards or niches. The roof and covering of all these buildings was of large beams without nails. The beams were attached with cords. Instead of tiles, the roofing was long, very well laid [bunches of] *hicho* grass. Therefore, all of the workmanship of these constructions was put in the walls, and truly, it was so great that an adequate description cannot be given to those who have not seen it.

In the first place, the walls were made partly of stone blocks and ashlars and partly of stones worked only on the face, with the edges also worked, though not perfectly even and straight. Second, in the parts of the walls that are still standing, stones made into blocks are seen so big that some of them are up to twelve, fifteen, and more feet in diameter. This clearly shows how very strong the people would have to be in order to carry them and place them where they are. In the third place, though these stones are of such extraordinary large size, they are very skillfully and elegantly worked, and so carefully fitted together one on top of the other without mortar, that the joints are hardly visible. Starting with the walls of irregular stones, even though they seem to be the coarsest, in my opinion, they were much more difficult to make than the ones of ashlar blocks. Except for the face, which they worked as well as the ashlars, the irregular stones were not cut even, and since it was necessary to fit them together so perfectly, it is easy to appreciate the work that it would take to make them fit the way we see them. Some of them are big and others little, and all of them of different forms and shapes; they are fitted together just as perfectly as the ashlar stonework. Thus, if the bottom stone has some bulge or peak, the stone placed on top has a space made in it that fits exactly into the other, and some of these stones have many jagged edges all around, and the stones that sit next to them are cut to fit perfectly. This work certainly is very hard and tedious. In order to fit the stones together, it was necessary to put them in place and remove them many times to check them, and since the stones are very big, as we see, it is easy to understand what a lot of people and suffering were required. The majority of these stones were flat and straight, set vertical, although some were a little inclined inward.

The walls and ramparts of ashlar blocks were more common than those of irregular stones, and generally they were built straight, with uniform-sized stones from the ground up to the top, fitting them together one on top of the other so perfectly that in some buildings not even a pin will fit into the joint. Apart from these straight walls, which, though ordinary among them, were as well made as our very finest, they made others with higher workmanship. One example is an entire section of a wall that still remains in the city of Cuzco, in the Convent of Santa Catalina. These walls were not made vertical, but slightly inclined inward. The stones are perfectly squared, but in such a way that they come to have the same shape and workmanship as a stone for a ring of the sort that jewelers call "faceted." The stones have two sets of faces and corners, so that a groove is formed between the lesser faces of the fitted stones, separating the faces in relief. Another skillfully made feature of this work is that all of the stones are not of the same size, but the stones of each course are uniform in size, and the stones are progressively smaller as they get higher. Thus the stones of the second course are smaller than those of the first, and the stones of the third course are also smaller than those of the second, and in this way the size of the stones diminishes proportionately as the wall becomes higher. Thus the above-mentioned wall of the structure, which remains standing to this day, has a lower course of ashlar blocks of more than one cubit in diameter, while the stones of the upper course are the size of *azulejos* [ornamental tile]. This wall is two or three *estados*[40] high. It is the most skillfully made of all the Inca structures that I have seen. We said that the Indians did not use mortar in these buildings, that all of them were made of dry stone; the first reason for this is that they did not use lime and sand for construction (never having discovered this type of mortar), and the second reason is because they set the stones together with nothing between them on the exterior face of the structure. But this does not mean that the stones were not joined together on the inside with some type of mortar; in fact it was used to fill up space and make the stones fit. What they put in the empty space was a certain type of sticky, red clay that they call *llanca*, which is quite abundant in the whole Cuzco region. I was able to see this for myself while watching as part of that wall of the Convent of Santa Catalina was being torn down for the construction of the church that is there now.

What amazes us the most when we look at these buildings is to wonder with what tools and apparatus could they take these stone [blocks] out of the rocks in the quarries, work them, and put them where they are without implements made of iron, nor machines with wheels, nor using either the ruler, the square, or the plumb bob, nor any of the other kinds of equipment and implements that our artisans use.[41] Thinking about this truly does cause one to marvel, and it makes one realize what a vast number of people were necessary to make these structures. In fact, we see stones of such enormous size that a hundred men could not work even one of them in a month. Therefore, what they say becomes believable, and it is that when the fortress [Sacsahuaman] of Cuzco was under construction, there were normally thirty thousand people working on it. This is not surprising since the lack of implements, apparatus, and ingenuity necessarily increased the amount of work, and thus they did everything by sheer manpower.

The implements that they had to cut the stones and work them were hard, black cobblestones from the rivers, with which they worked more by pounding than cutting. The stones were taken to the work site by dragging them, and since they had no cranes, wheels, or apparatus for lifting them, they made a ramp of earth next to the construction site, and they rolled the stones up the ramp. As the structure went up higher, they kept building up the ramp to the same height. I saw this method used for the Cathedral of Cuzco which is under construction. Since the laborers who work on this job are Indians, the Spanish masons and architects let them use their own methods of doing the work, and in order to raise up the stones, they made the ramps mentioned above, piling earth next to the wall until the ramp was as high as the wall.

Chapter 13: Of the bridges that they made over the rivers

Necessity moved the Indians to invent strange things which are quite different from the things that we use for the same purpose that they invented them. They never found out how to make stone bridges over the rivers because they had no knowledge of the mortar made from lime and sand, nor did their architecture include construction of the arch. Moreover, some of their rivers had such powerful currents and turbulent floods and overflows that posts could not be set in them nor could they be crossed in balsas or any other kind of boat. Therefore, they sought and found other unusual ways to cross them, according to the river's size and the lay of the adjacent land. As a result, by applying their ingenuity to the task, they were able to overcome even the widest, largest, and swiftest rivers. They navigated and crossed the placid rivers in their boats, even the ones that were very large and deep. On the other rivers, it was a problem, but they solved it with their ingenuity and work. If a river was lined by boulders and had a narrow enough channel for long beams to reach from one side to the other, they put some long ones across. After being covered with thin poles and branches, these beams served as bridges. On rivers too wide for beams to reach across, they used two unusual ways of crossing, or kinds of bridges; one was called *oroya*, and we use the name *crizneja* [twisted cable or suspension] bridge for the other one. These bridges are still used today to cross almost all the rivers where they had them formerly. And the government makes every effort to have the same Indians who used to do it in Inca times continue now to repair and maintain them. Without these bridges, it would be impossible to travel over most of this kingdom.

The *oroya* is a cable or rope the thickness of a leg made of *hichu* straw or of reeds. This cable is stretched and tied to both sides of the river between two boulders, if there are any, and if not, between strong pillars or supports made of stone. Sometimes the cable is as high as ten or more *estados* [42] [over fifty-five feet] above the water, according to the way the river banks are situated. To this cable they hang a basket like those for harvesting grapes, with its round, looped handle, by passing the cable through the handle. A man is put in the basket, and they pull from the other side with a rope that is tied to the basket, which slides across the cable until it reaches the other side. Not only men cross in these baskets but also bundles of clothing and whatever else they want. Other *oroyas* have no baskets. They just tie the man securely so that if he becomes alarmed and faints, he cannot fall, and hanging in the air from the cable by a large wooden hook which runs over the cable, the man is pulled from one side to the other. I have crossed rivers in both kinds of *oroyas*. I crossed the Apurimac River in the first kind, and in the second kind, I crossed the Jauja River, by the town of San Jeronimo de la Oroya, in this Archbishopric of Lima. Shortly after I passed by this town, an amusing incident took place there, and it was as follows. Traveling through this kingdom, there was an acrobat who made his living by doing somersaults on a cable. On his way he came to the town mentioned above, and he wanted to cross over the *oroya*, but the Indians in charge of the bridge were slow in coming. For this reason, the acrobat climbed up on the cable and went straight across on it just as if he were walking on land. The Indians of the town who saw him do this were astonished to see such a thing, and they became so frightened of the acrobat, thinking that he was some kind of spirit in human form, that they ran away.

The commonest type of bridge is the one we call a *crizneja* [twisted cable or suspension] bridge. It is made in the following way. On both sides of the river, they construct two large pillars or supports of stone on the same model as the walls that were discussed in the last chapter, except that the foundations are made very deep and strong; the wall is thicker and inclined a little toward the ground; it is about thirty or forty feet long and about the same height, or higher, according to the height of the ravine. A pair of walls of the same material extend inland from the corners of each pillar, leaving a space in between like a square room with only three walls, since the wall on one side was missing. Between those two walls on each pillar, they put four to six large beams crosswise, in the same order as those for the roof of a large room; the bridge is tied to these beams. When they find living stones on the banks of the river, they use them for the pillars. The bridge is made of thin, supple branches like wicker, by weaving thin plaits or twists, and three of these twists are made into another, thicker one. They continue in this way until the final cable or twist is as thick as the body of a boy. Five of these thick cables are used to make a bridge, and in order to take the cables across from one bank of the river to the other, a thick rope is tied to each cable, and a thin cord was tied to each of these ropes. One Indian swims across with the cord or takes it across in a balsa. The cord is used to pull the thick rope across, and a great many people pull on it to get the cable across, but since the cable is very heavy and the current pulls it, great strength is needed to make it stand up. After the five cables are pulled across, they are thrown over the pillars and tied to the beams that I mentioned; each cable is wrapped around each of the beams, so the cables will stay tight and not loosen. However, no matter how much the cables are stretched, the bridge sags into a bowlike curve. Thus, on starting across the bridge, one descends down until reaching the middle, and from there one continues going up to the end of it. When a strong wind blows, the bridge sways back and forth. Three of the five cables mentioned are used for the floor; the other two cables are the guard rails, one on each side. Over the three floor cables, and securely tied to them, they put poles as thick as an arm crosswise in the form of a wattle that extends the width of the bridge, which is about six or eight feet; over these poles, they place other thinner ones or fine branches. From the bridge floor up to the cables that serve as guard rails, they cover and intertwine the sides the whole length of the cables with branches; this makes two walls that serve more to keep those who cross from getting frightened than as a support. This construction makes these bridges strong and safe to cross for both men and beasts carrying loads, although the bridges swing and sway. It is true that, in order to avoid a disaster, cautious people unload the beasts and have Indians carry the load over on their shoulders, and travelers get off their horses and lead them across on foot. The longest of these suspension bridges that I have seen are the one over the Vilcas River, Diocese of Guamanga [Ayacucho], and the one over the Apurima River, Diocese of Cuzco; the longest one is about two hundred feet across. It is necessary to rebuild these bridges every year, and the people of the nearby towns come out to do it. I am not going to describe here the bridge at Desaguardo, on Lake Chucuito [Titicaca], which is similar to the bridge at Seville, though it is very unusual; this will be done in the description of that province, which will go in the second part of this *Historia*.[43]

Chapter 14: Of their boats

The people of this New World lacked ships and the art of navigating on the high seas with the ease and skill that we navigate. Nevertheless, they were compelled by necessity to invent several kinds of small boats; each nation made these boats out of the materials available in their land, without searching beyond there for this purpose. Though they did not use these boats to ply the great seas and trade in remote ports of the distant places, nevertheless, they used them for fishing on the sea, lakes, and rivers, for their limited exchanges on the shores of friendly nations nearby, and to rob from the shores of their enemies, for their wars and attacks, and especially to cross rivers, lakes, sounds, estuaries, and bays. It is also true that there is a great diversity of boats that the inhabitants of different regions used. Still, since the great empire of the Incas included so many provinces and nations, within its borders we find all the different kinds of vessels and boats that are made in the other parts of the Indies.

The boat most generally found all over America is the canoe. It is used by the *yunca* Indians who inhabit the woodlands, rich in the big trees used to make the canoe. It is a small, one-piece boat or ship, made of a huge log hollowed out in such a way as to take on the shape of a trough, except that inside it is like a ditch dug in the ground so as to be uniform, deep, and narrow, and outside it is round, almost in the same form as the tree trunk from which it was made. The bottom is somewhat flat, and there is no keel; the thickness of the sides all around is no more than two or three finger widths. Since the wood of which it is made is light (because normally it is a tree called *ceiba* [cottonwood]), it is enhanced so much by the form and shape that a little force from the wind or the oars will make it fly over the water, which accounts for the well-known fact that it is swifter than other kinds of boats. But at the same time that it is very swift, it is also a very dangerous boat. Therefore, it can only be used when the weather is fair; if any storm comes up or if the passengers rock it at all, it will turn over as easily as a round stick floating in the water. This is caused by the following factors: the boat's lack of ballast, its round shape, and its light weight. As a consequence, all those who use this type of boat should be good swimmers, and the Indians are such good swimmers that when the canoe turns over, they jump into the water and, while swimming, they turn it right side up again. Since it is so light it never sinks, even though it fills up with water. But the Indians empty out the water with gourds which they carry for this purpose. Then they get back into the canoe and continue their trip and their activities.

They make canoes as big as is permitted by the size of the log that is hollowed out. Some are so big that they are fifty or sixty feet long, and so wide that a wine cask would fit in it crosswise. Other canoes are so small that only two people can ride in them. The canoes were sailed, rowed, and propelled with poles. Only a small sail, normally made of cotton, can be used. Oars are the most common, and since these boats are made in a particular way, the oars are also. We call them paddles; they are made from one stick; the paddles are larger or smaller in proportion to the size of the canoe. The paddles are shaped like a baker's peel about two hands thick, with a ridge down the middle like a sword, thinner toward the edges and pointed. The largest paddles are about one *estado* [5½ feet] high; half of it is the blade, and the other half is a round pole which is attached to the blade itself; the pole is the size and shape of a crutch; in fact, on top there is a crosspiece exactly like the one on a crutch. The oarsmen stand in line along the sides of the canoe, and the movement of their arms as they row is like someone digging with a hoe.

Making these canoes is very difficult for the Indians; they dig them out by pounding on the logs with stone-headed axes and by burning out the parts that are roughhewn. Thus by dint of pounding and burning the logs are hollowed out, but after they are finished, there is no more work to be done; it is not neecessary to calk them or to perform any other maintenance. These boats are used by Spaniards in many places, and I have ridden in them many times. The word canoe [Spanish *canoa*] is taken from the Indians of Hispaniola Island, although there are different names for it in the languages of other lands. The Indians of Tierra Firme[44] call it *piragua*, and these are the only two names that we use ourselves, although we make the following distinction. We only use the name *piragua* for a certain kind of large canoe; although the part of these canoes that enters into the water is made of one log, on the sides they add boards or cane wattle covered with pitch; this makes them higher and wider than the common canoes.

The Indians from the southern part of the Kingdom of Chile make canoes out of three boards, one on the bottom and the other two on the sides. They make the bottom board a little cured with the ends bending up somewhat. The two side boards are adjusted

by twisting them and applying fire until the edges are even with
the bottom board. The boards are kept together and sewn with
thick thread made by pounding certain giant bamboos; the tooth of
an animal is used to make the holes where the thread goes through.
But now that they have our implements of iron, they bore holes in
the boards with an auger. They make oakum by pounding tree
leaves; it is used to seal the seams and boreholes. But since these
boats are not very well calked, they take on so much water that it
is always necessary to take a boy along to bail it out on the way.
When they reach land, they beach the boats so they will not sink.
These three kinds of boats are the only ones we find among the
Indians that have sides and are hollow inside. All the other boats
that they use are flat balsa rafts, of which there are many different kinds.

Where good wood for making balsas is lacking, the Indians
make them of other materials, which do not seem to be very appropriate for such use. The most common ones in this kingdom are
made of dry bulrush or some other kind of reeds. These balsas are
made in the following way. They bind two bundles of reeds, which
are the same size as the boat will be; the bundles are compact and
round, with the bow end pointed. Thus the bundles are thicker in
the middle and from there gradually get thinner toward the ends,
but not equally thinner because the end that serves as stern is
thicker, unless both ends are to be shaped like the bow, as in many
balsas; in this case, the bundles get equally thinner. The two
bundles are joined together by pairing them up from stem to stern,
and they are securely lashed together. With no further cost or work
the balsa is perfectly constructed; the bottom that sits on the water
is flat, or in the form of a channel, so that it will not turn over so
easily, and the top side is the same shape, where the cargo is placed.
The stem or bow curves upward more than the rest of the balsa,
and when it has two bows, both of them are shaped the same way.
The smallest of these balsas are a little more than four cubits long,
and the size around it at the thickest point is such that a man can
put his arms around it. The biggest ones are fifteen to twenty feet
long and ten or twelve feet around. The small ones will only carry
one or two people, and some of the bigger ones will carry twelve
people, and two big ones lashed together make one large enough to
carry beasts and cattle.

Both kinds are used on the sea, rivers, and lakes. However, the
big ones usually serve only for crossing rivers and lakes, and the
little ones are for fishing in the sea. Neither kind are suitable for

sails because they are so light that they overturn with a very light wind, and so they are propelled with oars and poles. The fishermen of these Peruvian coasts go out on the open sea four to six leagues on balsas that are so small that when they leave their homes they each carry their balsa on their back to the sea, and throwing them in the water, they get on. Seated in the middle of the balsas, they go very fast in groups of twenty, forty, and more Indians together, each one on their own balsa. Seen at a distance, they look more like big fish than boats. They row with a piece split from a big bamboo, about one hand wide and one *braza* [5½ feet] long; they grip it in the middle with both hands, holding it crosswise over the balsa, with one end on one side and the other end on the other side; alternately pulling in the water they propel the little balsas so swiftly that they sail over the water like birds. But if the waters get a little choppy, the fishermen and whatever they are carrying get soaked because the top of the boat is no more than one span above the surface of the water. When the fishermen return to shore, they beach their balsas, and they each carry their own balsas home, where they take the little boats apart and set the reeds in the sun to get dry for the next day. Therefore this boat is made so simply (leaving aside its reliability, which is very great) that it is constructed in the morning, and after traveling across the water most of the day, in the afternoon it is taken apart.

Similar to these in shape, though not in the material, are other balsas used by the Indians of the province of Arica. They make them of two inflated sea lion hides, which are lashed together like the bundles used in making the reed balsas. Each one is used by only one Indian, and he goes out on the sea as far as the others. But since these balsas usually deflate on the water, to avoid sinking each Indian carries a small tube, and out on the sea, from time to time he loosens them and blows in the air to reinflate them, as if they were inflated balls. These balsas are as light and swift on the water as the material of which they are made, which is air. Sails are never used on these, and they are also propelled only with oars, the same as the reed balsas.

There is another type of balsa used only for crossing rivers which is even simpler in design and construction. These balsas are made of many gourds which are dried and whole; all they do is put a large number of these gourds into a net, and each netful is a balsa. The people who are going to cross ride on top, and the ferrymen swim, one or two ahead pulling the balsa with cords placed around their foreheads, like horses pulling a carriage, and others behind, also swimming, who place their hands on the stern of the balsa and push ahead by kicking with their feet in the water. This type of balsa is generally used to cross the Santa River, which is one of the largest and swiftest rivers of this coast that drains into the South Sea [South Pacific].

Solely for this same purpose of crossing rivers, in other places balsas are made of cane in the form of wattle one or two spans thick; many small bundles of cane are lashed over several poles set crosswise which form the base of the balsa. This boat is as safe as those mentioned above, but the passengers do not remain dry. If a heavy load is put on this balsa, it will sink down to the level of the water or even sink under if the load is too heavy. When I came to the Apurima River in the year 1616, the bridge had been damaged and the river was being crossed on some of these balsas and by *oroya*. Although I was displeased by both of these methods of crossing, I decided to get into the basket and cross in the air by *oroya* rather than run the risk of getting wet, which is what I saw happen to others who crossed that way.

The largest balsas are used by the Peruvian Indians who live near woodlands, such as those of the ports of Payta, Manta, and Guayaquil. These balsa rafts are made of seven, nine, or more balsawood logs in the following way. These logs are placed on top of others set crosswise and all lashed together with lianas or cords; since the middle log is the bow, it is longer than the others, which are gradually shorter toward the sides; thus the bow takes on the shape of a person's fingers when the hand is laid out flat, but the stern is square. On top a platform is made so that the people and clothing on board will not get wet with the water that splashes up between the logs. Sails and oars are used to navigate out to sea, and some of them were big enough to hold fifty men comfortably. This kind of boat can be dangerous if the Indians on board plot a treacherous scheme, which can be carried out unexpectedly by unlashing the logs on the sly and letting them come apart. Since the Indians are excellent swimmers who wear little or no clothing, they escape by swimming, and those who do not know how to swim die by drowning. This is exactly what the people of the Island of Puná did to the Inca's soldiers when he tried to conquer them.

Chapter 15: Of the silversmiths that the Incas had, and of the other occupations that the Indians learned and used

Among these Indians we find things of silver and gold made by them long ago with such skill that we are amazed, especially considering the limited number of tools and implements that they had to make them. They did not have the forge; all they did was put the charcoal on the ground. In place of bellows, they blew through copper tubes three or four spans long. They also lacked tongs, hammers, files, chisels, burins, as well as the other implements used by our silversmiths. The Indians used only three or four types of stone and copper tools to do all their metalwork. They used very hard, flat stones for anvils. The hammer was a square piece of copper the size of a fist, shaped like a die with the corners rounded, and it had no wooden handle; they pounded silver with the hammer like we do when we split or crush something with a stone. The hammers came in three or four different sizes; the biggest were the size already stated, others were middle sized, others small. They did not have the lathe, and still they did not seem to need it. Finally, with such a small number of implements and equipment, they made excellent pieces of gold and silver. They did not discover many of our techniques. The most that they did was chisel, shaping and sculpting in their pieces animals, flowers, and other things that were imperfect in form and design. Nor did they learn how to overlay their silver pieces with gold, emboss them or add materials on them. They did not work standing up, but seated on the floor. The Inca kings had a large number of silversmiths throughout all the provinces of their dominion. Many successors of the craftsmen who were there when the Spaniards came are still in the same places, and to this day they work with the same implements and in almost the same way as in earlier times, but more skillfully because their work has been much perfected with the implements and techniques that they have learned to use from our silversmiths.

It must be pointed out here that these artisans who with study learned and practiced these occupations were not ordinary craftsmen who did business with anyone willing to pay for their services, as our craftsmen do; they worked only in the service of the Inca and the great lords and *caciques,* doing their works exclusively for them. And there were only three or four of these occupations, namely, *cumbi camayos* or *cumbi* weavers, stonemasons, and silversmiths, which were learned and practiced by persons who dedicated their entire lives to them and, as has been said, practiced them in the service of the nobility. The rest of the Indians of the community, except for the lords and nobles, knew how to make everything they needed in their lives, from the shoes that they wore to the headgear that they used, the house where they lived, and the food that they ate; everyone did all these things with their own hands, from shearing the wool off their sheep to making their clothing from it; thus they had no need for anyone to help them or do any of these things for them. Therefore, that maxim of Plutarch which says, "there is no one who has no need of another man's skills" does not apply to these people. Any of these Indians knows how to sow his fields and make the implements and equipment necessary for farming, prepare their food, weave their cloths, make their shoes, beds, beverages, and everything pertaining to this. Finally, there was nothing, not any of the valuables in their homes nor any of their necessities, that they did not make with their own hands. And this was not so much because they were industrious as because they were content with little. Their intellect, which was limited and not very inventive, was the reason why all of these jobs were done at such a rudimentary level. Anyone who tried to do them would learn shortly as well as their inventor. Their houses were no more elaborate than the huts or cabins of shepherds, and their clothing, their shoes, and everything else was made in the same rudimentary fashion.

Since they had no knowledge of iron, the implements that they used for doing all of their artisan work were made of copper, wood, and very hard stones. They discovered very little about weights and measures; they had no liquid weights or measures. They measured maize and all kinds of grains as by *almudes* [approximately four quarts] with a measure called *collo,* which they usually made with a dry gourd, although they had silver and wooden ones. What they measured with the most precision was agricultural fields. They measured them by *topos,* as we do by *hanegadas* [approximately 1.6 acres], and the *topo* was fifty *brazas* long and twenty-five wide.[45]

Chapter 16: Of the hunting and fishing of these people

These Indians did not go hunting or fishing simply for amusement or recreation; they did it out of necessity and for profit. These activities were not as frequent and common among them as among the nations of Europe. Hunting was very hard work for the Indians because they lacked skill, diligence, and training for it, and they did not make use of animals trained to hunt with them. To catch birds, they used nets and birdlime, which they got from certain types of trees. They hunted birds more for the feathers than for meat.

They killed dangerous animals with arrows and other missiles; these were also used for wild animals that they took to eat and for the skins and wool. They also made snares and traps. But the most common hunting method used by the Peruvians was the one called *chaco* in their language. It was always done by a large group of people and with the permission of the Inca or his governors. When the Inca himself wanted to go on a *chaco* or royal hunt, he ordered ten or twenty thousand Indians to assemble, or as many as he thought necessary, according to the size of the area that they were going to encircle. All together they would surround a large piece of land, which was sometimes ten, twenty or more leagues[46] around. They started somewhat separated from each other, and from there, little by little, in an orderly fashion, they came together, driving the game by beating the bush, and closing ranks until they could join hands. As they squeezed more tightly together, closing in on the game that they had encircled, they formed various lines, one man behind another, in order to better head off the animals and encircle them, and so that none would escape. Once the game was penned in this way with a thick wall of men, another group of Indians went into the circle and with clubs and other weapons, they caught and killed the number of animals that the Inca wanted, which normally was ten or fifteen thousand head; they released the rest and let them go free.

In this same way the people went out periodically to hunt from the provinces and from entire towns on the orders of their governors and *caciques*. The animals that they took in these *chacos* were vicuñas, guanacos, and deer. However, along with these, they would take some dangerous animals, which they would kill. Vicuñas were shorn for their fleece, then released. And they dried the meat from the animals that they had killed in the round-up. Also the animals rounded up in the way just stated were often enclosed in corrals that they made in gorges and narrow places. This method of hunting was called *caycu.*

While the Marques Francisco Pizarro was engaged in pacifying this kingdom, on his return from Cuzco to the Valley of Jauja, an impressive *chaco* was held by order of Manco Inca in Pizarro's presence; over eleven thousand wild animals were killed, including vicuñas, deer, foxes, and some birds; the shouting of the Indians stunned the birds, and they were killed. Ten thousand Indians participated in this *chaco,* and they surrounded many leagues of land.

They had several methods and implements for fishing. They generally went fishing with hooks, traps, and nets, whether they fished on the sea, rivers, or lakes. They made the hooks of copper and the nets of cotton thread. The nets were small enough to be cast by two persons. Thus when fishing on the sea, they went in groups or in pairs, each one on his own little balsa. Once the net was set, two men would pull it in by the ends, and as they were pulling, they would approach each other until their two balsas came together. Therefore, normally these nets cannot be used for fishing with less than two balsas, and big fish are not taken in them.

On the seacoasts, river mouths, and estuaries, where the water rises and falls a great deal, they make corrals of dry stone and stakes driven into the ground close together; these walls are low so that the incoming tide rises some distance above them; therefore, fish swim through the sea right over these walls, and when the tide goes out, a large number of the fish are trapped inside. Since the fish are left on dry land, they can be taken by hand with little effort. On the rivers, fishing with *barbasco,* which is a plant like a liana, is very common; when *barbasco* is pounded and put in the water, it stupifies the fish in such a way that they float on the water as if dead. On the rivers of the coastal plains, mainly to take crayfish, they dry a section of a river or all of it by changing its course, which leaves the catch on dry land, and in some parts of the Sierra, they do the same thing to take *armadillo* fish, *sabalos,* and *dorados.*[47]

On the deep, placid rivers there are Indians who go into the water with a fish spear in their right hand, while swimming very swiftly with only the left hand; they dive after the fish, following until they overtake it and spear it; then they pull the pierced fish out to shore. These are the most common fishing methods in this whole kingdom. However, the inhabitants of other regions and provinces have different methods of their own.

Chapter 17: Of the games that they had for their amusement; their musical instruments and

dances Although these Indians were barbarians, they invented some clever games that correspond to dice and other games of ours. But they played them more for entertainment than out of lust for winnings. Nevertheless, at times there were some prizes involved, such as blankets, livestock, and other things; still this was in small amounts and did not affect the game much. *Piscoynu* was a game that corresponds to whipping and spinning a top. The game called *pichca* was like dice; it was played with one die marked with five points, which was the highest number on the die. Another game called *chuncara* was played with colored beans and a flat stone or board that had five small holes carved in it. The die was thrown and according to the number to come up, the beans were moved from one hole to another until reaching the end; the first hole was worth ten points; the other holes were progressively each worth ten more up to the last which was worth fifty. Another type of game was called *tacanaco*, and it was played with the same die and colored beans as the board game. Apart from these, there were other less important games such as the one called *apaytalla*, *puma*,[48] and others.

The Indians were much given to their *taquis*, which is what they call their songs and dances. They celebrated happy events as well as sad, gloomy ones by singing, dancing, and drinking their wine or *chicha*. For these celebrations they had many musical instruments which were played only at their dances and drinking bouts. The sound of all their instruments was rather harsh and not very artistic. In just one lesson, anyone will learn to play their instruments like an expert. Their most widely used instrument is the drum, which they call *huancar*. They made their drums, both large and small, of a hollow log covered on both ends with llama hide, like thin, dry parchment. The largest ones are like our war drums, but longer and not as well made; the smallest ones are like a very small box of preserves, and the medium-sized ones were like our timbrels. The drum is played with a single drumstick, which is sometimes decorated with wool thread of different colors, and the drums were usually painted and adorned. The drum is played by both men and women, and there are dances done to the rhythm of a single drum and other dances in which they each carry their own little drum, dancing and playing at the same time. They also use a certain kind of tambourine, called *huancar tinya,* and a fife called *pincollo.* The *antara* is another kind of flute which is short and wide. The *quenaquena* is made of one single piece of cane like a flute for singing dirges. *Quepa* is a kind of small trumpet made out of a long gourd. In their dances they generally also play an instrument made of seven little flutes, more or less, placed together and of different lengths, like organ pipes; the longest one is about one span long, and the others progressively shorter. This instrument is called *ayarichic,* and it is played on the lower lip by blowing through the small pipes, which makes a muffled, somewhat harsh sound. They also play snail-shells and other instruments of less importance.

Apart from the adornments that they put on for their dances, they put strings of little round bells, that come in two or three different kinds, on the instep of the foot. Formerly, the Incas used certain little bells made of large, colored beans that are found in the eastern provinces of the Andes, and these little bells were called *zacapa. Chanrara* are another type of bells that were made of silver and copper like little cup-shaped bells. The most common ones were those called *churu,* which were long shells of sea snails in a variety of colors. Now they hardly use any of these bells because they prefer ours, which sound better to them, and they are very fond of them.

Almost all of their dances were accompanied by singing, and thus the name *taqui,* which means dance, signifies both song and dance at the same time. For every different kind of song, there was a dance to go with it. The Indians of Cuzco had their own songs and dances for their work, and every province throughout the whole Inca Empire had its own special dances, which were never exchanged. However, now in the church festivals, any nation will imitate the dances of the other provinces, and thus the many and diverse dances that they do in the procession of the Blessed Sacrament and in other big festivals are really worth seeing. Once while I was at a town in the province of Collao during the procession of Corpus Christi, I counted forty of these dances there, each different, which illustrated the dress, songs, and dancing of the Indian nations where they were from.

One of the most common dances that they performed was called *guacon;* it is restricted to men who wear masks and go jumping around while carrying in their hand the skin or dried-out body of a wild animal.

Another dance is called *guayayturilla;* it was danced by both men and women with their faces painted and a gold or silver ribbon across the nose from ear to ear; the tune was played on the dried head of a deer whose horns served as a flute. One dancer led off the dance, and the others followed with perfect rhythm.

The farmer's dance is called *haylli;* both men and women take part with their farming implements, the men with their *tacllas,* which are their plows, and the women with their *atunas,* which are wooden implements like a carpenter's adze, with which they break up the dirt clods and level the ground. They have other dances that represent their wars, and the men carry their weapons while doing them. The dance called *cachua* is very important, and in earlier times they only did it at very important festivals. Men and women join hands and form a circle or ring and go dancing around. The Inca's own dance is called *guayyaya.* Formerly this dance was restricted to people of royal Inca lineage, and they carried the royal standard or pennant with the *champi,* which were the king's insignias. They danced to the tune of a big drum, which a plebeian carried on his shoulders, and a woman beat it. The tune and the dance are solemn and dignified, without any hopping or jumping. In doing it, men and women join hands and form a line. Sometimes two or three hundred persons, more or less, take part, according to the solemnity of the occasion. Sometimes men and women dance together, and other times they divide up forming one line of men and another of women. They started this dance at a distance from the Inca or the *cacique* who was presiding over it, and they all began together by taking three steps in time with the music, one step backward and two steps forward, and in this way, they progressed forward until reaching the Inca. Sometimes, on very solemn occasions, the Inca himself took part in these dances. Another Inca dance was truly worth seeing, and in my opinion it was the most elaborate and entertaining of all the dances that I have seen these people perform. Only three people participate, an Inca in between two *pallas,* who are noble women; they join hands as they dance, doing innumerable turns and loops with their arms, without ever letting go, and rhythmically moving toward and away from the same place. They had songs composed to go with the rhythm of each of these dances. The happy, festive songs were called *arabis;* in them they told of their exploits and events of the past, and they praised the Inca. One person would lead the song, and the others would harmonize. All of these dances were so easy to do that anyone who tries can learn them as well as their most experienced dancers. Finally, they alleviated the fatigue of their dancing and recreation by drinking to excess.

Chapter 18: Of the different types of tombs that they had

A universal custom among all of the Indian nations was to pay more attention to the dwelling that they were to have after death than to the one they had during their lifetime. For their living accommodations they were satisfied with small, humble houses, which is clearly evident on the basis of what has already been stated in this book. Though they made no effort to have big attractive houses, they took great care in building and adorning the tombs where they were to be buried, as if all of their happiness resided there. These Peruvians observed the same custom, and with more care, style, and skill than any of the other peoples of this New World. Their pride and glory was to have the most lavish, impressive, and pompous burials and tombs possible, according to the importance of those to be buried. Most of the tombs were built in the countryside, some in their fields and others in the uninhabited pasturelands where their livestock grazed, and in some provinces in their own houses. The form of the tombs was not the same throughout the whole kingdom. Since the provinces and nations were diverse, they also had different types of tombs. However, we can assign them to two groups. The first, those that were dug out underground and the second, those that were built above ground. Within the first group, some were very deep; many steps were provided for going down into them, and others were at ground level. Both types were hollow like vaults; their size and elaborateness depended on the status of the one who had them made. The majority of these were square, and some were as large and deep as an ordinary room, with stone walls as well built as the finest Inca buildings. The doorway was narrow, and it was covered with a single stone slab, and some had a second slab under the first, and sometimes two more, very close together.

Tall tombs built above the ground were more common. But we also find a great variety of these because every Indian nation sought a new style of making them. In this respect, there was a great difference between the Indians of the plains along the seacoast and those of the sierra. The tombs of the coastal Indians were unusually large; we see some of them that seem to be medium-sized hills, like the ones that still remain in this Valley of Lima. Such is the one we see in the ancient settlement of the town of Surco and in the ruins of Maranga, between this city of Los Reyes [Lima] and the port of Callao. These tombs were made with thick high earthen walls, in the same form and design as the main houses of their *caciques*, on a square plan with many divisions and rooms. In some of them, the walls were very close together in the form of narrow passages; within the square of the above-mentioned walls, they made another square of the same dimensions with the same amount of space on all sides. Apparently they made these passages so as to easily cover them with stone slabs placed crosswise from one wall to the other. These large *guacas* or tombs located on the plains are filled with earth, and some of them are even covered with large piles of small stones; as they buried their dead in them, they filled them in, as we see, where many of them have been destroyed by the citizens of this city as they seek to use the earth for making adobes for their buildings and even search for treasure. Tombs like these are so numerous throughout all of the valleys of this coast that we are just as amazed by the vast number of them as by their size, and more than anything else, the infinite number of dead bodies found in the tombs is astonishing. Although one hundred twenty years have gone by since the Spaniards entered into this land and almost as many since the Indians have been converted to our holy faith and have stopped performing pagan burial ceremonies, in digging by hand one finds skeletons and dead bodies at a depth of less than a cubit in any of these tombs. Many of the bodies are uncovered and in plain sight; since it never rains here and many tombs are covered with sand, the winds blow the sand away, uncovering the dead bodies with the clothing and shrouds in which they were buried. Also because of the dryness of the sand, we find many bodies intact and dry; the skin is touching the bones; the hair, clothing, and implements of their occupations are intact also.

And for this reason, in a dramatic presentation on the [final] judgment that we put on in this Jesuit College of San Pablo for the Viceroy Luis de Velasco, the year 1599, in order to reinact more realistically the resurrection of the dead, we had many skeletons and bodies of Indians intact and dry taken from the ancient tombs, and this astonished all of us who were present. And it happened to me once while I was digging with a small stick in one of these tombs, after going down less than a span, I found the body of a child with his *quipe* still on his back, which is what we would call his knapsack; in it he has some small gourds and other toys and

trinkets with which he had been buried. Another time, in one of
the tombs of the old part of Surco, among the jars and things that
were with a dead body, I found an ear of maize with its kernels so
well preserved that the people to whom I showed it were amazed.
Based on the calculations we made, the maize must have been buried for more than seventy years.

The Indians of the sierra did not make such big tombs as those
of the coast. Nevertheless, the sierrans did not let the Indians of
the coast outdo them in either the number of tombs or the skill
with which they made them. They made them in the pastures,
grasslands, and uninhabited areas, some close to their towns, others
far from them. All the tombs were made in the form of small towers; the smallest ones were one *estado* [5½ feet] high, more or less,
the size of our fireplace chimneys, but a little larger, and the largest ones were four to six *estados* high. The doors on all of them
face east, and these doors are as small and narrow as an oven door,
for it is impossible to enter through them without touching your
chest to the ground. The Colla Indians used these large tombs, and
there are so many of them in the provinces of the Collao that it is
amazing. In their fields they normally made rows of tombs with six
in a row, ten, or more or less. Some of the tombs were so close
together that a person could hardly fit between them. We find the
largest number of these tombs on the royal road to Potosi, in the
province of Caracollo, between the towns of Calamarca and Hayo-
hayo, and also next to the town of Oruro in the Tambo de las Sepul-
turas [Station of the Tombs], which was given this name because of
the many tombs present in that place; and along the road to Oma-
suyo there are so many next to the town of Achacache that at a
distance, the place looks like a large town. Most of the tombs are
made only of earth, in the form of a square, with their four corners
or sections of equal length, of the height already mentioned, from
six to twelve feet wide on each side from corner to corner, straight,
even, and well made. Inside, the tombs are hollow up to about one
estado, like a vault, which is covered by some flat, wide stones.
From there on up, the tombs are solid; the top is covered with slate
or thin stone slabs, with its kind of cornice made of the slabs themselves, like the eaves of a tiled roof, which makes them more attractive. Many of the tombs are still so well preserved that they
seem to be new; it appears that they will last a very long time, and
I have no doubt that the ruins of these tombs will last for many
centuries. Other tombs of this same form and size are made in the

provinces of Collao, but these are made only of stone, some of ashlar masonry and others of irregular stonework, and in both kinds
the stones are skillfully fit together. They also made some of these
stone tombs round, although most of them are square, as has already been stated.

Chapter 19: Of the rites and ceremonies that they performed for their burials

When an Indian died, his relatives performed great lamentations and ceremonies before the burial, and if it was a lord and *cacique*, all of his vassals participated. These lamentations or funeral rites were longer or shorter according to the social status of the deceased. For the death of a great lord, the rites lasted eight days; during this time they made much *chicha* to drink; the more honored the deceased was, the more *chicha* they drank. The lamentations were performed by dancing to the tune of their drums and singing sad, plaintive dirges. While the lamentations lasted, no fire was lit in the house of the deceased. The relatives and friends of the person who died gave food and drink to all those who came to these funerals. When someone died, the relatives and friends went into mourning by wearing black cloaks for some time, and the nobles wore them for a whole year. During the days of the lamentations up until the burial, those who participated covered their heads with their cloaks, and at the death of the lords, many of their wives would cut their hair as a greater demonstration of sadness. Every day the procession went out dancing with drums and flutes, singing with sad voices; they visited all the places where the deceased enjoyed himself most often during his lifetime; in their songs, they told about all the incidents in the life of the deceased, recounting his heroic deeds, if he was brave, and all of his most remarkable achievements, in order to cause those present to grieve.

After mourning the deceased in this way, they performed their sacrifices and superstitious acts; at this time part of the property left by the dead man was burned, and if he was a true noble, some of his wives and servants were killed, and others were buried alive in the tomb with him so that they could serve and accompany him in the other life. Dressed and adorned in his finest garments and jewelry, he was buried; next to him were placed other new garments that were folded, much food and drink, and with him they also buried his weapons, the implements of his craft and occupation, and all of his wealth and valuables. Silver and gold were usually placed in his mouth, hands, and bosom, or other places. They celebrated the anniversary of the man's death by coming at certain times to the tomb. Opening it, they put new clothing and fresh food in place of what had been put there before, and they offered some sacrifices. As soon as they entered into this land, the Spaniards were possessed by the lust to have the treasures buried with the Indians. The Spaniards were moved to search for and open the tombs. In some instances, they have taken much wealth in gold and silver from them. The way of putting the body into the tomb was not the same everywhere. In the Valley of Jauja, the body was placed in a fresh llama skin, and it was sewn up so as to show the face with the nose, mouth, and the rest. In Chincha, the burial was performed with the bodies placed on *barbacoas*, a cane framework of a bed. But most of the kingdom followed the custom of the Incas and natives of Cuzco, who buried their dead seated on the ground, the head over the knees, and if they were lords, they were placed on their *duhos* or low benches. After the burial was finished, the deceased's wives and servants who were not buried with him cut their hair short and dressed in the most ordinary and shabby clothes that they had, with little care for their personal appearance.

The funeral rites and burial of the king were celebrated in the same way, but with a large and magnificent gathering. At death, his family unit took charge of him, and before all else they took out his entrails and put them in a safe place with great solemnity and public lamentations, which lasted many days. At this time they had great drinking bouts with dances and mournful songs. They visited the places where the deceased usually went for his recreation; his relatives would carry in their hands his garments and weapons, telling in the dirges and sad songs of the heroic deeds that he had done with his weapons, and the victories and trophies that he had achieved, recounting his laudable customs, his virtues and his generosity with everyone. They killed the wives whom he liked the most and the servants whom he seemed to need here in this world as well as different officials and servants from each occupation. Their love for their king was so sincere that they willingly offered their lives, considering themselves fortunate to accompany their king, and if someone refused to accompany the king, he was considered to be an infamous traitor, and such women were held to be adulteresses. For this [funeral ceremony] they did a solemn dance; for it all those who were to die dressed in their most elegant garments and adornments, and they danced and drank wildly, and when they were quite drunk, they were strangled, and with songs made up for this purpose, they were told that since they served the lord Inca in this life, they should serve him in the other life [also]. They say that the reason for introducing such a cruel

custom was so that the souls of the kings would not go alone without anyone to accompany and serve them. And the devil, being so
fond of shedding human blood, in order to establish the custom
more firmly, would sometimes appear in the countryside in the
form of the dead lords and kings accompanied by their wives and
servants.

The dead body was embalmed with great skill; much time was
spent in preserving it; this was done with such care and skill that
two hundred years after death when some of them were found in
Cuzco, the bodies were so complete and the hair so well fixed and
preserved that it seemed that they had died less than a month before. The faces were always kept covered, wrapped in a large
amount of cotton, and they were richly dressed. At first the bodies
were not kept with so much adornment because some very old
bodies found had been placed in small copper bars covered on the
outside with woven *cabuya* fiber in such a way that the only part
visible was the face. They handed over to the servants all of the
service of gold and silver and all of the clothing that the deceased
had accumulated in his lifetime; with this clothing the body was
always kept very well dressed, and the servants wore it also; none
of it was given to the heirs. Part of this treasure was kept with the
body, and part of it was buried in the places where the deceased
usually went to enjoy himself. They said that since these things
were made for the Inca's use when he was alive, no other person
should use them after his death; these things should always be
known as his property and remain at the service of their owner.

Notes

FOREWORD

1. J. H. Rowe, "An Account of the Shrines of Ancient Cuzco," Ñawpa Pacha 17 (1979): 1–80 (Berkeley: 1980); Institute of Andean Studies, "La constitución inca del Cuzco," Histórica 9, no. 1 (July 1985): 35–73 (Lima).

BOOK I

1. See Father Cobo's History of the Inca Empire, pp. 43–46, where he classifies the Indians of the New World into three types of barbarians or primitive people, according to their social and political organization: small loosely organized groups of hunters and gatherers, larger communities of farmers under a single cacique, and the highly organized states under a powerful ruler such as the Inca Empire.
2. See Chapter 5 ahead for a description of the Inca sun worship.
3. See Chapter 3 ahead for a description of Viracocha, the creator god.
4. The Quichua word guaca or huaca designates anyone or anything sacred or believed to have some supernatural power. It was applicable to certain objects, shrines, and people. See ahead especially Chapters 7–11.
5. The Biblical chronology most likely used by Cobo puts Creation around 4000 B.C. and the Flood at about 2300 B.C.
6. The word guacamaya refers to the macaw.
7. See History of the Inca Empire, pp. 103–107.
8. Viracocha is probably best analyzed as a title with no secondary meaning. Thus, Viracocha Yachachic would be rendered as "Viracocha the Creator." For a discussion of the titles of the Creator, see John H. Rowe's article, "The origins of Creator worship among the Incas," in Culture in History, ed. Stanley Diamond (New York: Columbia University Press, 1960), pp. 408–429.
9. Inca Yupanqui refers to Pachacutic Inca Yupanqui, ninth Inca.
10. As John H. Rowe pointed out in the "Foreword" to the History of the Inca Empire, Cobo was mistaken in placing the Chanca attack during the time of Viracocha Inca. Both the victory over the Chanca and the elevation of Viracocha to the status of supreme god should be attributed to Pachacutic.
11. Father Cobo evidently did not check out these references to his own work because the first should be Chapter 10 and the second Chapter 12; see History of the Inca Empire, pp. 128–129 and pp. 134–135.
12. See above note 9.
13. The mamaconas were cloistered women who served the Inca gods. For more details, see ahead Chapter 37.

14. This image was probably placed on the exterior of the east-facing wall located now in the courtyard of the church of Santo Domingo.
15. The Quichua term *ceque* means a line of any kind.
16. See ahead Chapters 13–16 for an account of the shrines of Cuzco.
17. The *ayllo* was an extended family or lineage believed to have a common ancestor.
18. This refers to the Aristotelian or scholastic divisions used in natural philosophy. The simple bodies or elements were air, water, earth, and fire. The perfectly mixed elements were divided into inanimate, including stones and metals, and animate, including plants and animals. This can be diagrammed as follows:
    Elements
    I. Simple: air, water, earth, and fire.
    II. Perfectly mixed
        A. Inanimate: stones, metal, etc.
        B. Animate
            1. Plants
            2. Animals
                a. Rational: man
                b. Irrational: all others
19. Father Cobo evidently did not check out this reference because it should be Chapter 10. See *History of the Inca Empire*, pp. 128–129. See also glossary under *pururaucas*.
20. See ahead Chapters 13–16 of this book.
21. The *orejon* was an adult male of Inca nobility privileged to wear large ear spools. The term is a Spanish nickname meaning "big ears." Spanish writers commonly equated the *orejones* with European knights.
22. See above note 4.
23. The Thunder, a major Inca deity, is described in Chapter 7 of this book.
24. The piles of stones located at the *apachitas* were accumulations of offerings made by travelers.
25. The word *coya* properly means a vein or lode of ore in this context.
26. The word *mama* means nugget here, and *corpa* refers to a large piece of ore.
27. *Soroche* designates a lead ore containing very small amounts of silver which was mixed with silver ore in the process of extracting the pure silver.
28. This refers to the Huatanay River.
29. This square was called Limapampa.
30. Chapters 13–16 are an account of the shrines of Cuzco. For a thorough analysis and translation, see J. H. Rowe's "An Account of the Shrines of Ancient Cuzco," in *Ñawpa Pacha* 17 (1979): 1–80 (Berkeley: Institute of Andean Studies, 1980).
31. Pacaritampu, located southeast of Cuzco, is a prominent place in the origin myths of the Incas. See *History of the Inca Empire*, pp. 103–107.

32. The fortress is Sacsahuaman, located on a hill just north of Cuzco.
33. See ahead Chapter 25 of this book for a description of this festival.
34. The word *buhio* is used in Spanish to designate a one-room native hut with a thatch roof.
35. The sheep used for sacrifice were llamas or alpacas. There were no sheep in South America until the arrival of the Europeans.
36. Huanacauri or Guanacauri was a major Inca deity associated with a hill of the same name located south of Cuzco. See ahead Chapter 15, Co-6:7.
37. The Spanish word *cesto* means literally basket, but as applied to units of coca leaves, it refers to a package or closed unit for shipping, usually by llama. The exact size is unknown, but several *cestos* were carried by a llama.
38. The terms *puna* and *paramo* are synonyms meaning high altitude grasslands in Cobo's usage. *Puna* is from Quichua and *paramo* from Spanish.
39. See above note 34.
40. Cobo's description is of the Pachacama Temple of the Sun. The term Pachacama was applied to the entire complex by Cobo, as it still is today. However, there is a separate Temple of Pachacama at the site not described by Cobo. See Max Uhle, *Pachacama*, report of the William Pepper M.D., LL.D., Peruvian Expedition of 1896, translated by C. Grosse (Philadelphia, 1903), especially pp. 10–11, note 9.
41. Each *estado* equals the height of the average man, about five feet six inches. This term is used for vertical measurements.
42. The Castilian league used here equals about three miles.
43. *Mitimaes* or *mitima*, anyone living in someplace other than his or her place of ethnic origin, anybody who was moved to a region or province of a different ethnic group, sometimes even applied to Spaniards.
44. *Chicha* was an alcoholic beverage made by fermenting maize, other seeds, or fruits.
45. Since the alder (Alnus family) is not an indigenous tree in the Lake Titicaca area, the term is used here as a general reference to a shade tree.
46. Father Cobo refers to his geographical study of the Andes. He made a classification of some six zones according to differences in flora, fauna, and climate. The first zone is the puna, the highest lands of the Andes. The second level is the high plain known as the altiplano. See *Historia del Nuevo Mundo*, Book 2, Chapters 10–17, not translated.
47. See *History of the Inca Empire*, p. 141, where Father Cobo states that the Inca Pachacuti first saw Tiahuanaco and ordered his men to take note of the building method used there.
48. Father Cobo had good reasons for believing in the existence of giants. Genesis 6 states that "giants were upon the earth" before the Flood. Many classical authors also mention giants, and some of the most respected chroniclers state that giants were present in America. Chroniclers such as Pedro Cieza de León said the fossil bones at Punta Santa

Elena, on the coast of modern Ecuador, were from giants.

49. See *History of the Inca Empire*, p. 95, where Father Cobo tells how he measured the head of one of these statues.

50. The encomendero or grantee was authorized by the Spanish Crown to require the Indians of a certain place to perform labor service and give tribute. The encomendero was supposed to Europeanize the Indians.

51. See Chapters 13–16 of this book.

52. The *sisa* was an excise tax on foodstuffs.

53. See above Chapter 1, where Father Cobo explains that the first cause is God, who created all things, and the second causes are the sun, water, earth, etc., which are necessary for sustaining life.

54. See *History of the Inca Empire*, p. 252, where Father Cobo describes the function of these pillars which were called *sucanca*.

55. The *apachitas* were high places and hill tops found along a road. See note 24 and Chapter 11.

56. The Inca calendar was a day-count calendar of twelve months of 30 days each, some of which had extra days added to make up a total of 365 days in the year. The length of the year was determined by solar observation at the solstices, and an extra day was added to adjust for leap year. Information provided in personal communication by Professor John H. Rowe, correcting an earlier section of his article "Inca Culture at the Time of the Spanish Conquest," in *Handbook of South American Indians*, ed. Julian Steward, vol. 2 (Washington, D.C.: Smithsonian Institution, 1946), pp. 327–328.

57. *Cabuya* is a fiber made from agave or maguey cactus.

58. *Quinua* refers here to a tree of the Peruvian highlands (*Polylepis australis*) which is about the size of a European olive. See Cobo's *Historia del Nuevo Mundo*, Book 6, Chapter 128. The word *quinua* has a homonym which is the name of an Andean plant cultivated for its grain. In Spanish this tree is usually called *queñua*.

59. The *tocto* is probably a type of owl.

60. This refers to the Huatanay and the Tullumayo rivers, at the southeastern end of Cuzco.

61. *Yanaconas* were retainers or persons serving someone of rank.

62. The *aravi* or *yaraví* was a narrative song about some important event of the past. See ahead Book II, Chapter 17.

63. *Mamazara* is a compound word, *mama*, mother, and *zara*, maize, meaning the maize deity.

64. The *quishuar* tree (*Buddleia longifolia*) is found in the Peruvian highlands. See Cobo's *Historia del Nuevo Mundo*, Book 6, Chapter 39, where he says that it is similar to the European olive.

65. See above Chapter 10 of this book.

66. See *History of the Inca Empire*, pp. 103–107.

67. This reference is not found in the published works of the Licentiate Juan Polo de Ondegardo. Father Cobo had access to a report on Inca

religion that Polo wrote in 1559. All that remains is an extract with the following title: "Tratado sobre los errores y supersticiones de los indios"; it was published in the *Confesionario para los curas de indios* (Lima, 1585).

68. The term *vilca* here refers to a tree (*Anadenanthera colubrina*) and its seeds which were used in making this *chicha*. See Cobo's *Historia del Nuevo Mundo*, Book 6, Chapter 89.

69. *Ariolo* is a Hispanicized Latin term not found in Spanish dictionaries. The Latin is "hariolus" or "ariolus," a soothsayer or prophet. However, it has been translated as "oracle-monger" in a passage from Cicero's *De Natura Deorum*, Loeb Classical Library, pp. 54–55.

70. See *History of the Inca Empire*, pp. 236–238.

BOOK II

1. The eight parts of speech would be as follows: noun (substantive and adjective), pronoun, verb, adverb, participle, infinitive, preposition, and conjunction.

2. The reference here is to the *Doctrina christiana y catecismo para instrucción de los indios . . . compuesto por auctoridad del Concilio Provincial, que se celebro en la Ciudad de los Reyes, el año 1583* (Antonio Ricardo, primero impressor en estos Reynos del Pirú, 1584). This is a bilingual catechism in Spanish and Quichua. It is also the first book published in the Viceroyalty of Peru.

3. Father Cobo evidently did not check this out. The reference is actually found in Book 11, Chapter 3, of his *Historia del Nuevo Mundo*. For a translation, see *History of the Inca Empire*, pp. 13–16.

4. See *History of the Inca Empire*, p. 197.

5. *Usuta* is one of the Hispanicized versions of this word meaning sandal. The form used elsewhere by Cobo is *ojota*.

6. The *palmo* or span equals the length of the hand from the tip of the thumb to the tip of the little finger, roughly eight inches. The *vara* or Spanish yard equals four *palmos* or about thirty-three inches. These measurements refer to the size of the piece of cloth laid out flat on the loom. Thus the cloth for the average tunic would measure roughly twenty-four inches wide (three and one-half *palmos*) and sixty-six inches long (two *varas*). It was worn like a poncho with the sides stitched up. See John H. Rowe's "Standardization in Inca Tapestry Tunics," in *The Junius B. Bird Pre-Columbian Textile Conference* (Washington, D.C.: Textile Museum, Dumbarton Oaks, 1979), pp. 239–264.

7. The *tercia* is one-third of a *vara* or approximately eleven inches.

8. The *geme* is the distance from the tip of the outstretched thumb to the tip of the forefinger, roughly six inches.

9. *Galpon* is a large one-room storehouse or shed.

10. *Bahareque* refers to a house having walls of poles interwoven with slender branches or reeds.
11. See note 41 of Book I.
12. *Guaca* means shrine here. See note 4 of Book I.
13. *Buhio* means hut. See note 34, Book I.
14. *Hicho* is a type of coarse bunch grass common in the Andes.
15. *Chuño* is a freeze-dried potato food.
16. *Quinua* is a grain of the Andean highlands.
17. *Cabuya* is a fiber. See note 57 of Book I.
18. See *History of the Inca Empire*, pp. 27–28.
19. See above notes 15 and 16, Chapter 4.
20. See *History of the Inca Empire*, pp. 27–28.
21. Most Inca towns were divided into two sections called *hanansaya* and *hurinsaya*. For an explanation of this subdivision, see *History of the Inca Empire*, pp. 195–196.
22. *Acllas* were chosen women, selected at about eight or nine years of age. *Mamaconas* were cloistered women who trained the *acllas*. For more details, see Book I, Chapter 37, of this work.
23. See Book I, Chapter 10, of this work.
24. The Chunchos were a group located in the forests east of Lake Titicaca on the border of the Inca Empire.
25. The Spanish name *pege tamborino* or *tamboril* may refer to the puffer or globe-fish. See Cobo's *Historia del Nuevo Mundo*, Book 7, Chapter 34.
26. *Manzanilla* refers to the poisonous apple-like fruit of the tropical American manchineal tree. See Cobo's *Historia del Nuevo Mundo*, Book 6, Chapter 32.
27. The word *ayllo* used here for this weapon and the word for lineage are homonyms. The Spanish word for the weapon is *bolas* or *boleadoras*.
28. The *braza* is the stretch of a person's arms, about five and one-half feet.
29. Father Cobo refers to the Hippocratic theory of pathology. A healthy body has a balance of "hot" and "cold" essences contained in the four humors, phlegm, blood, black bile, and yellow bile. An imbalance of "hot" and "cold" essences causes illness. For more details, see George M. Foster, "Relationships between Spain and Spanish-American Folk Medicine," *Journal of American Folklore* 66 (1953): 201–217.
30. See Cobo, *History of the Inca Empire*, pp. 17–19.
31. See note 29 above.
32. An encomienda was a grant by the Spanish crown of Indian vassals. The Indians were required to perform labor service and give tribute. See also note 50 of Book I.
33. *Repartimiento* was the distribution of Indians for labor service. Often used interchangeably with encomienda, repartimiento refers only to the system of forced labor imposed on the Indians.

34. The term "llama" is used here to include both the common llama and the wooly alpaca.
35. See above note 6.
36. The term *yunca* refers to the humid lowlands east of the Andes.
37. The term *gorboran* apparently comes from *gorbion* or *gurbion*, a silk twist thread fabric of fine wool.
38. The *cumbi camayo* was a craftsman who made fine cloth for the Inca.
39. The *mamaconas* were cloistered women. For more details, see Book I, Chapter 38, of this work.
40. Two or three *estados* is about eleven to sixteen feet. See note 41 of Book I.
41. This is an exaggeration. Inca builders did use the plumb bob and perhaps other implements like a square.
42. See note 41 of Book I.
43. Father Cobo refers to a part of his *Historia del Nuevo Mundo* that has been lost.
44. Tierra Firme refers to the northern part of South America, including modern Colombia and Venezuela.
45. Each *braza* is about 5½ feet. This makes the *topo* about 275 feet long and 138 feet wide.
46. See above, Book I, note 42.
47. Father Cobo describes these fresh water fishes briefly in his *Historia del Nuevo Mundo*, Book 7, Chapters 39 and 43. The *armadillo* is a type of armored catfish up to about sixteen inches long. The *sabalo* is a medium-sized characin with large scales. The *dorado* is a large characin that resembles a salmon in form. See Gilmore, "Fauna of Neotropica," in *Handbook of South American Indians*, vol. 6, p. 413.
48. No information has been found about how these games were played.

Glossary Loan words from American Indian languages: Q, *Quichua*; A, *Aymara*; T, *Taino*; and N, *Nahuatl*

abasca. Q. The coarse wool cloth used for ordinary clothing.

aclla. Q. Chosen women. *Acllas* were selected at about eight or nine years of age.

acllaguaci. Q. House of the chosen women.

agi or *aji.* T. Capsicum pepper. A condiment like chile.

anacu. Q. Women's dress. It extended from the neck to the feet and was fastened with pins.

Ancochinchay. Q. A star of uncertain identification.

antara. Q. A small panpipe.

apachita. Q. High places and hilltops found along a road. *Apachitas* were considered deities and offerings were made to them.

apaytalla. Q. A game. There is no information about how it was played.

aporuco. Q. An old llama used for sacrifice.

apu. Q. Lord, a person of great power and authority.

apupanaca. Q. Commissioner assigned by the Inca to pick out the girls who were to fill the ranks of the *acllas.*

aravi or *arabi.* Q. A festive song that tells of someone's past exploits.

asiro. A. Serpent. A nickname for a boy. The Quichua term is *amaro.*

atuna. Uncertain origin. Wooden implement used by women to break up dirt clods.

ayarichic. Probably Q. A panpipe made of canes graded in length.

ayllo or *ayllu.* Q. An extended family or lineage believed to have a common ancestor.

ayllo. Q. A weapon made of cords with weights of stone or copper attached at the ends. It was used in war at fairly close range to entangle the enemy's feet. It was also used in hunting. This word and the word above meaning "lineage" are homonyms. The Spanish word for the weapon is *bolas* or *boleadoras.*

bahareque. Prob. T. A wall of poles interwoven with slender branches or reeds. A house with such walls.

barbacoa. Prob. T. A cane framework used as a bed. The same term is also applied to the grill used for roasting meat or fish.

buhio. T. House. Used in Spanish to designate an Indian hut with a thatched roof.

cabuya. T. Fiber of the agave or maguey cactus.

cachua. Q. The warrior's dance. Performed on solemn occasions by men and women with joined hands.

cacique. T. A native chief.

callacha. Prob. Q. The flat stone base of the grinding mill. See also *maray.*

camasca. Q. Healer or doctor.

camayo or *camayu.* Q. Official.

canipo. Q. Metal disk used as a chest or head ornament by soldiers.

canoe. T. Native boat made from a hollowed-out tree trunk or from three boards. The Hispanicized term used in the Cobo manuscript is *"canoa."*

caquingora. Uncertain origin. A bird like an ibis.

Catachillay. Q. The Southern Cross.

caycu. Q. Hunting technique. Animals such as the guanaco were driven into fenced-off gorges, where they were captured.

cayo. Uncertain origin. A certain dance.

ceiba. T. *Ceiba pentandra.* The large tropical silk-cotton or kapok tree. Spelled *ceyba* by Cobo. The standard spelling in both Spanish and English is *ceiba.*

ceque. Q. A line of any kind. Used specifically with reference to lines marking the shrines of Cuzco.

Chacana. Q. A group of three stars which make up the belt in Orion, called the Tres Marías in Spanish.

chacara. Q. A piece of ground or field under cultivation.

chaco. Q. Public hunt in which several thousand men made a great circle and drove wild animals toward the center; designated hunters would go in when the circle was small and kill as many animals as desired.

champi. Q. One of the Inca's royal insignias. A mace with which the Inca fought in wars.

chanrara. Q. Little copper or silver bells.

chaquira. Uncertain origin, but prob. from the Indians of Panama. Thin beads usually made from seashells.

charqui. Q. Dried llama meat.

chicha. Uncertain origin, but prob. from an Indian language of Panama. Any of various alcoholic beverages made by fermenting maize, other seeds, or fruits.

chipana. Q. Bracelet.

chonta. Q. *Bactris utilis.* The peach palm, a spiny-trunked palm with hard dark wood.

chua. Prob. Q. Medium-sized earthen casserole.

chuco. Q. A knitted cap. Called *chullo* in Spanish today.

chumpi. Q. Sash worn by women around the waist.

chuncara. Q. A board game played with beads.

chuño. Q. Freeze-dried potatoes.

Chuquichinchay. Prob. Q. A star of uncertain identification.

churu. Q. Snail-shell bells or rattle.

chusi. Q. Coarse cloth used for blankets. The Hispanicized plural is *chuses.*

chuspa. Q. A small square bag carried by men.

ciracuna. Q. Needle, usually made from a thorn, bone, or copper.

coa. T. A kind of spade. It was called *lampa* in Quichua.

coca. Q. *Erythroxylon coca.* A plant similar to a rosebush or the leaves of this plant, which contain a stimulating narcotic. The Andean Indians chewed these leaves. The word *coca* is used in both Spanish and English.

Collca. Q. The Pleiades.

collca. Q. A large storehouse. This word and the word above are homonyms.

collo. Q. A dry measure of approx. 4 quarts, usually a large calabash.

concho. Q. Dark *chicha.*

Coricancha. Q. House or enclosure of gold. Located in Cuzco, this was the most sacred Inca shrine.

coya. Q. Queen or principal wife of the Inca.

coya. Q. A vein or lode of ore. This word and the word above are homonyms.

cui. Q. *Cavia.* The common cavy or guinea pig. It was an important domesticated animal in ancient Peru.

cumbi. Q. The first quality of wool cloth made for the Inca.

cumbi camayo. Q. Craftsmen who made fine cloth and clothing for the Inca. *Cumbi* means "fine cloth" and *camayo,* "official."

cuntur. Q. Variant of the word *condor.* A nickname for a boy.

cuspar. Q. This verb is a Hispanicized form of the northern Quichua verb *cuspani.*

duho. T. A low stool or bench which was a symbol of high public office.

guaca. Q. Any object, place, or person worshiped as a deity. The Incas had numerous such shrines or sacred things, including temples, burial places, idols, stones, and springs.

guacamaya. T. Macaw. Large, bright-colored parrot.

guaci. Q. House.

guacon. Q. A common dance performed by men who wore masks and carried animal skins or dried animals.

guaman. Q. Hawk. A nickname for a boy.

guanaco. Q. *Lama guanicoe.* The larger wild species of llama.

guanco. A. *Cavia.* The guinea pig or *cui.*

guanear. Hispanicized verb from the Quichua *guano.*

guano. Q. A fertilizer from the excrement of seafowl.

guara. Q. Loincloth, a symbol of manhood that was put on at about the age of 14 as part of a maturity rite called Guarachicuy.

guaraca. Q. Sling. One of the major long-range weapons used by the Incas.

Guarachicuy. Q. Maturity rite held for boys. See above *guara.*

guari. Q. A certain dance performed as part of the boy's maturity rite.

guauque. Q. Brother. Also an image taken by the Inca emperors as their personal guardian.

guayara. Apparently a variation of *guayyaya;* see below.

guayaturilla. Q. A certain dance for both men and women.

guayra. Q. A furnace used to melt silver.

guayyaya. Q. Inca family dance. Men and women joined hands and formed long lines, doing a dignified step.

hammock. T. A hanging bed. The Hispanicized equivalent used in the Cobo manuscript is *hamaca.*

hanansaya. Q. Upper moiety or subdivision of most Inca towns and provinces. See also *hurinsaya.*

haylli. Q. Farmer's dance. Men and women participated while carrying their agricultural implements.

hicho. Q. Stipa. Puna grass. Coarse bunch grass common in the Andean highlands.

huacanqui. Q. A love charm.

huancar. Q. Drum.

huancartinya. Q. A tambourine or small drum. The term *tinya* has the same meaning. *Huancar* means drum.

huminta. Q. Small cakes made of maize flour.

hurinsaya. Q. Lower moiety or subdivision of most Inca towns and provinces. See also *hanansaya.*

Inca. Q. King or emperor. A member of the royal *ayllos* or nobility.

inti. Q. Sun, a major deity.

lampa. Q. A kind of spade with a narrow blade which was used for planting seeds and weeding.

llacta. Q. Town.

llallahua. Q. Potatoes of peculiar form which were worshiped.

llama. Q. *Lama glama.* The well-known domestic animal of South America, used as a beast of burden and a source of wool. It was also important for sacrifice in religious ceremonies. Cobo uses the term *llama* to include both domestic species: *Lama glama,* the common llama described here and *Lama paco,* the alpaca, used only for wool.

llanca. Q. Clay.

llauto. Q. A wool headband worn by the Indians of Cuzco and all those of Inca lineage. It was not a symbol of royalty but was used to support the royal fringe which was called *maxcapaycha.*

lliclla. Q. A large mantle worn by women over the dress.

llimpi. Q. Mercuric ore or vermilion.

locro. Q. A stew of meat, potatoes, *chuño,* vegetables, and lots of capsicum peppers.

macana. T. A sword-shaped double-edged war club made of hardwood.

Machacuay. Q. A star of uncertain identification. This is also a general term meaning "snake."

maize. T. *Zea mays.* The native name for the corn of America. The Spanish equivalent used in the Cobo manuscript is *maiz.*

mamacona. Q. Cloistered women dedicated to the service of the Inca gods. These women also trained the newly chosen girls, the *acllas,* in household occupations such as spinning, weaving, and cooking. The word *mama* meant mother, and the suffix *cona* can mean either plural or a member of a class. Cobo uses the Hispanicized plural *mamaconas.*

Mamana. Prob. Q. A star of uncertain identification.

mamazara. Q. Maize mother, a special storage bin made of maize stalks; it was a deity.

mani. T. Peanut.

maray. Q. A stone mill for grinding grain.

marca. A. Town.

mati. Q. The calabash. Used as a vessel or bowl.

meca. Q. A wooden plate.

Miquiquiray. Prob. Q. A star of uncertain identification.

Mirco. Prob. Q. A star of uncertain identification.

mitimaes. Q. The Hispanicized plural of the term *mitima*. Anyone living in some place other than his or her place of ethnic origin, even sometimes applied to Spaniards.

motepatasca. Q. A stew made from maize, herbs, and capsicum peppers.

napa. Q. The sacred white llama of the Inca.

ojota or *usuta.* Q. Footwear of sandals.

oroya. Prob. Q. A type of bridge made of a single rope. Passengers or goods were pulled across in a basket.

palla. Q. A woman of the Inca nobility.

pampacona. Q. A fine piece of cloth used as a headdress by women.

papa. Q. Potato.

pata. Q. Agricultural terrace used for farming hillsides.

petaca. N. Case or chest.

pichca. Q. Five. A game scored with a single die marked with one to five points.

pilcopata. Prob. Q. A feather diadem worn above the forehead.

pincollo. Q. A small flute.

piraguas. Prob. from a Caribbean language. A large canoe.

pirua. A. A small bin made of maize stalks plastered with mud. Grain was stored in it.

piscancalla. Q. Toasted maize.

pisco. Q. Bird, especially a small one.

piscoynu. Q. A spinning top.

pisqui. Q. A stew made with *quinoa* grain and vegetables.

pitahaya. T. A type of cactus pear.

pucu. Q. An earthen plate.

puma or *poma.* Q. Mountain Lion. A nickname for a boy. This same term is also the name of a certain game.

punchao. Q. Day. Also the name of an image of the Sun god.

puñuna. Q. Bed.

puquiu. Q. A spring or fountain.

pururaucas. Q. Name given to certain stones that were worshiped and believed to act as soldiers for the Inca. According to Cobo the term means "hidden thieves." *Auca* means "enemy, soldier," or possibly "thief," but the sense of "hidden" is not found for *puru* in any of the Quichua dictionaries or vocabularies.

quenaquena. Q and A. A flute made usually of a joint of cane. The abbreviated form *quena* is used today in Spanish.

quencha. Q. A wall of poles interwoven with slender branches or reeds. A house with such walls. This is the Quichua term for *bahareque.*

quepa. Q. A gourd trumpet.

quero. A. A wooden drinking tumbler.

Quiantopa. Prob. Q. A star of uncertain identification.

quilla. Q. [*sic; aquilla*] A silver drinking tumbler.

quinua. Q. *Polylepsis australis.* A tree of the Peruvian highlands which is about the size of the European olive.

quinua. Q. *Chenopodium quinoa.* A plant cultivated for its seeds in the higher lands of the Andes, where it replaces maize. Usually spelled *quinoa* in English, it is a homonym in Quichua for the word above meaning a certain tree.

quipe. Q. Knapsack.

quirau. Q. Cradle.

quishuar. Q. *Buddleia longifolia.* A medium-sized tree of the Peruvian highlands which resembles a European olive.

sanco. Q. A porridge of partly ground maize.

savanna. T. Grassland, open plain. The Spanish equivalent used in the manuscript is *sabana.*

soncoyoc. Q. Stout-hearted man. Healer or doctor.

soroche. Q. A lead ore used in extracting pure silver.

sundorpauca. Q. This appears to be a misnomer in the sense of "pouch." See below *sunturpaucar.*

sunturpaucar or *sundorpauca.* Q. A staff covered from top to bottom with small feathers of different colors; three of the feathers rose from the top. This staff was one of the royal symbols of the Inca.

suyu. Q. A section or division of land assigned to one man and his family for their share of agricultural labor. This same word is also used in the toponym Tahuantinsuyu, "Land of the Four Quarters," the Inca name for their empire.

tacanaco. Prob. Q. A game played with a single die and beans.

taclla. Q. Foot plow.

tambo. Q. A station with shelter or lodging and storehouses. *Tambos* were located at convenient intervals along the Inca roads.

tanay. Q. The top stone of the mill for grinding grain. See also *maray.*

taqui. Q. Dance and song. The term refers to both activities. Almost all Inca music included singing and dancing.

tiana. Q. Chair.

tocto. Q. Little white feathers used in a ceremony. Also means a type of owl.

Topatoraca. Prob. Q. A star of uncertain identification.

topo or *tupu.* Q. Large pins of copper, silver, or gold used by women to fasten their clothing.

topo. Q. Measurement of farm land. An area 50 *brazas* long and 25 wide. Each *braza* equals the stretch of a man's arms or about 5 feet 6 inches. This word and the word above meaning a pin are homonyms.

tuna. T. A type of cactus pear. See also *pitahaya.*

umu. Q. Diviner.

uncu. Q. Tunic worn as a sleeveless shirt by men.

Urcuchillay. Q. The constellation Lira.

usuta. Q. A variant of *ojota,* sandal.

uta. A. House.

vicuña. Q. *Lama vicugna.* The smaller wild species of llama. See also *guanaco.*

vilaoma. Q. Hispanicized version of *villac umu.* See below.

vilca. Q. Anything regarded as a deity. See *guaca,* which is a synonym in more common use.

vilca. Q. *Piptadenia colubrina.* A tree and its seeds which are used in making a type of *chicha* or alcoholic beverage. This word and the word above meaning a deity are homonyms.

vilca camayo. Q. Religious official responsible for the *guaca* or *guacas* at a certain place.

villac umu. Q. High priest. *Villac* means, "he who speaks," and *umu* means "diviner."

vilque. Q. Large drinking tumblers made of gold or silver.

vincha. Q. Headband about the breadth of a finger worn by women.

Viracocha. Q. Creator of the world. He was the Inca's major deity, and he was also known as Viracocha Yachachic, "Viracocha the Creator," or Pachayachachic, "Creator of the World." After the arrival of the Spaniards, the term *viracocha* was applied to the Europeans in contrast to the Indians, who were known as *runa,* person.

yacarca. Q. Diviner by fire.

yacolla. Q. A large cloak or mantle worn by men over the tunic.

yaguayra. Prob. Q. A certain dance.

yanacona. Q. Retainers. As officials of the Inca government, they were exempt from the *mita* labor service. *Yana* means "retainer"; the suffix *cona* can indicate either plural or a member of a class.

yauri. Prob. Q. A palm wood staff. See also *champi,* which was similar.

yunca. Q. Hot, humid lowlands. The term is applied to the lands east of the Andes. It is used as an adjective: *temple yunca* and *provincias yuncas.* Unlike a number of other writers of the Sixteenth and Seventeenth Centuries Cobo never uses *yunca* to refer to the coastal desert of Peru. In Cobo's usage, *yunca* Indians are those who inhabit the eastern Andes.

yutu. Q. A type of partridge present in the Andes.

zacapa. Q. Little bells that the women wore on their ankles.

zupay. Q. Devil.

Index

Indexes for the Shrines of Cuzco
BOOK I: *Chapters 13–16*

Modified from J. H. Rowe, "An Account of the Shrines of Ancient Cuzco."

Index of *Guaca* Names

The alphabetical order is that of Spanish: *ch* follows *c*, *ll* follows *l*, and *ñ* follows *n*. For two *guacas* in the list, no Inca names are given in the text; these *guacas* will be found under "*pared*" (wall) and "*quebrada*" (ravine). In the case of "Piccho," it is not clear from the text whether this place name is also the name of the *guaca*.

Acoyguaci, Co-6:3
Achatarque Puquiu, Cu-1:9
Amarocti, Cu-4:2
Amaromarcaguaci, An-1:7
Anaguarque, Cu-1:7
Anahuarque Guaman, Cu-1:10
Anaypampa, Co-3:5
Ancasamaro, Co-5:5
Apian, Cu-6:1
Apuyauira, Ch-9:6
Aquarsayba, An-5:7
Araytampu, Ch-4:1
Arosayapuquiu, An-5:6
Aspadquiri, Ch-8:11
Ataguanacauri, An-9:5
Atpitan, Co-1:6
Auacospuquiu, An-8:4
Aucanpuquiu, An-4:5
Aucapapirqui, An-2:6
Aucaypata, Ch-5:4
Aucaypata [Paccha], Ch-8:3
Auriauca, An-6:1
Autviturco, An-1:4
Ayacho, An-3:3
Ayavillay, Co-4:5, Co-4:6
Ayllipampa, An-7:1
Aypanospacha, Ch-9:1

Cachaocachiri, Co-9:11
Cachicalla, Cu-8:7

Cachipuquiu, An-5:2
Cajana, Ch-6:5
Calispuquio, Ch-3:8
Calispuquio Guaci, Ch-3:7
Callachaca, An-4:3
Callancapuquiu, Ch-7:6
Cancha, Cu-10:3
Canchapacha, Ch-3:2
Capi [Çapi], Ch-6:7
Capipacchan [Çapi Pacchan], Ch-6:6
Caquia Sabaraura, Cu-3:2
Caribamba, Co-1:4
Caripuquiu, An-3:7
Caritampucancha, Cu-5:1
Cariurco, An-4:1
Caruinca Cancha, Cu-7:3
Cascasayba, An-2:9
Catachillay, Ch-8:10
Catonge, Ch-6:1, Co-5:1
Cauadcalla, Cu-8:14
Cauas, Cu-8:3
Cayallacta, Cu-5:3
Cayaopuquiu, Cu-4:3
Cayascas Guaman, Cu-3:3
Caynaconga, An-2:7
Cicacalla, Co-5:4
Cicui, Cu-8:10
Cinca, Ch-5:9
Cirocaya, Ch-1:4
Coapapuquiu, Co-8:6

Vilcaraypuquiu, Co-7 : 6
Viracocha, An-4 : 4
Viracochacancha, Co-6 : 5
Viracochapuquiu, An-6 : 5
Viracochaurco, Cu-10 : 4
Vircaypay, Co-7 : 4

Viroypacha, Ch-2 : 4

Yamarpuquiu, Cu-1 : 11
Yancaycalla [Yuncaycalla], An-3 : 9
Yuncaypampa, An-3 : 8
Yuyotuyro, Ch-9 : 10

Index of *Ayllus*

Ayllus *in Charge of* Ceques

Ayllu	Ceque	Classi-fication	Other Ayllus and "Indios"
Aguini Ayllu	Co-1	Cayao	Acabicas [Alcabiças], Co-9 : 1
Apu Mayta	Co-4	Cayao	Andasaya (*ayllo*), Ch-4 : 4
Aucailli Panaca	An-4	Collana	Ayamarca (*indios*), Ch-5 : 9
Capac Ayllu	Ch-7	Cayao	Ayavillay (*ayllu*), Co-4 : 5
Cari	An-9	Cayao	Chachapoyas (*indios*), Co-7 : 4
Cubcu [Çubçu]			Goalla (*indios*), An-1 : 4
Pañaca Ayllu	An-1	Collana	Inacapanaca (*ayllo*), Ch-5 : 1
Chima Panaca	Cu-5	Cayao	Maras (*ayllo*), Ch-9 : 5
Goacaytaqui	Ch-1	Cayao	
Haguayni	Co-2	Payan	
Quisco	Cu-2	Cayao	
Usca Mayta	Co-7	Cayao	
Vicaquirao	Ch-2	Payan	

Index of Named Places

Named places that are *guacas* are listed as such in the index of *guaca* names.

Acoyapunco (cf. Angostura), An-9 : 2
Alca, Cu-9 : 3
Anaguarque—*cerro grande,*
  Cu-1 : 14, Cu-4 : 4
Andamacha (cf. Undamacha),
  An-8 : 9
Angostura (cf. Acoyapuncu), An-9 : 3,
  Co-1 : 7, Co-1 : 8; Co-1 : 9, Co-3 : 9
Aytocari—*poblezuelo,* Cu-4 : 2

cabildo—casas de, Ch-5 : 5, Ch-8 : 3
Cacra—*pueblo,* Co-1 : 4, Co-2 : 6,
  Co-2 : 7, Co-4 : 6, Co-5 : 8, Co-5 : 9,
  Co-6 : 10

Cachaocachiri—*cerrillo,* Co-9 : 11
Cachona, Cu-7 : 5, Cu-8 : 3, Cu-8 : 4,
  Cu-8 : 10, Cu-8 : 11, Cu-8 : 12
Cajana, Ch-6 : 4
Calispuquio—*llano,* Ch-3 : 6
Callachaca, An-5 : 6, An-5 : 8,
  An-6 : 2
Capi [Çapi], Ch-6 : 6; *cerro de,*
  Ch-6 : 8
Cariurco—*cerro,* An-4 : 1, An-4 : 2,
  An-4 : 3
Carmenga—*barrio,* Ch-0, Ch-7 : 3,
  Ch-7 : 4, Ch-7 : 5, Ch-7 : 7, Ch-8 : 5,
  Ch-8 : 6, Ch-9 : 3

Sunchupuquiu—*cerro*, An-2 : 5
Suriguaylla—*llano*, Co-3 : 6

Tambo (cf. Pacaritampu, Tampu),
  Co-6 : 8, Cu-2 : 2, Cu-3 : 4, Cu-4 : 5
Tambo Machay, An-1 : 8, An-1 : 10,
  An-2 : 7, An-2 : 8
Tampu (cf. Pacaritampu; Tambo),
  Cu-1 : 4, Cu-5 : 1
Temple of the Sun (cf. Corican-
  cha; Santo Domingo), Ch-2 : 1,
  Ch-3 : 1, Ch-6 : 1, Ch-8 : 1, An-1 : 1,
  An-1 : 2, An-3 : 1, An-6 : 1, Co-9 : 1,
  Cu-4 : 1, Cu-7 : 2

Ticcicocha—*laguna, adoratorio*,
  Ch-6 : 5
Ticutica [Ticatica], Ch-7 : 6
Totocache—*barrio*, Ch-2 : 3; *cerro*,
  Ch-1 : 1
Toxan—*cerro*, Ch-7 : 4

Undamacha [Andamacha], An-9 : 1

Yaconora—*pueblo*, An-5 : 3, An-5 : 4
Yancacalla—*quebrada*, An-4 : 5 (cf.
  An-3 : 9)
Yucay, Ch-5 : 7, Ch-5 : 9, Ch-6 : 9,
  Ch-6 : 11, Ch-7 : 7

Index of Persons in Spanish Cuzco

Altamirano, [Antonio]—*chacara*,
  Cu-2 : 1
Bachicao, [Hernando]—*chacara*,
  An-3 : 2
Carrasco, Pedro Alonso—*calle*,
  Ch-9 : 1; *molino*, An-8 : 1
Cayo, [Diego]—*casa*, An-2 : 2
Figueroa, [Juan de]—*casa*, Ch-7 : 1;
  solar, Co-8 : 1
Gama, Licentiate [Antonio] de la—
  casas, Ch-5 : 2
Garcilaso [de la Vega]—*casa*,
  Ch-8 : 4; *llano*, Co-2 : 5
Gil, Diego—*chacara*, Co-2 : 1
Gualparocas (unidentified)—
  chacara, Cu-14 : 1
[Hojeda], Juan Julio [de]—*molino*,
  Ch-8 : 12
Maldonado, Diego—*calle*, Ch-3 : 2;
  casa, Ch-3 : 3, Ch-4 : 2; *chacara*,
  Co-3 : 3, Co-4 : 2, Co-4 : 3, Co-8 : 2

Mesa, [Alonso de]—*chacara*,
  An-7 : 1
Moreno, Francisco—*chacara*,
  Co-2 : 4, Co-7 : 1
Paullu Inca—*casa*, Co-6 : 7
—, descendants of—*chacara*,
  Co-2 : 3
Peces, [Francisco]—*plaza*, An-3 : 1
Peña, Benito de la—*casa*, Ch-4 : 1
[Pereira], Don Antonio—*solar*,
  Co-9 : 2
Pizarro, Hernando—*encomienda*,
  Cu-5 : 3
Ruiz, Anton—*casas*, Co-1 : 2
Salas, Juan de—*casa*, An-2 : 1
Serra, Manso [Mancio Sierra de
  Leguizamo]—*casa*, Co-1 : 1,
  Co-3 : 1, Co-6 : 1
Sona, Juan—*casa*, Co-5 : 1
Sotelo, [Cristóbal de]—*casa*, Co-4 : 1
Toro, Alonso de—*llano*, Co-9 : 3